PENGUIN ⬤ CLASSICS

# THE BACCHAE AND OTHER PLAYS

EURIPIDES was an Athenian born in 484 BC. A member of a family of considerable rank, he avoided public duties as far as possible, and devoted his life to the work of a dramatist. His popularity is attested by the survival of seventeen of his plays and by abundant other evidence; though it was partly due to his audience's inability to penetrate the irony of his character-drawing. His unpopularity is equally clear from the constant attacks made upon him in the comedies of Aristophanes, and by the fact that in fifty years he was awarded first prize only four or five times. At the age of seventy-three he found it necessary to leave Athens; he went into voluntary exile at the court of Archelaus, king of Macedon. It was during these last months that he wrote what many consider his greatest work, *The Bacchae*. When news of his death reached Athens in 406 BC, Sophocles appeared publicly in mourning for him. Euripides is thought to have written about ninety-two plays of which seventeen known to be his survive.

PHILIP VELLACOTT translated the following volumes for the Penguin Classics: the complete plays of Aeschylus, the complete plays of Euripides, and a volume of Menander and Theophrastus. He was educated at St Paul's School and Magdalene College, Cambridge, and for twenty-four years he taught classics (and drama for twelve years) at Dulwich College. He lectured on Greek drama on ten tours in the USA, and spent four terms as Visiting Lecturer in the University of California at Santa Cruz. He wrote a number of books including *Sophocles and Oedipus* (1971), *Ironic Drama: A Study of Euripides' Method and Meaning* (1975) and *The Logic of Tragedy: Morals and Integrity in Aeschylus' Oresteia* (1984). Philip Vellacott died in 1997.

EURIPIDES

# THE BACCHAE
## AND OTHER
## PLAYS

ION
THE WOMEN OF TROY
HELEN
THE BACCHAE

★

TRANSLATED BY
PHILIP VELLACOTT

PENGUIN BOOKS

PENGUIN BOOKS

Published by the Penguin Group
Penguin Books Ltd, 80 Strand, London WC2R 0RL, England
Penguin Putnam Inc., 375 Hudson Street, New York, New York 10014, USA
Penguin Books Australia Ltd, 250 Camberwell Road, Camberwell, Victoria 3124, Australia
Penguin Books Canada Ltd, 10 Alcorn Avenue, Toronto, Ontario, Canada M4V 3B2
Penguin Books India (P) Ltd, 11 Community Centre, Panchsheel Park, New Delhi – 110 017, India
Penguin Books (NZ) Ltd, Cnr Rosedale and Airborne Roads, Albany, Auckland, New Zealand
Penguin Books (South Africa) (Pty) Ltd, 24 Sturdee Avenue, Rosebank 2196, South Africa

Penguin Books Ltd, Registered Offices: 80 Strand, London WC2R 0RL, England

www.penguin.com

This translation first published 1954
Reissued with a revised text and new introduction 1973
37

Copyright 1954 by Philip Vellacott
Copyright © Philip Vellacott, 1973
All rights reserved

Printed in England by Clays Ltd, St Ives plc
Set in Monotype Bembo

The terms for performance of these plays
may be obtained from The League of Dramatists,
84 Drayton Gardens, London SW10 9SD
to whom all applications for permission
should be made

# CONTENTS

# PREFACE TO THE SECOND EDITION

THE principal changes which this new edition has made possible are in *The Women of Troy* and *The Bacchae*, where I have entirely re-written the dialogue in 'verse', using the relaxed six-beat line which I have used in the volumes called *Medea* and *Orestes*. My hope is that the change from prose has led to greater economy and tautness of expression. In *Ion* and *Helen*, however, which are comedies, prose remains, as probably the most flexible medium for pure entertainment. The lyrics in all four plays I have left almost untouched. The Introduction badly needed revision, and about half of it has been re-written; the Notes too have been considerably altered.

P. H. V.

# INTRODUCTION

EURIPIDES was born in Athens probably a few years before
the decisive battles of Salamis and Plataea (480 and 479 B.C.)
which, by putting an end to the menace of invasion from
Persia, inaugurated for many of the Greek states, and par-
ticularly for Athens, that astonishing period of political
activity, artistic creation, and intellectual brilliance, which we
refer to as 'fifth-century Hellas'. During the first fifty years of
Euripides' life Athens won for herself the position which
Pericles described as that of 'the school of Hellas'. (For those
to whom fifth-century Hellas is an unknown or shadowy
world, the most direct way of beginning to discover it, and
to see what that phrase of Pericles meant, is to read the
passage where it occurs – Thucydides, Book II, chapters 34 to
46, and allow the rest of that work to exert its alluring power
without resistance.*) We have one play, *Alcestis*, written by
Euripides in his forties; another, *Rhesus*, also from that decade,
is of doubtful authorship. His first surviving tragedy, *Medea*,
appeared when he was just over fifty, in 431 B.C.; his last,
*The Bacchae*, was written after he had retired, in 407, to
voluntary exile in Macedon, and was produced in Athens
some time after his death in 406. The year 431 also saw the
beginning of the war between Athens and Sparta known as
the Peloponnesian War; and the other fifteen plays of Euri-
pides which remain to us were all produced under the deepen-
ing shadow of this desperate struggle, which ended in 404
with the total defeat and humiliation of Athens.

The performance of a tragedy on a Greek stage was an *agon*,

* Thucydides, *History of the Peloponnesian War*, translated by Rex
Warner, Penguin Classics.

a struggle or issue. In Euripides' day it reflected, more than ever before, the experience of an agonizing audience; a nation of people tied by training and sentiment to a set of values, assumptions, and ideals which the facts of war-time living seemed to make irrelevant; a nation whose more thoughtful citizens were convinced that man is his own moral measure, yet bewildered by the conclusions to which this conviction led. An Athenian dramatist was expected to be the teacher of the citizens, to have a message. It was his duty equally to entertain the masses and to provide men of his own mental calibre with food for thought. To write about Euripides' message is hazardous; there is so much that even the most learned do not know about life in those times; and the few who understood Euripides in his own day failed to transmit their understanding to subsequent generations, so that even Aristotle, a century later, sometimes appears obtuse. The effort, however, is worth making. One experience which we have in common with that world is the suffering and the guilt of war. In this volume, *The Women of Troy* is entirely about war, and *Helen* has much to say on the subject; while *The Bacchae* was written between *Orestes* and *Iphigenia in Aulis*,* two plays obsessed with the war-mentality, and is conspicuously an *agon*, and an essay on the psychology of violence. Another experience uniting us with Euripides' audience is the progressive loss of faith in any agency external to man himself which man might look to, either for aid in confronting the dangers of life, or for guidance in solving moral problems. The modern world has derived its traditional code of behaviour even more specifically from divine injunction than did ancient Greece; and today's irrational search for credible sources of guidance suggests parallels with that addiction to imported religions which made *The Bacchae* a topical piece. In fact, we today may well be in a better position to read and properly value Euripides' plays than any

* Both are included in *Orestes and Other Plays*, Penguin Classics.

other generation in recent centuries. The reader who comes
fresh to these plays ought not to feel that he treads by suffer-
ance on ground already surveyed, mined, and recorded; but
rather that he is entering a world whose mysteries are infinite
because they are the simple ones of common human experi-
ence.*

I

The first play, *Ion*, has sometimes been regarded as an attack
on religious belief, particularly belief in Apollo. Ancient
religion, however, had very little that could be called dogma;
and Greeks did not in general assume that gods must be
morally perfect, though it was natural on occasion to wish
that they were. 'If the gods do evil they are not gods' is a
much-quoted line from a lost play of Euripides, and certainly
represents a view which some people held; it was equally
certainly not the view of the dramatist. It was probably true
then, as it often is still, that people need only slight or occa-
sional encouragement to persist in the religious beliefs in
which they were brought up. When Apollo deceives Xuthus,
quibbles with Creusa, and lies to Ion, the average member of
Euripides' audience would simply recognize that this was his
own experience in dealing with that part of our human en-
vironment over which we have no control – the unknowable
future, the barriers of time and distance, the perversity of
chance events. It is true that in this play the supernatural
element in the myth – Apollo's paternity – is given, by the
psychological pattern of the action, the simplest possible
rational explanation; but this is because the central figure,
Ion, has a character which belongs to the younger generation
of the poet's own day. It is set off by its contrast with the
fanatical and incurable believer, Creusa – a figure probably as
familiar in contemporary Athens as that of the young ration-

* For a fuller general account of the work of Euripides see the
Introduction to *Alcestis and Other Plays*, Penguin Classics.

alist. In fact, theology is not the issue in this play; the entertainment is a melodrama, and the interest a conflict not of ideas but of two persons who are among the most lively characters in Euripides' work. At the same time there is also an element of theological interest, because the play allows of two alternative interpretations, suited to different sections of the audience. Those who are like Creusa can assume that Ion is in fact Creusa's son by Apollo, and that he was miraculously conveyed to Delphi by Hermes. Those who are like Ion can, with Xuthus as their ally, reject the supernatural, and recognize sinister undertones in the superficially happy ending.

One of the high points of interest in this play is that it shows a distinct development of its chief character in the course of the action – a feature which in many Greek plays is precluded by the convention of building a whole play round a single central event. Ion first appears as boyish, humbly pious, content and kind-hearted. His sympathy quickly responds to Creusa's sad tale; his piety equally quickly perceives the impossibility of pressing Apollo for an answer he did not want to give. In his soliloquy after Creusa and Xuthus have gone out, he shows that he has always accepted as pleasant myths the promiscuous loves of the gods; but that it is a severe shock to meet for the first time the personal story of a human victim, for whom the consequences have proved less pleasant. He concludes that 'the gods are to be blamed' for their behaviour. He has begun the process of growing up, of reconciling religious faith with the facts of human life. By the time of Euripides it was for educated Athenians no longer a question of believing or disbelieving in myths or miracles; that question the Athenian intellect could settle for itself. But the uneasiness of superstition survives the victory of intellect – Thucydides provides examples. And further, the intellect which rejected supernatural interference in mundane matters could, in both personal and political complications, use a hard-dying superstition for disingenuous ends; precisely as

Creusa, with belief and determination nicely mixed, offers Ion pious but quibbling explanations which he cannot for a moment accept. Against this corruption the only defence is individual integrity; and it is this integrity which Ion shows from the outset, by which he claims the alliance of the intelligent in the audience, and dominates the play.

Several remarks of Ion show how integrity and intelligence combine in his search for the truth. His immediate reaction to the story of Apollo's rape is, 'Nonsense! Of course it was a man.' When he sums up the discussion he says, '*If* it were proved that Apollo had behaved so badly ...' – in no way committing himself to believe Creusa's story. Yet he is shaken. His soliloquy is a genuine soliloquy, arising spontaneously from the situation he has just been faced with. It is entirely in character that he puts into plain words the dilemma inevitably produced by the mistaken assumption that gods are a source of moral guidance, and naïvely concludes, 'I must remonstrate with Apollo.'

Next comes his interview with Xuthus. He does not take to Xuthus, whose brusque tone has already suggested what his later behaviour confirms, that he is a hard-boiled egoist. However, Ion's rationalist instinct receives encouragement from Xuthus' blunt statement that 'the earth does not bear children'; which reminds us that in a few minutes we shall be confronted again with a woman who really believes that her grandfather was born in that picturesque manner. This comedy scene is richly entertaining; and the rest of what passes between Xuthus and Ion makes it clear that, whether Ion is Xuthus' son or not, he is almost certainly the son of some visitor to the Bacchic mysteries. Indeed we surmise that there must have been an annual crop of chance babies, most of them reared at home by their young mothers. Naturally Ion is not enthusiastic over the discovery; but when Xuthus overrides his objection, he suddenly resolves to cooperate with Fate, accept his father's will, and change Delphi for

Athens, boyhood for manhood, with adventurous courage and a bumper feast. So one exciting scene follows another; until in due course Ion finds himself questioning Creusa about her past sex-life, just as he had earlier catechized Xuthus. When Creusa on Apollo's behalf explains to him the superior value of expediency over truth, Ion shows how much has happened to him since the play began, and resolves to do what in the opening scene he had forbidden as impious. 'I will ask Apollo himself whose son I am.' He strides to the temple door; but before his challenge is uttered Apollo retires from the contest; and Athene appears, as in *Iphigenia in Tauris*, to give his answer.

And that is as far as a play can take the matter. For the answer Athene gives is in fact that same quibble which Creusa has just advanced, and which Ion has rejected as un-worthy of his own self-respect – to say nothing of the honour of Apollo. To Creusa this answer seems, for the moment, to provide the one happy ending. For Creusa does not look beyond the moment; each successive scene has made more evident the credulity, or rather suggestibility, which has been her character and her curse ever since the first weakness eighteen years ago. She accepts Athene's fatuous last words as Peleus accepts a comparable utterance from Thetis at the close of *Andromache*.

But Ion has his answer too. It is that he may look for guid-ance only to the honesty of his own heart. His father is Xuthus or some counterpart of Xuthus; but that does not really matter. He still has pity and affection for Creusa; perhaps he is even sorry for Xuthus. But his long speech to Xuthus has already told us that he knows what life in Athens will be like; and it included his picture of the unpleasant situation he is now about to enter in the royal palace of Athens. A little while ago, when the great feast was beginning, he had felt a zest for this dangerous new life. But since then Apollo has vanished, or diminished; the child of the temple has lost his home and gained neither father, mother, nor friend; he is alone. He will go – not because he must, but because he has no wish to stay.

An interesting point of criticism concerns the last few exchanges before the Chorus-Leader's closing lines. Scholars have disagreed over the ascription of the lines, since the MSS leave room for question. Interpretation partly depends on the untranslatable word *axios*, usually rendered 'worthy'. In the first edition I translated it 'just and honourable', and assumed that Creusa was thinking of the son she had gained. But the preceding line, 'Sit upon your ancient throne', must be addressed by Athene to Ion; and I now think that the words 'That possession is for me a worthy one' are Ion's reply. If so, it is a formal and meaningless remark and is intended as such. Ion's previous statement, 'Even before you came, that was not incredible', was equally ironical (it must surely imply 'Not incredible to Creusa'; since in the course of the play he has twice tried to persuade Creusa not to believe that her son's father was Apollo); and the result is to show him leaving Delphi for his dubious destiny still alone in his integrity, unable to speak a plain word because he knows that truth is of no concern either to Creusa or to Athene.

Though the play is more concerned with character than with ideas, there is one further idea which is here given a brief but positive statement. The readiness of the Greek male to set the blame for everything upon a woman was a fact of which Euripides constantly, though nearly always ironically, re-minded his contemporaries. Because he recognized that this attitude was not without excuse he was called a misogynist. But it was Greek society that was guilty of misogyny, not Euripides. In this play the last stanza of the third stasimon specifically denounces poets who slander women. The story of the play presents a girl raped, a wife tricked and deceived, a group of women slaves threatened with death – not by a barbarian but by a king of Athens. The theme of women's wrongs is not an important part of this play; it is heard more distinctly in *The Women of Troy* and in *The Bacchae*; it is a major concern in *Medea* and *Andromache*, and an ironical undertone in several other plays. In this point as elsewhere, Euripides' use of irony shows his grasp of a truth which every prophet must face: you can only persuade people of that which they are now ready to accept.

## II

More than one third of *The Women of Troy* is written in lyrical metres; and much of the dialogue is static. The play itself contains little that can be called either action or plot. The traditional tragic pattern showed an heroic figure in a position of greatness, an act of pride arising from weakness or excess, a catastrophe, and death. That pattern can be found here. The 'tragic hero' is the Greek army; their sin is the desecration of temples and the murder of the innocent; the catastrophe is the storm promised by Poseidon in the prologue and heard rising as the ships weigh anchor at the end of the play – a storm to shatter the returning fleet. But the bulk of the play consists of an enlargement to life-size of a single moment in this moving pattern – the sufferings of a small group of women from the captured city as they wait for their departure into slavery. The play's denunciation of such horrors stirs the conscience and the fears of our own century with enough force to place it among the most often performed of Euripides' plays. Its relevance to the situation of its original audience was more urgent and more specific; so that its failure to win the prize at the Great Dionysia in 415 B.C. may have been due as much to its emotional effect as to intellectual dissatisfaction with its form.

At the time of its production the Athenians had been at war with Sparta, with one brief interval, for sixteen years. Five times during that period a Spartan army had invaded Attica early in the summer and destroyed the crops. In the second

summer of the war, when the country population was
crowded between the Long Walls that ran from the city to
Peiraeus – a space of three and a half miles by three hundred
yards – plague had ravaged Athens, causing frightful suffering.
During these sixteen years success by land and sea had varied.
The Dionysiac festival at which this play was produced took
place only a month or two before the largest expedition ever
equipped by a Greek state sailed from Peiraeus for Sicily, to
win the alliance of the Sicilian states. Clearly by this time
feeling in Athens for or against continuing the war was
intense. For there was, and continued to be until the very end,
a Peace Party; and Athens insisted on hearing their views, just
as Hecabe insists that Menelaus shall hear Helen. Clearly, also,
the fortunes of the Peace Party were lowest when hopes of the
Sicilian expedition were so high. But the morale of the citizens
on the launching of this vast enterprise was impaired by a
sense of guilt at their action the previous year in the matter of
the island of Melos. The Melians, having a tradition of friend-
ship with Sparta, refused the Athenian demand for a contribu-
tion of men or money for the war, and asked to be allowed to
remain neutral. The Athenians rejected this reasonable plea.
They attacked Melos and ultimately captured it; they then
put to death all the male inhabitants, sold the women and
children as slaves, and colonized the place with some of their
own citizens. In the Athenian Assembly there had been bitter
controversy over a method of warfare regarded by many as
needlessly rigorous even in the case of a barbarian enemy, and
outrageous when practised against fellow Greeks. There can
be no doubt that Euripides meant in *The Women of Troy* to
give his fellow citizens a picture of what they had done to
Melos, as well as a warning (in the mouth of Cassandra) of the
folly of far-flung aggression. So topical a performance would
certainly hold attention without the help of a plot; and the
author evidently felt free to develop a reflective theme unen-
cumbered by suspense or surprise.

Euripides himself proved a Cassandra. Within eighteen months retribution had come to Athens; the whole of her Sicilian armament, supplemented by a second almost equal supply of men, ships, and equipment, was lost. Not till many months later did a few survivors straggle home. Even then the warning of this play was not heeded. For a further nine years the Athenians continued the war; then at last they surrendered to Sparta, and the Long Walls were demolished. But by that time Euripides had died in Macedon.

The prologue establishes the formal pattern by conversation between a pair of deities, whose character conforms to the type conceived in Homeric times, and developed by Euripides for his special purpose of representing the intangible forces which govern human life: natural cause and effect, moral impulse both good and bad, and unpredictable chance. Like Death and Apollo in *Alcestis*, Aphrodite and Artemis in *Hippolytus*, they are egotistic and amoral; self-conscious puppets expressing emotions which they seem to assume as a sort of solemn game; illuminating by their very pettiness and falsity the dignity and reality of the human figures whose fates they control.

The action comprises four episodes, concerned respectively with Cassandra, Andromache, Helen, and the dead Astyanax. Hecabe is on the stage from beginning to end. She, the Chorus, Cassandra and Andromache are all dishevelled and ragged; they have been dragged from their beds, hurried through burning streets, and kept for a couple of days in a ruined room under military guard. The excitement and pathos of the first two scenes are set off by this drabness of colour, while Hecabe's authority and dignity bind the episodes together. Then, after the 'Salamis Ode', comes the kind of change which offers great scope to an imaginative director. First, the emotional pressure is punctured by the self-satisfied pomposity of Menelaus. Then the mysterious utterance of Hecabe makes us look to see if we still recognize her; faced at last with the man who made the war – and a Spartan – has she no curse, but only praise of Zeus? Finally, into a sordid half-light which has accustomed the eye to greyness bursts, in all the radiance of her divine beauty, Helen.

Euripides' treatment of the figure of Helen is a fascinating study for which there is little room here. Certainly the words he gives her in this scene are puzzling enough at a first reading; more insight is likely to result from trying to see what lies under the irony, than from uncritical acceptance of the superficial meaning. In the first place, it should be remembered that this play was the third of a trilogy in which the first was *Alexander* (the other name of Paris); and it is at least possible that the part of Helen's speech which refers to the Judgement of Paris assumes a knowledge of what happened in the earlier play, and of the character of Paris there shown. The lines are extremely condensed, even to obscurity, and this points to the same conclusion. Suppose, for example, that Euripides presented Paris, not as the rather flat and colourless lover described in the Iliad, but as a natural genius who, conscious of his capacity to attain the summits of glory in the arts of government or war (the prizes offered by Hera and Athene), had deliberately set them aside and chosen instead the pursuit of beauty (and what symbol of eternal beauty should Greek folklore find, if not the face and form of a living woman?) – if, when the third play began, Paris was established in the minds of the audience as a real man with qualities on the heroic scale, the first half of Helen's speech would take on a clearer meaning. Let us now look at it in more detail.

'It was all Hecabe's fault, and Priam's, for not killing Paris at birth.' Thus begins the central speech in the central scene in the play. Such an opening is either infantile, or pregnant; it is spoken either out of vulgar ignorance, or like a daughter of Zeus. If the latter, the speech could mean something like this:

'You are trying to fix the blame for all this suffering – on me. You made the war; I was the cause of your action; Paris was the cause of my action; his parents were the cause of Paris – where are we to stop? Of course Hecabe and Priam are innocent; no parents would kill their child for fear of a prophecy. Paris rejected the sceptre and the sword. If he had chosen them, the result would have been the same – war between East and West; but victory might have gone to the other side. As it was, Fate prepared the situation; all that was needed was the opportunity. This you, Menelaus, provided, by going away and leaving me alone with Paris.' She might have added, that many husbands had been made cuckold before Menelaus: was it because he was the slave of Ares that he alone made his plight the excuse for a ten years' war?

For nine years, until Paris was killed, Helen had lived with him as his wife. What is there either improbable or unworthy in her statement that after Paris's death she tried to get back to the Greek camp, but was forcibly held by Deiphobus? Hecabe's contradiction (as we shall see presently) will hardly pass muster; and Hecabe's speech is, in general, on a less serious level than Helen's. Helen concludes by telling her husband that his view of the whole matter is too simple, that he is dealing with realities which he cannot understand – the power of gods. Helen says about Aphrodite what the poet said about her in *Hippolytus*: that the goddess does not forgive, but that mortals who encounter her must forgive. She makes no defence of adultery; but refuses to pretend to feel guilt, when she knows only that she, Menelaus, Paris, and everyone else, have from the beginning been at the mercy of mysterious and incalculable forces; that folly urges revenge, and wisdom forgiveness.

Euripides was throughout his life's work a master of irony. If this scene contains no irony except the obvious hollowness of Menelaus, then the poet intended Helen to be the vulgar, shallow person that most readers have assumed her to be. If

that is so, then not only is the play weak at the very point
where we should expect it to be strong, but we find here the
sole instance where Euripides portrays a contemptible
woman. The common view of Helen in *Orestes* merely re-
flects the common interpretation of this scene in *The Women
of Troy*. Even Alcmene (in *Children of Heracles*) is too for-
midable, even Hermione (in *Andromache*) too miserable, to be
an object of contempt. Euripides presents men who are con-
temptible; not women. He regularly shows the weakness of
heroic figures traditionally honoured; but women traditionally
execrated for their crimes – Clytemnestra, Medea, Phaedra –
are treated by him with neither extenuation nor malice, but
with sympathetic impartiality. The onus of proof is with
those who assert that he treated Helen otherwise. Greek
society, in which for centuries men claimed power and
privilege, while women had what men allowed them, used
the name of Helen as a proverbial stigma. To deny this fact
in a tragic play was impossible (what he did with it in *Helen*
we shall consider presently). To question its justice with
veiled irony is what we should expect Euripides to do.

We must now look at Hecabe's part in this scene. She has
greeted Menelaus' arrival and his announcement of his inten-
tions with a fervent thanksgiving. The man who more than
any other made the war and destroyed her city, she welcomes
as an ally. She begs the privilege of helping Menelaus to pass
a just judgement on his wife. When Helen has finished speak-
ing, the Chorus show that they are of one mind with Hecabe;
they share in the fantastic change that has come over their
queen with the appearance of Helen. 'There is something
sinister here,' they say; but the most sinister thing is the united
venom with which all the women present close ranks and face
the woman they hate.

Hecabe begins her reply. It is absurd to suggest, she says, that
Hera would be ready to bargain away her own city of Argos
for the sake of a beauty-prize. Unfortunately, however, this

play opened with Athene announcing her resolve to withdraw her favour from the Greeks and destroy them on the way home, from personal pique. It is natural to conclude that here Euripides is deliberately putting into Hecabe's mouth an argument which he has already shown to be groundless. Hecabe ridicules the notion that three goddesses would have any reason for rivalry in beauty – an entirely unconvincing contention. She ridicules the very mention of the goddess of love, saying that people will call any lasciviousness Aphrodite. The love of Paris and Helen, she declares, was Helen's enterprise alone, and she allows Paris no initiative. Her next point is: 'You say that my son took you away by force.' In fact Helen has said nothing of the kind, but rather the opposite. Next, dealing now with a point which Helen made, she answers it with an irrelevant question: 'You say that after Paris's death you tried to escape from Troy. Why did you not commit suicide with rope or dagger? I told you myself to leave Troy; my sons could find other brides.' Then we hear the betraying accusation, 'You come out here beautifully dressed!' Helen has been dragged through charred streets like the others; but she has somehow, unforgivably, found a clean dress, washed her face and combed her hair. Finally Hecabe appeals to Menelaus to 'crown the victory of Hellas' by condemning Helen to death – Hecabe, queen of Troy. If Euripides had wished to write for Hecabe in her anger a speech vibrant with dignity and truth, he could have done so. Instead he has written a speech at which the exact listener blushes for the miserable queen – and this situation is brilliantly characteristic of Euripides' drama.

It is remarkable that this pathetic display of blind jealousy, stronger than all the sorrow and all the love hitherto shown, has so often been accepted as in no way derogating from the dignity of Hecabe. The truth is that in this scene she throws away all the sublimity so far achieved, and shows a glimpse of that element in her nature which Euripides treats more fully in the play called by her name. The still deeper truth is, that sublimity seems to us most vivid when exhibited as the achievement of an imperfect character; and that the pathos of the gall of hate poured from so noble a vessel is more effective than any other kind of pathos could be, in establishing the humanity, the naturalness, the inevitability, of those complexes of human suffering which Helen was trying to describe in her speech. Hecabe's burst of viciousness cancels the unreal pattern of black and white, villain and victim, and shows instead the balanced group of imperfect individuals, caught together in the noose of a relentless Fate, which is Euripides' habitual way of exhibiting the human tragedy.

The summing-up of the debate is again ironical. Menelaus in two short sentences shows that he has not listened to a word spoken by Helen, and could not have understood it if he had. Helen's 'The gods are to blame, not I!' comprises in fact the philosophical truth of the matter. She will not admit guilt or remorse; but she will ask forgiveness – the constant and universal claim and duty of man; and the creed of Euripides. The Chorus beg Menelaus to be worthy of his family; and we think of Atreus and Thyestes and the murdered Iphigenia. Hecabe kneels to speak for the Greeks dead in battle and their children; and we reflect on this broad sympathy that springs from an intimate hatred. Most ironical of all, the braggart Menelaus leaves behind him the certainty that he will not have the strength to carry out his intended revenge; that he will be as good as his reputation, and live a woman's man.

Now the play is out of balance; for the moment it has no central figure. Once Helen has gone, Hecabe must be raised again to dominate as before by native moral strength. This is supremely achieved by the mourning over Astyanax. After that the crescendo never relaxes until, in gathering darkness deepened by Troy's last flames, the final overwhelming crash of Pergamus merges in the howl of the rising storm.

## III

It is possible to enjoy a work of art for the successsion of
moving or delightful moments it provides, together with a
vague impression of design and a strong sense of atmosphere,
without troubling to acquire that knowledge of detail,
association, and source which was assumed by the author as
necessary to its full comprehension; as, for example, many
English readers have enjoyed and will continue to enjoy such
works of art as *Gulliver's Travels* or *The Waste Land*. In this
way a reader may find great enjoyment in *Helen*, while
allowing numerous questions to remain unanswered. It is
impossible to miss the attraction of Helen herself – her grace,
wit, lightness of touch; for gravity to remain proof against
the sublime absurdity of Menelaus, his courage and his loin-
cloth; or for one's sense of theatre not to respond to the play's
racy, confident invitation to suspend now disbelief, now
belief, as each quick-moving development may require. It
was written in a good humour which is infectious, and in a
poetic mood which quickens both eye and heart.

But it is in fact a play full of puzzles. Its plot is largely
modelled on that of *Iphigenia in Tauris*, with an opening
taken from *Andromache*, a lyric strophe and an entrance from
*Hippolytus*; there are also very many verbal echoes, mainly
from *Iphigenia*. Every dramatist sometimes repeats himself;
but not to this degree, except in deliberate parody. It seems
likely that this play was first written for private performance
on the occasion of the festival of the Thesmophoria, when
rites attended only by women were performed in honour of
Demeter the Great Mother and her daughter Persephone. As
Euripides had been taxed with never showing any virtuous
woman in his plays, such a festival, dedicated especially to
women, would be a suitable occasion on which to present at
last the perfect woman, and in doing this to concede so much

to his critics as to make fun of some of his previous work, to compliment his friends, and to include a splendid poem in honour of the two goddesses. (This interpretation was first put forward more than sixty years ago by A. W. Verrall in his chapter on *Helen* in *Four Plays of Euripides*.) This explanation accounts credibly for the otherwise inexplicable irrelevance of the fourth Ode (the 'Demeter Ode'), and for the burlesque based on this play which appears in Aristophanes' *Thesmophoriazusae*, produced in the year after the public production of *Helen*; and indeed for the choice of subject and the use of parody.

On any showing, the machinery of the play must be admitted to bear a somewhat makeshift appearance, suggesting that nothing here is as serious as it pretends to be. The arrival of Teucer is given only the most perfunctory explanation; he has not been caught, nor has his ship – presumably at anchor – been sighted by Theoclymenus' guards; he seems to have missed Menelaus and his crew entirely; he departs – without his fair wind for Cyprus – into the nebulous exile from which he appeared. His sole function is to provide the dramatic machinery for giving Helen news which she might in fact have got from Theonoe any time in the last seven years.

After the first Ode comes Helen's soliloquy, very similar to Andromache's in *Andromache*. The tragedy of her life, Helen says, has been that she is reputed to have been born in an egg, and has therefore always been known as a freak. And she contemplates suicide, remembering, perhaps, the heroic fortitude of Iocasta, Eurydice, Phaedra. But fortitude is not enough. 'I will not be seen dangling in a rope!' The Chorus have a better suggestion: 'Go and see Theonoe.' So Helen, whose position in Theoclymenus' palace is so desperate that she has taken sanctuary, and brought a mattress – Helen now abandons the protection of Proteus' tomb, taking opportunity again to toy prettily with heroic fantasies of suicide. And meanwhile the power of poetry holds the feelings in so perfect a balance, that she can pass straight from false tragedy and romantic gesture to 'Weep for the tears of Troy', and the topical seriousness of 'Through Hellas too the same river of weeping runs' (an echo of an Ode in *Andromache*); and end with some charming lines about other mythical beauties who suffered from the jealousy they aroused.

By this time the blend of comedy and poetry has established itself securely; and Menelaus enters wearing his rag of sail. A passage in Aristophanes' *Acharnians* tells us how celebrated was Euripides' tendency to exhibit his heroes in rags (chiefly in plays now lost, such as *Telephus*); and the reiterated insistence on this detail in *Helen* sounds like a joke with richly enjoyed personal references. But on his first appearance Menelaus, for the moment disregarding his attire, introduces himself, as all members of the House of Pelops introduced themselves on the Attic stage, with reminiscence of an incident in the gruesome family history; though the exact reference he selects was probably used on this occasion only. From it he proceeds to a few self-commendatory and quite irrelevant remarks which would give the actor scope for impersonating any tedious political orator of the day.

After the recognition, poetry and true sentiment hold the stage for a while, and the old servant delivers some home truths about oracles to Athenians who were always too ready to use them. Then, after a prolonged 'build-up', Theonoe enters; and proceeds at once to demonstrate her omniscience – by *telling Helen* that the man standing there in rags is her husband. This neat device removes all needless terror from the figure of the formidable prophetess, whose initial unkindness is only for the sake of the scene – and, as the Chorus say, because we all want to hear Menelaus plead for his life. Menelaus does so, and satisfies every expectation; and Theonoe, in agreeing to help him escape with Helen, once again balances the comedy with a tender seriousness, speaking of the dead Proteus in terms which seem to anticipate the voice of Socrates in his last days, and which may well have referred to some person known and mourned by the play's first audience.

The next Ode, the 'Nightingale Ode' (corresponding to the 'Halcyon Ode' of *Iphigenia in Tauris*), contains a direct appeal to the makers of war to cease their competition in bloodshed; and to philosophers to turn their attention from academic speculation to the needs of mankind; and then enters the barbarian king, who, by being several degrees more comic than Thoas, maintains the essential difference between this play and its more serious model. From here to the end the action pursues its obvious course; with a last mention of Menelaus' rags, a barrage of double meanings, a 'suspense Ode', a Messenger's speech and closing theophany both modelled on those in *Iphigenia*, and the tail-piece familiar from *Alcestis* and found again in *The Bacchae*.

The play, then, is rightly known as a comedy and, as such, it adds something special to our knowledge of the poet. It was first publicly acted in 412 B.C., less than a year after news reached Athens of the catastrophic defeat of the Sicilian expedition; and, woven into the fabric of the comedy, are some of Euripides' most forthright criticisms of the war. The famous statement quoted by Helen in her prologue from the *Cypria*,\* that Zeus caused the Trojan War 'to ease the earth of her burden of men', might be acceptable to an audience who were thinking of the twelfth century B.C.; but its effect on Athenians in 412, when there can hardly have been a family that had not lost a man at Syracuse, is difficult to imagine. Just before Menelaus enters, comes the passage already referred to:

---

\* A post-Homeric epic poem surviving only in fragments. This statement is quoted also in *Electra* and in *Orestes*, in each case in the epilogue.

But listen! Loud and full
Through Hellas too the same river of weeping runs,
And hands are clasped over the stricken head,
And nerveless fingers clutch and pull
The unfeeling flesh till the nails are red.

And again in the first stasimon:

... ten thousand Hellenes dwell with death,
Leaving heart-broken wives to mourn shorn-headed
In empty chambers ...

There are other passages equally poignant. But the poet's condemnation of the futile war which Athens repeatedly refused to end is most powerfully conveyed by his use of the contrived tale, invented by Stesichorus a few generations earlier, that Paris went off to Troy with a phantom Helen, while Helen herself spent seventeen years in Egypt. By accepting this tale as true, he shows the greatest war in ancient history as a disastrous error from beginning to end, all its crimes and agonies a purposeless performance, its heroes puppets, its achievement nothing. It was nineteen years since Athens first went to war with Sparta; if her motives were clear then, and her purpose intelligible, in 412 only a phantom was left, and reason and motive had yielded to helpless paranoia:

CHORUS: You are all mad, who seek warlike reputation in the clash of spear with spear ... If a bloodthirsty struggle is to be the only solution, war will never leave the cities of men. (Lines 1151 ff.)

Euripides has made yet a further use of Stesichorus' rather naïve invention; though there is room here only to suggest it, since the evidence lies in all eight of the extant plays dealing with the Trojan War. The commonly accepted picture of Helen as a shallow, worthless creature, her name a term of abuse, her life the sole origin of a thousand crimes – this figure is a phantom; Helen herself – whatever her acts – was a different person in the poet's mind. Such an interpretation cannot be established from this single play, nor can it be proved from the considerations noted above in connection with *The Women of Troy*. But when all the references to Helen in eight plays are contemplated together, the reader is faced with two alternative views: either Euripides did not know when he was being tedious, and had no firm standards as a dramatist, or he had, underlying this repetitiveness, an ironic intention and a positive meaning. But that is as far as the matter can be taken in this context.

## IV

*The Bacchae* was one of Euripides' last two plays (the other being *Iphigenia in Aulis*), written when, past seventy years of age, he had at last left behind the hectic, exhausted, war-obsessed city of Athens, and escaped from a quarter-century of siege into the mountain-freshness of Macedon. The emotional experience involved in this change is hard for us to imagine; the painful act itself may have followed some years of hesitation; there was no prospect of return. The stimulus of new air and scenery is felt at work in the vividness of many lines describing the power and mystery of mountain solitudes. The theme of the play, the Dionysiac cult, is new for Euripides; but the material in which the theme is worked out, the nature of human character and its relation to natural environment – this has the familiar stamp; and it is almost certain that so intense and complete a work was the result not of a sudden new inspiration, but of many years of thought. The play grew out of the Athenian world, out of the despairing follies of a disillusioned people, and was addressed to them as the last testament of a man who knew them and their need better than any other man except Socrates. Much, though not all, of what I have to say in this section is owed directly to Professor R. P. Winnington-Ingram's fascinating and comprehensive exposition of the play, *Euripides and Dionysus*; and any student of this work must be equally indebted to Professor E. R. Dodds's indispensable edition.

The play sets forth two opposite sides of man's nature. First there is the rational and civilized side, on which a large community like a city depends for its stability. Since Pentheus is a king, he is in Thebes the official representative of this side, which is concerned with law, the conventions of sex and property, the organizing of war. Then there is the instinctive side, which by its simplicity by-passes all the errors of rational man, enjoys the life of the senses without the ability or desire to analyse it, is vividly conscious of unity with the animal world, and contains within itself that potential of divinity and supernatural power which Greeks always recognized in animals. Each side of man's nature tends to fear and despise the other; both may be manifested at different times in the same person or the same society. When the civilized grows arrogant and masterful, it is betrayed from within by the bestial, as Pentheus is betrayed by his own instinctive fear and violence. When the Maenads are free and undisturbed they are gentle and pure. Dionysus is terrifying; but what he did to Pentheus is not altogether out of proportion to what Pentheus was ready to do to the Maenads and their leader; the god claims to be not only terrifying but also 'most gentle to mankind'. We are not to regard Dionysus with unmixed repulsion; he only exists because he is a part of the world, and in particular he is a part of the world's most complex product, man. The play is not a 'condemnation' of Dionysus or of his religion.\* The 'worship' which Greek gods required was not adoration, nor gratitude, nor even unreserved

---

\* The matter is particularly well stated by Professor Dodds on page 14 of the Introduction to his edition: 'As the "moral" of the *Hippolytus* is that sex is a thing about which you cannot afford to make mistakes, so the "moral" of *The Bacchae* is that we ignore at our peril the demand of the human spirit for Dionysiac experience. For those who do not close their minds against it such experience can be a deep

approval; and was thus quite unlike what 'worship' means in a Christian context. It was simply a recognition that they existed, that they were an integral and immutable part of human nature, of human society, of the natural world, or of the physical cosmos; and that as such they had an inherent rightness, and an unquestionable beauty (an exception was Ares, whom both gods and men were at liberty to abhor). *The Bacchae* is – among other things – a demonstration that the consequences of refusing 'worship' in this sense to Dionysus are disastrous, since such refusal is a denial of undeniable fact; it is a 'condemnation', if you will, of intolerance, violence, and cruelty, all of which are generated when humanity tries to deny either of the two sides of its nature. Thus there is no place for the view once held by a number of scholars, that the play was the poet's 'recantation' – that after a lifetime of intellectualism and disbelief Euripides repented and wrote this play to express and encourage reverence for the gods, by showing the fate of those who oppose them. The question of 'believing in' Dionysus was irrelevant.

By the time the cult of Dionysus made its first appearance in Greece – at what date is not known – the Olympian gods were already firmly enthroned. Dionysus, however, seems to have taken his place among them within a very short time; he was accepted as son of Zeus, and given a place alongside Apollo at Delphi. He was primarily a spirit of life, and of all that produces or liberates life; liberates it from pain or fatigue, from tedium or ugliness, from the bonds of responsibility, law, pity or affection. One of his most obvious and popular gifts was that of wine; but his exclusive association with wine was a later development. Music, dancing, and above all the excitement of group-emotion, of worshipping in a company distinguished by dress, secret rites, and a con-

---

source of spiritual power and *eudaimonia*. But those who repress the demand in themselves or refuse its satisfaction to others transform it by their act into a power of disintegration and destruction . . .'

sciousness of power residing in mass-surrender to the super-
natural – these were all means by which this cult attracted
not only the more excitable Oriental, but the Greek who for
one reason or another found the demands and restrictions of
civilized life profitless and irksome.

Indeed it seems possible that the first rise of such a move-
ment, whenever it may have occurred, was an instinctive
reaction of the healthy, freedom-loving mind and flesh of
humanity against the curbs applied by the spread of civilized
communities and law. Greek common-sense recognized the
necessity of such reaction, and provided a safety-valve by
sanctioning Dionysiac rites at certain periodic festivals. But
at the end of the fifth century the problem was showing a
new urgency. For three generations, ever since the repulse of
Persian power, many Greek states had tried in varying de-
grees to order their public life according to reason; autocracy
had given place to assembly, debate, and the vote. This
change had been followed by a generation of war; it had led
to a degree of organization which had taken from life much
of its liberty and beauty and joy and given anxiety in return.
The life of reason was proving a heavy strain. Dionysiac
worship offered an escape from reason back to the simple joys
of a mind and body surrendered to unity with Nature.

The characteristic Dionysiac experience is fully described
in the Herdsman's speech on p. 215. It begins with a large
band of worshippers enjoying a delightful picnic in the moun-
tains, all cares and responsibilities of domestic and city life
left behind; they sing and dance in a modest and orderly
manner. But at the first shock or stimulus excitement leaps
up; they begin running; they find themselves endowed with
enormous physical strength, released from inhibitions and
impelled towards violence; as oneness with Nature has been
the object of their surrender, they merge themselves in the
larger life of the animal creation and act towards other species
as animals do – with murderous ferocity; they hunt goats and

cattle and tear them in pieces; the hunt may be followed by a feast of raw flesh. Then, the ecstatic impulse fulfilled, they relax, wash themselves, and become again quiet and orderly human beings. In their peaceful moments they suckle young animals; in their ferocity they tear them. This combination of opposites is an essential feature of Bacchic madness; and Agauë shows it in precisely this form, for she was Pentheus' mother. There seems also to have been a belief that the prey they pursued and caught embodied the god himself; so that it was the god who was eaten, and thus entered into all his worshippers. This is illustrated by Pentheus; for it is only when his own personality has abdicated, and the god has entered into him, that he becomes a ritual victim.

In other plays, such as *Hippolytus*, Euripides shows gods as representing certain given elements in the natural or the social world. Unless we wish to court disaster, we must come to terms with Aphrodite, Artemis, Hera, Poseidon; and the terms will be theirs, not ours. We cannot expect the universe to be on our side, or even to be impartial; moderation, humility, a readiness to endure, and, above all, human kindness – these are the keys to a tolerable life; and the amorality of divine omnipotence cannot impair the ultimate dignity of man. But the presentation of Dionysus in *The Bacchae* is different. He is not a formally personified background, but the character who dominates the action. Aphrodite and Artemis are powers whose service, while not perfect freedom, is at least compatible with moderation, and whose resentment is only aroused by outspoken contempt. Dionysus on the contrary is himself the embodiment of excess; and while in the play no conditional way of accepting his divinity is proposed as an alternative to Pentheus' insane attempt to expel him by force, it is made clear that the attempt to ignore or banish him will render his nature not merely amoral but bestial, and hostile to the highest human values which the slow progress of man has won to distinguish him from beasts.

In all mystery religions, with their secret rites and initiations, the central notion is that of manifesting the nature of the god to his worshippers. In the prologue Dionysus announces his intention of manifesting himself as a god to those who at first have rejected him. Throughout the action the verb 'to show', and its correlatives 'to recognize' and 'to understand', are constantly repeated. And two distinct processes are implied: first, the acknowledgement of Dionysus' existence as a divinity; and secondly the understanding of the potential nature of this divinity – of the lawless and pitiless cruelty latent in human nature, which may be liberated when man's 'rational' part labours to produce violence rather than gentleness, organizes war instead of peace. In the course of the manifestation the language of the play presents as it were a series of moral claims made by the new cult, and the different appearance of these claims when revealed in the actions of Bacchic worshippers.

It is as though the Dionysiac apostle said to the world of Euripides: 'Civilization is diseased; get away from civilization, and have a *sound mind*. Your search for cleverness is relative and conventional; discover your oneness with Nature, and possess absolute *wisdom*. Civilization is responsible for ugliness, anxiety, and malice; escape from it to *beauty, peace, and gentleness*. The civilized world is unjust; Nature is *just*. A city life is materialistic, inhuman; go to the mountains and discover that man is divine.' The play shows how each of these claims, if scorned or opposed with violence, develops its own perversion. Rigid resistance evokes a like response: soundness of mind is revealed as imperviousness to pity; wisdom as knowing how to take revenge; beauty as natural, i.e., fortuitous and amoral; gentleness and peace as liable without warning to give place to ferocious violence; justice as personal vindictiveness; divinity as being superhuman in power, sub-human in nature, showing that the *beast in man* is worse than bestial, that the horned god is no other than a fiend.

The difference which *The Bacchae* shows in the treatment of the divine character is accompanied by a difference in the treatment of the central human figure. Outwardly Pentheus is at once recognizable as the king who yields to the temptation of power, commits *hybris* against man and god, and is overtaken by catastrophe. In the traditional pattern an heroic character is betrayed by a weakness which the particular occasion renders fatal. But Pentheus on his first appearance has already lost what heroic quality he may have had; he is 'extremely agitated', and his rational control is imperilled. His strength appears as obstinacy, his courage as plain folly, while his indignation is suspect, being coloured by an interest in the practices he condemns. Once rational control has left him, this interest becomes the craving which leads him to his doom. And the Fate which pursues him differs from that of other tragic heroes in that the element of chance is missing; as Professor Winnington-Ingram points out in his book, the word for 'chance', so constant a refrain in other plays, does not occur in *The Bacchae*. Pentheus is limited man confronting an irresistible force; since he will not bend, he has no chance.

There are two words which indicate how and why Pentheus has lost his battle, his *agon*, before it begins. The first is the verb 'to hunt'; Pentheus intends to hunt the Maenads and catch them. The idea of the hunt has already been mentioned by the Chorus in their opening song; the imagery of the hunt, which is unbridled violence, runs right through the action, until Pentheus himself is hunted and torn to pieces. The other significant phrase is used by Pentheus near the end of his first scene; in fury at the caution and the rebukes of Teiresias, he gives orders that his place of prophecy shall be 'turned upside down'. This very phrase is used three times more in the course of the play (see *Euripides and Dionysus*, p. 55, note) to describe the indiscriminate destruction which is characteristic of the violent phase of Bacchic possession. So here in his first appearance Pentheus shows that, when opposed, his instinctive recourse is to the same kind of 'berserk' behaviour which he is proposing to check and punish. This is the one point in the play which shows the fatal operation of that 'chance' which may await every man as a final test; Pentheus' curse, like Hamlet's, is 'that ever he was born to set it right'. For Pentheus is a Dionysiac by nature. His half-consciousness of this, his fear of what he is, produces his crude puritanism. This weakness, hinted at in the first half of the play, comes suddenly into full view when Dionysus seizes upon it as the means by which he will finally subjugate Pentheus. 'Do you wish *to see* those women . . .?' And Pentheus, already weakened, now collapses, and the god enters into him.

In this final state he achieves two stages of understanding of which he was incapable while still 'sane'. First, he perceives that Dionysus has horns like a bull – the horns which were mentioned in the opening song of the Chorus. That is to say, he perceives that Dionysus stands for man's whole animal nature – its splendour, strength, freedom and truth, and equally its imperviousness to human sensitivity, the pitilessness of a beast of prey; that he belongs to that mysterious world of experience around which the whole fabric of 'black magic' has been constructed. But Pentheus has already crossed from this world to that, and feels no horror. Secondly, in the last moments of his life, when his mother stands over him and grips him, 'he understood what end was near'. He awakes from his trance to see in a flash of time the meaning of his struggle and his folly; the only true perception he ever achieves.

A further respect in which this play differs from others is its use of the Chorus. Whereas in plays like *Medea* the existence of a Chorus is almost an embarrassing concession to necessary form, the Chorus of *The Bacchae* is collectively a chief character and always concerned in the action. The nature of Dionysus is expressed in deeds by the women of Thebes, whose activities on the mountain are successively reported in words by the Chorus. Their first song (the 'Parodos') describes rapidly all the essential features of their worship, its delight and its terror, its beauty and its cruelty, but all conveyed in decorous phrases which help the pious mind to skim happily over the contradictions involved. The first Ode emphasizes the joy, gentleness, good sense, and peace which are the gospel of Dionysus. This is their answer to the violence which Pentheus is showing towards the meek and smiling god. In the second Ode they express indignation at their rejection by Thebes, and faith in the saving power of Dionysus, followed by a violent outcry against Pentheus and an appeal to the god to restrain him. There follows the scene in which Dionysus asserts his power, and baffles and humiliates Pentheus. After this episode the Chorus carefully avert attention from the violence and cruelty whose operation is now becoming evident, and sing of peace, justice, and the law of Heaven; but in a brief refrain they avow that for them the noblest of all things is the joy of revenge. Finally, when Dionysus has departed with his victim to the mountain, they throw off all restraint, and call for Pentheus' blood in words of pure savagery. When Agauë returns with her son's head they acclaim her; and their hesitation when invited to 'join in the feast' springs not from pity but from contempt.

Cadmus and Teiresias are both detailed and vivid studies. Cadmus, the wreck of a hero, obsessed with his family's reputation, who has learnt as a ruler to recognize strength when he meets it, and make terms in good time, finds that all his shrewdness cannot save either him or his family. Teiresias begins by disowning sophism, and proceeds to use little else. He speaks of wine as a necessary opiate for sorrow (an argument he can hardly have taken seriously), touches on the connection of Dionysus with war and prophecy (both purely academic or decorative points), and in general indicates the accommodating spirit in which Greece did in fact receive this new element in her religious life.

It remains to suggest very briefly a line of reflection about the place which this play holds among the other works of the poet, and especially those written in the last six years of his life: *The Phoenician Women* (about 410 B.C.), *Orestes* (408), *Iphigenia in Aulis* (406).★ Among these *The Bacchae* (406) stands alone. *The Phoenician Women* and *Iphigenia in Aulis* are unsparing denunciations of the way men behave when committed to a war; *Orestes* is a numbing picture of the mental state from which such behaviour springs. In *The Bacchae* we find no realistic treatment whatever of war, politics, or ethics. In their place we have a lyrical and symbolic ritual. This ritual includes in its pattern allusions to three themes which Euripides' plays have treated again and again: the destructive folly of violence; the sordid ugliness of revenge; and the subjection and suffering imposed upon the female by the injustice of the male. But these are allusions, not the main concern. The central theme of the play is the nature of the human soul and human society, presented in a world of legendary miracle where gods and men speak together. Athens and Sparta and their particular and contemporary agonies are forgotten; yet these particular and contemporary themes, which filled the action of *Medea*, *Andromache*, *The Women of Troy*, and the three late plays just mentioned, are also all here in *The Bacchae*, lifted to an abstract plane, their limited conflicts quieted and subsumed in the profounder contemplation of man himself. The more formal structure of this play, its more traditional language and metre, are not accidents due to the author's mood. *Iphigenia in Aulis* shows us that in the remoteness of Macedon he could still write as though he were among his besieged and desperate friends in Athens; but he could now do what was impossible there: choose a timeless theme and clothe it in a timeless form.

NOTE
The line numbers in this edition refer to the lines of the original Greek text.

★ These three are included in *Orestes and Other Plays*, Penguin Classics.

# THE PLAYS

# ION

\*

## Characters:

HERMES, *Messenger of the Gods*
ION
CHORUS *of women slaves of Creusa*
CREUSA
XUTHUS, *her husband, King of Athens*
OLD MAN, *slave of Creusa*
MESSENGER, *another slave of Creusa*
THE PRIESTESS *of Apollo at Delphi*
ATHENE

\*

*Scene: The forecourt of the Temple of Apollo at Delphi. The play
opens just before sunrise.*

HERMES *enters from a grove of laurels and olives beside
the temple porch.*

HERMES: I am Hermes, servant of the Immortals. Almighty
Zeus was my father; my mother was Maia, and she too was
daughter of a goddess, and of Atlas, whose brazen shoulders
wear the weight of the resting sky, the ancient home of gods.
This place is Delphi, the centre and navel of the earth; and
here Apollo prophesies to mortal men, chanting continually
from his holy seat oracles concerning what is and what is to
be. My reasons for coming here I must now explain.

You have all heard of Athens, known as the city of Pallas
of the golden spear. There, at the foot of the mountain of
Pallas, near a north-facing cliff called by the rulers of Attica
The Long Rocks, Creusa, daughter of King Erechtheus, was
found and raped by Phoebus Apollo. She said nothing to
her father – Apollo wished it so; but carried her body's

burden in secret until her time came. Then she bore her son in her own home, and afterwards conveyed him to the same cave where Apollo lay with her; and there, in a deep rocking-cradle, she left him to die.

There was a tradition in her family which said that when Erichthonius was born of his mother Earth, Athene set a pair of entwined serpents as his bodyguard to watch him, and so entrusted him to the care of the daughters of Agraulus; and from that time to the present day the descendants of Erechtheus duly adorn their children with a necklace of golden serpents. Creusa observed this custom; she also wrapped round the infant a rich shawl woven by herself as a girl; and so left him to die.

Then Apollo – who is my brother – came to me with a request. 'Go, brother,' he said, 'to the race that sprang from the soil of Athens – you know the fame of their city; there in a rocky cave lies a new-born child; bring him to Delphi – cradle, infant-clothes and all – to my oracle there, and put him down right at the entrance to my temple. The rest you may leave to me; for the child, you must know, is mine.'

So, to oblige my brother, I took the basket-cradle and brought it, and laid the child here on the temple-steps; leaving the curved lid wide open, so that he might be seen. Now it happened that just as the sun rode up the morning sky the Prophetess was entering the temple. She saw the infant, and was astonished that any Delphian girl should be so bold as to cast her secret labour at Apollo's door. Her first thought was to put it outside the precincts; but pity overcame sternness, and Apollo too moved her to let the child stay. She took him and brought him up, not knowing either that Apollo was his father, or who his mother was; and the boy knows no more than she. So the temple became his home, and here as a child he wandered unrestrained. When he grew up, the Delphians appointed him guardian of the temple gold and steward in general to Apollo; and so to this day he leads a consecrated life here in the temple.

His mother Creusa meanwhile was married to Xuthus. It happened in this way: Athens became involved in a serious war with the Euboeans, who are descended from Chalcodon. Xuthus fought as an ally of the Athenians and helped them to victory; and he received in acknowledgement the hand of Creusa, though he is no Athenian but an Achaean descended through Aeolus from Zeus. After many years of marriage he and Creusa still have no child; and it is this, their longing for children, that has now brought them to the oracle of Apollo – who, on his part, has not abandoned them as they suppose, but is guiding their destiny to fulfilment. When Xuthus enters the oracle, Apollo will give his own son to him, and will tell him that he, Xuthus, is his father; so that the boy may come to his mother's house, and be recognized by her, and receive the position due to his birth, without any exposure of her union with Apollo. He is to be called Ion; and Hellas shall know him as the founder of the Ionic settlements in Asia.

Now I'll retire into the laurel-grove, to see what Fate has in store for him. Here he comes, the son of Apollo, with his broom of laurel-twigs, to sweep the porch clean. I am the first of the gods to call him by the name he is to receive – Ion!

*Exit* HERMES. *Enter, from the temple,* ION, *with several temple attendants.*

ION:

    The dazzling chariot of the sun
    Now lights the earth; and every star
    Flies from that fire's fierce rising ray
    Behind the night's mysterious bar.
    Smoke of Arabian frankincense
    Streams upward to the temple's height.
    Parnassus' pathless peaks grow bright

With welcome to the new-born day.
Now on the holy tripod-seat
The Delphian priestess takes her place,
And daily to the Hellene race
  Her chanting tones repeat
  What her own ears have heard –
The thunders of Apollo's word.

    Servants of Delphian Apollo!
    Go to the Castalian spring;
    Wash in its silvery eddies,
    And return cleansed to the temple.
    Guard your lips from offence;
    To those who ask for oracles
    Let the god's answer come
    Pure from all private fault.
                    *Attendants go out.*

    Now I will sweep the temple –
    My duty here since childhood –
    With a broom of laurel-branches,
    And purify the entrance
    With holy wreaths of flowers;
    Sprinkle the floor with water;
    And with my bow and arrows
    I'll send the wild birds flying
    That foul our temple treasures.

    I have no father or mother;
    All I would owe to them
    I give to Apollo's temple,
    Which nursed my orphan childhood.

Come, little broom, of fresh and lovely leaves
Gathered from the immortal laurel-groves,
Sacred foliage fed by unfailing waters

That gush from myrtle-thickets – come, my broom,
Used for Apollo's sacred hearth within,
Used for the cleansing of this holy floor,
When, as the swift sun wings the morning sky,
This ritual task I offer to Apollo.
    Apollo, Lord of healing,
    Apollo, son of Leto,
    Blest be thy name, Apollo!

Phoebus, the service of thy temple-court,
The stewardship of thy prophetic seat,
Is honourable. Slave to no mortal master,
But an eternal god, I am exalted,
Toil without weariness in praise and prayer.
Apollo's temple nursed my infancy;
He by his kindness made himself my father;
I bless him by that name – I am his son.
    Apollo, Healer, Saviour,
    Apollo, son of Leto,
    Blest be thy name, Apollo!

Enough of sweeping; rest, my laurel-broom.
Now with pure hands knowing no carnal touch
From golden jars I sprinkle earth's pure dew
Fresh from the swirling fountain of Castalia.
So may I live always Apollo's servant,
Or, if I cease, good fortune be my guide!

Ha! See, from their nests on Parnassus the birds come
    flocking!
Keep clear of the temple walls and the golden roof!
An eagle! Herald of Zeus,
With talons stronger than all other birds,
Take care! I will shoot again!
And there – a red-foot swan! Away, away!

Though Apollo himself played his lyre to your song,
That would not save you from my arrow!
Away, fly on! Alight on the lake of Delos!
If you will not obey me,
The sweet notes of your song will drown in blood!
Why, now! Another still? What bird is this?
Ah! Do you want to build under these eaves
And rear your young? My twanging bow shall scare you.
Away to the banks of Alpheius, and there toil
To feed your family, or to the Isthmian wood.
These are the holy precincts and the treasures
Of Apollo! There must be no uncleanness here.
    And yet I hate to kill you –
    You bring God's word to mortals.
    I am Apollo's servant
    And he is my protector;
    Then I will do his bidding
    And never cease to serve him.

*The attendants now return and perform sacrifice; then exeunt with*
    ION. *Enter the* CHORUS; *they walk to and fro admiring the*
    *buildings. Until* ION *re-enters they speak severally.*
CHORUS:
So holy Athens is not the only place
Where the gods have pillared courtyards
And are honoured as guardians of the streets.

– Apollo's temple too has the twin pediments,
Like brows on a smiling face.

– Look – look at this! The Lernian snake
Being killed by Heracles with his golden falchion –
Do look, dear!

           – Yes, I see.
But who is this other next to him

Waving a flaming torch? Is it the man
Whose adventures we are told at weaving-time,
The brave fighter Iolaus
Who went with Heracles to his labours,
And stayed with him to the bitter end?

– Oh! and look here
At Bellerophon astride his winged horse
Killing the monster with three bodies
And fire belching from its nostrils!
– I am looking eagerly on every side.
See, carved on the marble wall,
The Giants overcome by the Gods in battle!

– Yes, we can see it from over here.
Ah! but behold her there, brandishing
Her Gorgon shield over Enceladus –

– I see her, my own Pallas Athene!

– And the thunderbolt, smouldering and irresistible,
Which Zeus holds ready to hurl from heaven!

– I see huge Mimas fiercely raging,
Charred with the flame of the thunderbolt.

– Here's yet another earth-born giant
Destroyed by Dionysus with no weapon
But his thyrsus wreathed with ivy-shoots.

*Enter* ION.

CHORUS: You, Sir, by the doorway – may we take off our
shoes and go into the sanctuary?
ION: It is not allowed, friends.
CHORUS: Then I would like to ask you a question.

ION: What do you want to know?

CHORUS: Is it true that Apollo's temple stands at the centre and navel of the whole earth?

ION: Yes, the Navel-stone is here, hung with wreaths, and the carved Gorgons on either side.

CHORUS: Just as we were told!

ION: If you have made your sacrifice of oil and honey, and wish to ask Apollo some question, you may come up to the altar; but you may not go inside the temple unless you have sacrificed sheep.

CHORUS: I understand. We only want to do what is allowed. We like looking round outside.

ION: Yes, look round at everything that is open to the public.

CHORUS: Our mistress gave us permission to come and see the temple.

ION: Who is your mistress? Of what family?

CHORUS: A royal family. My mistress's home is the home of Athene. But here comes the Queen herself.

*Enter* CREUSA.

ION: Whoever you are, my lady, I can see at once you are noble both in birth and nature. Royal blood shows in the face and bearing. – What? Oh, my lady, what is the matter? Who do you hide your eyes? Your cheeks are wet! The sight of Apollo's oracle has made you weep! What can be making you so unhappy? To see this temple gives joy to everyone else, but you – weep!

CREUSA: Young man, you are surprised at my weeping: that is no discourtesy in you. At the first view of this house of Apollo I retraced the path of an old memory. My mind strayed – far away from here. Oh! the wrongs of women! the wickedness of gods! When our oppressor is all-powerful, where shall we fly for justice?

ION: I don't understand you, my lady. What distresses you?

CREUSA: Nothing. I have shot my arrow. From now on I will be silent – think no more about it.

ION: Who are you? Where do you come from, and what is your family? What name may I call you?

CREUSA: My name is Creusa. I am the daughter of Erechtheus, and my native land is the city of Athens.

ION: My lady, I reverence you both for the famous city which is your home and for the great king who was your father.

CREUSA: Yes, I am fortunate in them − not in other things.

ION: Now, in Apollo's name tell me − is the common story true −

CREUSA: What story, young man? What is it you're asking?

ION: That your father's ancestor was born from the earth?

CREUSA: Erichthonius, yes. My descent from him has not helped me.

ION: And did Athene really take him up out of the earth?

CREUSA: She did. But she was a virgin; she was not his mother.

ION: And then, as we see in so many paintings −

CREUSA: She gave him to Cecrops' daughters to keep, but forbad them to look at him.

ION: And they, naturally, opened Athene's box, I have heard−

CREUSA: And for that they met a bloody death on the sharp rocks.

ION: Oh! ... There is another story −

CREUSA: What do you want to ask? I have time enough.

ION: Is it true, or merely a tale, that your father Erechtheus killed your sisters in sacrifice?

CREUSA: It was for Athens that he steeled himself to it − children as they were.

ION: And how did you escape their fate?

CREUSA: I was a mere baby in my mother's arms.

ION: And is it true that your father was engulfed in a chasm which opened in the ground?

CREUSA: The sea-god's trident struck the earth − that was his grave.

ION: In your country there is a place called The Long Rocks?

CREUSA: Why do you ask that? – You reminded me of something.

ION: It is a place honoured by Apollo; he reveals himself there in lightning-flashes.

CREUSA: Honoured by ... Honoured! If only I had never seen it!

ION: It is a place Apollo loves dearly. Why do you hate it?

CREUSA: It is nothing. The caves there hold a certain shameful secret that I know of.

ION: What Athenian is your husband, my lady?

CREUSA: No Athenian; I am married to a foreigner.

ION: Who is he? No doubt a man of royal blood?

CREUSA: Xuthus; son of Aeolus and descended from Zeus.

ION: How could a foreigner win a wife of the true Athenian blood?

CREUSA: Athens was at war with the neighbouring city of Euboea –

ION: A city divided from you by an arm of the sea – yes?

CREUSA: Xuthus fought on our side and conquered Euboea.

ION: And then your ally became your husband?

CREUSA: I was the prize awarded for his valour.

ION: Are you making this pilgrimage with him or alone?

CREUSA: With him. I left him at the precinct of Trophonius.

ION: Has he come sightseeing, or for consultation?

CREUSA: He has one question to ask both Trophonius and Apollo.

ION: What is it about? His harvests? Or about children?

CREUSA: We have no children. We have been married a long time.

ION: You mean that you never bore any child all your life?

CREUSA: Never any child – Apollo knows how true that is!

ION: How sad! So much happiness – yet so great a sorrow!

CREUSA: But who are you? I am sure your mother is to be envied.

ION: They call me Apollo's slave, my lady; and so I am.

CREUSA: Did some State present you, or were you bought?

ION: I know nothing except that I am said to belong to Apollo.

CREUSA: Then it is now my turn to pity you!

ION: Yes, I know neither my father nor my mother.

CREUSA: Have you a home, or do you live in the temple?

ION: My home is any part of the temple buildings I happen to sleep in.

CREUSA: Were you a baby when you came here, or older?

ION: A baby, they tell me. I don't remember.

CREUSA: And so some Delphian woman suckled you and reared you?

ION: I was never nursed at the breast.

CREUSA: Poor child! You have suffered as I have.

ION: I was brought up by Apollo's priestess. I think of her as my mother.

CREUSA: And how have you been kept all these years?

ION: There were always the altar-offerings, and gifts from visitors.

CREUSA: Your poor mother! I wonder who she was.

ION: I am the child of some woman who was wronged, perhaps.

CREUSA: You are handsomely dressed. You must be well provided for?

ION: I am Apollo's slave; these clothes are all his.

CREUSA: But did you not do all you could to trace your parents?

ION: No, my lady. I have no evidence at all.

CREUSA: None at all! ... [*Then, with hesitation*] There is someone who has suffered the same fate as your mother ...

ION: Who is she? I would gladly find someone to share my sorrow.

CREUSA: It is for her sake I came here before my husband.

ION: What is it you want, my lady? I will help.

CREUSA: I want an answer from Apollo on a secret matter.

ION: Tell me. I will lay your question before him.

CREUSA: Listen, then. – But the shame is too much.

ION: Then you will get no answer. Shame never helped any-
one.

CREUSA: She says – this friend – that Apollo lay with her . . .

ION: Apollo! With a mortal woman? You must not say it!

CREUSA: Yes! And she bore him a child, and kept it secret . . .

ION: Impossible! Some man wronged her, and she is ashamed
to own it.

CREUSA: No, it was no man, she says; and she has suffered
bitterly since.

ION: Suffered! With a god for her lover?

CREUSA: She took it – her own child – out of the house, and
left it . . .

ION: Where is it, then? Is it alive?

CREUSA: No one knows. That is what I want to ask.

ION: What could have happened to it?

CREUSA: Poor little child! She thinks wild beasts killed it.

ION: What reason has she to think that?

CREUSA: She went back to where she left him – and he was
gone.

ION: Was there any blood on the ground?

CREUSA: She says not; and she searched again and again.

ION: How long is it since the child was lost?

CREUSA: If he were alive he would be a lad of just your age.

ION: And since then she has had no other child?

CREUSA: Apollo cheats her of that too: she is childless and
miserable.

ION: But – suppose that Apollo took him and has brought
him up secretly?

CREUSA: Is that any more just – to enjoy alone what he ought
to share?

ION: How sad! What you tell me echoes my own sadness.

CREUSA: You too – yes! Some poor mother must be longing
for you.

ION: Do not revive a grief I had forgotten.

CREUSA: I will not. Tell me more about the question I asked you.

ION: Well: do you see that your case is very weak in one point . . .

CREUSA: Is there any point in which – her case is not weak, poor woman?

ION: I mean this: is Apollo to reveal what he intends should remain a mystery?

CREUSA: Surely his oracle is open for every Greek to question?

ION: No. His honour is involved; you must respect his feelings.

CREUSA: What of his victim's feelings? What does this involve for her?

ION: There is no one who will ask this question for you. Suppose it were proved in Apollo's own temple that he had behaved so badly, he would be justified in making your interpreter suffer for it. My lady, let the matter drop. We must not accuse Apollo in his own court. That is what our folly would amount to, if we try to force a reluctant god to speak, to give signs in sacrifice or the flight of birds. Those ends we pursue against the gods' will can do us little good when we gain them. What heaven gives us gladly will bring blessing.

CHORUS: You may meet people in every variety of fortune and condition; but happiness in human life is hard to find.

CREUSA: Apollo! To the absent woman that I speak of, you were unjust then and you are still unjust. You ought to have protected your own son: you did not protect him. You are a prophet: yet you will not answer his mother's question, you will not help her to bury him if he is dead nor to see him again if he is alive. So I must go without the knowledge that I long for, since God denies it . . . Sir, I see my husband Xuthus arriving from the shrine of Trophonius. Say not a word to him about our conversation. I might incur some disgrace for undertaking my friend's cause without his knowledge, and the matter might be unravelled beyond what I have told you. Life is harder for women than for men: they judge us, good and bad together, and hate us. That is the fate we are born to.

*Enter* XUTHUS.

XUTHUS: My first greeting is to the divine Apollo. My next to you, Creusa. You look disturbed: were you anxious at my delay?

CREUSA: No. A little – but then you came. Tell me, what does Trophonius say? Are we to have children?

XUTHUS: He would not anticipate Apollo's answer; but he told me this: neither you nor I shall return home from this temple childless.

CREUSA [*turning aside*]: Leto, holy mother of Apollo, bring us home in happiness! All that your son has been to us in the past – turn it to good!

XUTHUS: Amen. – Now, who is the god's interpreter?

ION: I will take you to the sanctuary door; inside you will be guided by others, Delphian noblemen, appointed by lot to places near the Tripod Throne.

XUTHUS: Good; that is all I want to know before entering. I understand that a general sacrifice has been offered before the temple on behalf of all visitors, and that the day is auspicious. Today, therefore, I wish to receive the divine answer. Meanwhile, Creusa, go round all the altars and decorate them with laurel-branches, and pray that I may hear from Apollo the promise of children.

*Exit.*

CREUSA: I will, I will! – If Apollo now will at least put right past wrong, – that could hardly make him my devoted lover; yet as much love as he wishes to show I will accept. He is a god.

*Exit.*

ION [*alone*]: What are these ambiguous hints? Every word held

a veiled reproach against Apollo. Is it all love of this friend
for whom she asked her question? Or is she keeping back
something best left unspoken? The daughter of Erechtheus
is nothing to me. I will get the golden jars and fill the
purifying-bowls ... I must remonstrate with Apollo:
what can have come over him? He ravishes girls by force,
then abandons them? He begets children by stealth, then
leaves them to die? Apollo, no! Since you possess power,
pursue goodness! Why, if a man is bad, it is the gods who
punish him. How can it be right for you to make laws for
men, and appear as lawbreakers yourselves? Why, if –
suppose something impossible, for the sake of argument –
if you, Apollo, and Poseidon, and Zeus King of Heaven,
are to pay to men the lawful indemnity for every rape you
commit, you will empty your temples in paying for your
misdeeds. You put pleasure first and wisdom after – and it
is sin! It is unjust to call men bad for copying what the gods
find good: the sin lies with our examples!

*Exit.*

CHORUS:
  Come, my own Athene, who at Prometheus' touch
  Sprang in unlaboured birth from the helmet-crest of Zeus,
  Athene, holy victory, hear my prayer!
  Fly from golden chambers of Olympus
  To the streets where the prophetic temple stands,
  Where from the tripod seat, from the central altar of earth,
  Go forth unfailing oracles to the religious throng.
  Athene, come! Come, Artemis! Sisters of Apollo,
  Sisters in chastity and godhead, lend your untainted prayer,
  That the ancient house of Erechtheus may receive after
    many years
  A clear answer, and the promise of children!

  Happiness beyond measure, wealth inexhaustible,
  Belong to the man who guards in his father's house

A golden fruitful store of sons and daughters,
To inherit his possessions and bequeath them;
Defence in trouble, delight in peace;
A strong sword arming his native land.
Give me children of my own to rear and be proud of,
Rather than riches or a royal palace.
A life without children – I have no use for it,
No, nor for anyone who wants it.
I would rather be only moderately rich, and have a fine
   family.

I think of the Long Rocks,
The cliffs and caverns, haunts of Pan,
Where the ghosts of the daughters of Aglaurus
Dance on the grass before Athene's temple,
While fluttering flute-notes call
From Pan piping in the sunless cave!
There comes the girl Apollo loved,
Bringing his child, with bitter tears;
Leaves him as a feast for vultures, a prey to the bloody claw,
To mock the cruel moment that begot him!
Many a song and story I have heard
Of sons that mortal women bore to the gods,
And not one tells of happiness.

*Enter* ION.

ION: Women – you have been waiting here by the temple-
   steps watching for your master – tell me, has Xuthus yet
   come out from the oracle, or is he still there making his
   inquiry?

CHORUS: He has not come this way, Sir; he is still inside.
   But I hear a sound at the door; someone is coming out. Yes,
   here he comes; this is our master.

   *Enter* XUTHUS; *he sees* ION, *and runs up to him.*

XUTHUS: My son! All happiness to you, my son! Before
   anything else I must wish you joy.

ION: Thank you, I am quite happy. If you will behave sensibly
   it will be the better for us both.

XUTHUS: Let me kiss you and embrace you!

ION: Sir, are you in your right mind, or has some god sent
   you mad?

XUTHUS: I have found what I longed for. Is it mad to show
   my love?

ION: Stop! Take your hands away – you will break my wreath.

XUTHUS: What does that matter? I'm no pirate! I've found
   you, and you belong to me.

ION: Stand off, before you get an arrow between your ribs.

XUTHUS: Why do you run away from me? Doesn't instinct
   tell you to love me?

ION: I don't love teaching strangers good behaviour. You are
   being vulgar and crazy.

XUTHUS: Very well, kill me – but you will have to bury me
   too: I'm your father!

ION: My father? You? Is this a joke?

XUTHUS: A joke? No! Isn't that plain? Don't you understand?

ION: What do you mean?

XUTHUS: I am your father! You are my son!

ION: Who says so?

XUTHUS: Apollo! It was for me that he brought you up.

ION: So you say; but –

XUTHUS: I heard the divine oracle –

ION: You heard some riddle and misunderstood it.

XUTHUS: Then I must be deaf or silly.

ION: What was Apollo's oracle?

XUTHUS: He said, whoever met me as I came out of the
   temple –

ION: Whoever met you – yes: what about him?

XUTHUS: – is my son!

ION: Your son by birth, or merely by gift?

XUTHUS: A gift, yes; but mine by birth too.

ION: And I was the first one you met?

XUTHUS: No one else, my dear boy!

ION: How could such a thing happen?

XUTHUS: I know; it puzzles me too.

ION [*with a sudden cry of joy*]: Ah! Then you know my mother! Who is she?

XUTHUS: I have no idea.

ION: Apollo said nothing?

XUTHUS: I didn't ask him; I was too delighted –

ION [*bitterly*]: Ha! another child of the earth!

XUTHUS: The earth doesn't bear children.

ION: But how can I be your son?

XUTHUS: I don't know. I'll ask Apollo.

ION: No. Let us try to reason it out further.

XUTHUS: Yes, that would be better.

ION: Did you have some love-affair?

XUTHUS: I was young once, and foolish.

ION: Before you married?

XUTHUS: Yes; never since.

ION: So that would be how you begot me?

XUTHUS: The time tallies.

ION: But then – it's a long way to Delphi: how did I come here?

XUTHUS: I can't imagine. I feel bewildered.

ION: Were you ever in Delphi before?

XUTHUS: Yes, I came once for the Bacchic mysteries.

ION: Yes?

XUTHUS: And I was taken by my host, along with some Delphian girls –

ION: To the revels, no doubt?

XUTHUS: Yes. They were in a state of – religious frenzy.

ION: Were you sober or drunk?

XUTHUS: I had enjoyed the celebrations.

ION: So that was my beginning!

XUTHUS: That is how Fate appointed it, my son!

ION: How did I come to the temple?

XUTHUS: Probably the girl, to dispose of you —

ION: At least I am not slave-born!

XUTHUS: So now, my son, accept your father.

ION: Naturally one believes the god . . .

XUTHUS: It is only sensible.

ION: After all, what more could I wish for —

XUTHUS: Now you're seeing reason!

ION: — than a father who is descended from Zeus?

XUTHUS: Exactly!

ION: And since he is my father, I must take his hand . . .

XUTHUS: The gods command it.

ION [*stonily*]: Greeting, Father!

XUTHUS: I am happy to hear you say that.

ION [*unconvinced*]: This is a happy day.

XUTHUS: Happy indeed for me.

ION: My mother, my dear mother! When shall I find you too? Whoever you are, I long to see you now more than before. Perhaps you are dead, and it will never be possible.

CHORUS: We of course share in the family rejoicing. Yet I wish Creusa too had been given the child she longs for — a true heir for the house of Erechtheus.

XUTHUS: My son, Apollo has made good his oracle by uniting us: he has given you to me, and you now see your father for the first time. It is natural that you should want to find your mother. I share your feeling — I want to see who bore me my son. Well, we must have patience; perhaps we shall find her one day. But meanwhile you must not live in the temple on charity any longer. Come with me to Athens, and take the position that I plan for you, as the son of a rich and powerful king. It is true there is a cloud over your birth; but at least no one shall call you poor. Your wealth will establish your blood as royal. — Have you nothing to say? Why do you stare at the ground, lost in thought? What is it? Why do you change all my happiness into fear?

ION: Things have one appearance when far away, and quite another when looked at closely. I welcome the chance that has discovered you as my father; but there are certain facts that I realize now. The Athenians, I am told, are not settlers, but a race born of their own soil; and I shall arrive among them with two disadvantages – my father a foreigner, and myself born, as you say, under a cloud. So long as I remain without power, this disgrace will brand me as a nobody. If, on the other hand, I struggle to be somebody in politics, and reach the front rank, I shall be hated by those who have no ability – success is always unpopular; while those who have ability, and could rise, will be clever enough to sit back and look on, and laugh at me for a busy fool inviting the slander of the city. Established politicians will use their brains and their influence to frustrate my ambition. It is always so: place and power have no mercy on a rival.

Then, your home is not mine: I am an alien. Your wife has no child; now, instead of sharing her sorrow with you as before, she must bear it alone in bitterness of heart. She will hate me, and rightly. When she has no son, how could she endure to see me stand next to my father's throne? If you favour her, then you slight me; if you honour me, you have your house in an uproar. Many a woman, when driven to it, has used the knife or poison against her husband. Besides, Father, I pity her. She is your wife; she is growing old without any child. It is not right that she should have no heir to such a noble family.

As for being a king, it is overrated. Royalty conceals a life of torment behind a pleasant façade. To live in hourly fear, looking over your shoulder for the assassin – is that paradise? Is it even good fortune? Give me the happiness of a plain man, not the life of a king, who loves to fill his court with criminals, and hates honest men for fear of death. You may tell me the pleasure of being rich outweighs everything. But to live surrounded by scandal, holding on to your money with both hands, beset by worry – has no appeal for me. A simple, untroubled life is what I want; that is what I have here, Father; and I have been happy. I enjoy the prime blessing of leisure; I am free from most annoyances; the unmannerly jostling of a city street, the humiliation of having to make way for the low rabble – here, I escape all this. Whether at prayers, or in conversation, the people I help are happy, not miserable. I welcome new guests, and enjoy their company, as they do mine, because it is always fresh; then I say good-bye to them as friends. Duty and nature alike have kept my life innocent – as a man should pray to be, even if he prays reluctantly – and fit for Apollo's service. So, weighing everything together, I value this life more than what you offer me, Father. Let me choose my own way! To allow me the humble life that I love, is as generous a gift as the pleasures of greatness.

CHORUS: I am glad you want to stay here. That would certainly be the happiest thing for our dear mistress.

XUTHUS: No more of this: learn to accept good fortune. I intend to celebrate a public feast of thanksgiving, here where I found you, and to offer the sacrifices I did not offer when you were born. For the present I shall entertain you not as my son, but as someone I am taking home with me on a visit, to see the sights of Athens. I don't wish to upset my wife, now that she remains childless while I have got what I wanted. Later on I shall choose a suitable opportunity and persuade her to accept you as my heir. And I give you a new name, 'Ion', after our meeting, because you were the first to meet me as I came out of the temple. Now go and gather all your friends to the banquet, so that you may say good-bye to them before leaving Delphi. – You servants, say nothing about all this: if you speak one word to my wife, I will kill you.

ION: I will go. But there is one thing missing: I care nothing

for all this, Father, unless I can find my mother. And, if I
might choose, I would like her to be an Athenian; then I
should have free speech in my blood! A foreigner, coming
to a city of unmixed race, must curb his speech: the law can
enfranchise his name, but not his tongue.

*Exeunt* XUTHUS *and* ION.

CHORUS:
There will be tears for this! This day will cause
Gloomy rejoicings, tears among the applause,
When the Queen sees him happy with his son,
And knows herself left childless and alone.
Prophet Apollo, son of Leto! Why
Wrap up your chanted word in mystery?
Who is this youth reared in your temple halls?
In whose womb did he lie?
I do not like your answer: it rings false.
It is too simple. Where such chance may lead
I dare not think. This juggling makes no sense.
Why should chance choose this boy of alien breed?
There's trickery here! Who wants more evidence?

Women, shall we tell Creusa this?
Shout her husband's treason in her ear?
Every hope she had, poor soul,
Lay in him, was shared with him.
Now despair will drown her –
He sails on, successful!
She, his wife, dishonoured, sad,
Sinks to grey old age alone;
He, a wretch, an alien, came to Athens,
Walked into wealth, and gives no fair return.
Traitor to my mistress,
Curse him, traitor, curse him!
When he offers sacrifice and prayer,
When the holy flame flies up to heaven,

Then may gods ignore him,
May his prayer fall powerless!
He shall learn where my allegiance lies.

Now the time is near;
Soon the feast begins;
The new father comes with his new son.
Listen, peaks and ridges of Parnassus,
Enfolding high rock and cloudy seat,
Where Bacchus, with flaming torch held high in the
    night,
Swiftly leaps onward among his frenzied followers –
Let that boy never come to my city!
Let his new life be death to him!
Is Athens now so impoverished
That she welcomes foreign invasion?
Erechtheus founded our city,
And his family shall rule us!

*Enter* CREUSA *with an old* SLAVE. *They have to climb steps on
    to the stage, and* CREUSA *helps the old man up.*

CREUSA: Come on, old friend! When my father was alive he
trusted you to look after me; so you must come up to the
temple, to share in my happiness, if the oracle has promised
us children. When joy comes, it is good to have a friend to
share it; and if sorrow comes – which God forbid – the
deepest comfort is to see it reflected in the eyes of a friend.
Yes, I am your mistress; but I am only returning the kind-
ness you used to show my father.

SLAVE: My daughter, that's like you – and like your father.
Your father was noble, a true son of Greek soil; and you're
a credit to him. Yes, take my arm. Pull – pull me! Prophecy
lives up a steep hill, eh? I'm worn out; you must patch me
up. Your legs are young.

CREUSA: This way; mind where you place your foot.

SLAVE: There! I try to go faster than I can.

CREUSA: Feel the ground with your stick.

SLAVE: Well, if I'm short-sighted, my stick's blind!

CREUSA: Yes, I know. Don't give up, now.

SLAVE: Not if I can help it. But I can't use strength I haven't got.

CREUSA [*turning to the* CHORUS]: Women: we have so often worked together at our weaving, that I trust you as friends, though you are slaves. I see my husband has gone – tell me, what is appointed for us? What answer did he get to our question? Shall we have children? Make me happy with good news, and I will show you my gratitude.

CHORUS: Oh, gods!

SLAVE: That's a bad beginning.

CHORUS: My poor lady!

SLAVE: You mean the oracle gave my master bad news?

CHORUS: Well, what are we going to do? It means life or death!

CREUSA: Why do you say that? What are you afraid of?

CHORUS: Shall we tell her? Or say nothing? What shall we do?

CREUSA: Tell me. I understand: you have bad news for me.

CHORUS: You shall be told, even if I die twice over. My lady, you will never hold children in your arms or put them to your breast.

CREUSA: Oh! Let me die!

SLAVE: My daughter ...

CREUSA: This answer has broken my heart, I cannot bear it, I will not live!

SLAVE: Oh, my child, my child!

CREUSA: Despair stabs me through like a sharp pain.

SLAVE: Yet wait! Keep your tears till we know whether –

CREUSA: Now is the time for tears. What more is there to know?

SLAVE: Whether your husband has bad news too: does he bear this blow with you, or do you suffer alone?

CHORUS: Apollo has given Xuthus a son. He has his good
fortune to himself; Creusa is left out of it.

CREUSA: Oh! this is the bitterest of all! Why did you tell
me?

SLAVE: This son you speak of – did the oracle say he was to be
born of some woman, or is he born already?

CHORUS: He is already born and grown to manhood!
Apollo presented him to Xuthus here before our eyes!

CREUSA: What? Impossible! Incredible!

SLAVE: Impossible indeed! Tell me more exactly – how was
the oracle put into effect? Who is this young man?

CHORUS: Apollo promised to Xuthus, for a son, the first
person to meet him as he came out of the sanctuary.

CREUSA: His son! [*She sobs aloud.*] But I may go childless,
there is no son for me, my house remains an empty desert!

SLAVE: Then whom did the god mean? Who met him? –
My poor lady! – Where and how did he find him?

CHORUS: Dear Mistress, you remember the lad who was
sweeping the temple here? It is that same lad!

CREUSA: Oh! if I could but soar up through the melting sky,
far from the land of Greece, beyond the Western stars! . . .
Have pity on me, friends; you see what I suffer.

SLAVE: What name is his father giving him? Has he said, or
is it not decided yet?

CHORUS: Yes, he is calling him 'Ion', because he was the
first to meet him.

SLAVE: Who was his mother?

CHORUS: We don't know. But – I will tell you all I can –
Xuthus has gone now to have a tent set up and a banquet
arranged for his new son. He is saying nothing about it to
our mistress. He will entertain Ion as a friend; but in fact he
intends to offer the sacrifices due at the birth of a son.

SLAVE: My lady, I feel as you do: we have been betrayed by
your husband. This is a deliberate scheme to insult us and
oust us from Erechtheus' palace! I am not speaking from any

dislike of your husband, but because I love you better. Why, it's clear enough now: after coming and planting himself on Athens – a foreigner – and marrying you, and taking over your palace and everything you inherited, he goes and secretly breeds children with another woman, – yes, secretly. Listen: when he saw you were childless, he was not content to be childless too and share your misfortune. No, he went behind your back to some slave-woman, and from her got this boy; sent him away from Athens; gave him to some Delphian to bring up. For secrecy, the boy is dedicated to service in the temple, and is educated there. Now, when your husband knows him to be full-grown, he persuades you to come here inquiring about children. It was not Apollo who told lies, but your husband: he was rearing the boy all the time! And see the plot he laid so carefully: if he were found out – it was the god's responsibility; if not, if time went safely by, he would fetch him and invest him with the royal power of Athens; and his name, Ion, after all this time he passes off as a new name given because of the way he met him.

CHORUS: How I hate such men! They contrive malicious mischief, and cunningly cloak it over. Poor and honest makes a better friend than clever and treacherous.

SLAVE: Now, to crown all, you are to have this nobody, this slave's brat, brought along to lord it in your house! Why, it would at least have been a single insult if he had got himself a son and heir from a free-born woman – after asking your permission, and in view of your barrenness; and if you objected to that, well, he ought to have married one of his own race. Now you must do something: show yourself a woman! Kill your husband and his son, before they put an end to you! Either use a sword, or do it indirectly, or by poison. I mean it – if you flinch you will lose your own life. If two enemies come to live in the same house, it's bound to be the worse for one or the other. I'll help you do it: I can

slip in where the boy's preparing the feast and stab him.
You've been a good mistress to me, and I owe it to you, if it
costs me my life. Yes, it's only the name of slave that carries
disgrace with it; in every other point a loyal slave is as good
as a free man.

CHORUS: My dear mistress, I will be loyal too; I am with
you in this, whether for life or death.

CREUSA:

My soul, how can I keep silence?
Yet, how strip off shame, and show
That lustful act in open light?
What is left now to hinder me?
What prim glance now could make me blush?
My husband has turned traitor!
I have no home now, no child; no hope left now.
I thought, if I hid my ravishing,
If I hid my baby's birth, and all my tears,
I could bring those hopes to fulfilment;
But I could not. Now by the starry throne of Zeus,
By the Guardian of the Rock of Athens,
By the holy shore of the Tritonian Lake,
I will ease the load from my heart,
Hold my secret no longer.
With tears falling from my eyes, my soul tormented
By the scheming cruelty of man and god alike,
Who demand love and give treachery in return –
I will expose them!
Listen, Apollo, you who can wake to song
The seven strings of your lifeless lyre
Till they chant immortal music to lonely shepherds –
Here in the white light of heaven I denounce you!
You came to me, with the gleam of gold in your hair,
As I was picking an armful of yellow flowers
Whose petals, pinned on my dress, mirrored the same
   golden gleam;

You gripped my bloodless wrists,
Dragged me, shrieking for help, into the cave,
Bore me to the ground – a god without shame or remorse! –
And had your will – for the honour of Aphrodite!

I bore you a son; and, in dread of my mother's eye,
With many tears I laid him
On the same cruel bed where you ravished me.
Where is he now, our little child?
Torn and devoured! – and why should you
Lay down your bragging lyre, or stop your song?

Listen to me, Apollo, seated at the earth's centre,
Dispensing oracles from your golden throne –
I shout it in your ear: vile betrayer!
My husband never did you service,
Yet you give him a son to inherit his house,
While my child – yes, and yours – like a beast you leave to
    die,
To be torn by vultures from the crib where his mother laid
    him.
Your very birth-place hates you,
Your sacred laurel and soft palm-tree hate you,
Where Leto laboured in her holy labour
And bore you, the Son of Zeus!

CHORUS: What treasure of suffering is here laid bare! Who
    would not weep for her?

SLAVE: My daughter, the look in your eyes makes me grieve
    for you; but I do not understand. There I am, weeping be-
    cause you have no children, when you take me by surprise
    with a very different story; you leave today's unhappiness
    and wander off into the past looking for other trouble.
    What is this? What do you accuse Apollo of? You had a
    child, you say? What child? You left him somewhere in
    Athens, for beasts to bury? Tell me again.

CREUSA: I will tell you; though I am ashamed – you have known me so long.

SLAVE: I can sympathize all the better.

CREUSA: Listen, then. You know a cave on the north side of the Acropolis – a place called the Long Rocks?

SLAVE: I know; there is a temple of Pan and an altar.

CREUSA: It was there that I suffered a terrible ordeal.

SLAVE: Suffered? What? There are tears in my eyes already.

CREUSA: Apollo . . . raped me.

SLAVE: Oh my daughter! Then – that was what I noticed?

CREUSA: What did you notice? If you are right I will tell you.

SLAVE: You were ill and miserable, but you kept it to yourself.

CREUSA: That was what I tell you of now.

SLAVE: But – how did you hide what had happened?

CREUSA: I bore a child. – Why should you have to listen to all this? – but be patient!

SLAVE: Where? Who helped you? Or did you go through that alone?

CREUSA: Alone; in the same cave where –

SLAVE: But where is he now? You need not be childless any longer!

CREUSA: Dead. Given to the beasts.

SLAVE: Dead? Apollo was brutal enough to allow that?

CREUSA: He allowed it. My son has Death for a father.

SLAVE: Who exposed the child? Not . . . you?

CREUSA: Yes. In the night I wrapped him in a royal shawl; no one knew what I was doing; I was alone with Fate and darkness. I left him there in the cave – how could I bear to do it? I said my pitiful good-bye to him, steeling my heart to cruelty.

SLAVE: Cruel! but Apollo was crueller.

CREUSA: You would have said so, if you had seen him stretch out his hands to me, reaching for my breast, feeling for my arms, wanting his rightful place, which I took from him.

SLAVE: What were you hoping for when you left him?

CREUSA: That Apollo would care for his own son.

SLAVE: A noble, flourishing house – how it has fallen!

CREUSA: Friend, why do you cover your face and weep?

SLAVE: Because you and the royal line are brought low, and I have lived to see it.

CREUSA: That is our mortal fate. Nothing is permanent.

SLAVE: We must stop weeping, my dear. There are other things to think of.

CREUSA: What things? Misery drives out other thoughts.

SLAVE: The first to wrong you was Apollo. Take your revenge!

CREUSA: What can I do against the power of a god?

SLAVE: Set fire to this holy temple!

CREUSA: I dare not. I suffer enough already.

SLAVE: If that's impossible – kill your husband!

CREUSA: No; he has been a good husband to me in the past.

SLAVE: Well, then: this boy who is foisted on you!

CREUSA: If I could ... How? ... Yes!

SLAVE: Provide your servants with swords –

CREUSA: I will. Where shall they do it?

SLAVE: In the tent where Ion's entertaining his friends.

CREUSA: No: too open, and – with slaves – too uncertain.

SLAVE: If you're afraid, I give it up. Think of something yourself.

CREUSA: I have a way – secret and certain.

SLAVE: Both good things – and I'll help.

CREUSA: Listen, then. You have heard of the war of the Earth-born Giants against the gods, among the Thracian volcanoes?

SLAVE: Yes.

CREUSA: At that time the Earth, to help her children and dismay the gods, produced that fearful monster, the Gorgon, which was killed by Athene, daughter of Zeus. Now this fierce and terrifying beast was armed with a snake which coiled round it like a breastplate –

SLAVE: I remember the story – Athene wears the skin of this snake on her breast, and they call it the Aegis, or Athene's robe, since the day she won it in the battle of the gods – well, how can that injure your enemies?

CREUSA: Erichthonius – you know whom I mean? – my grandfather, first of my race, born from the earth, – when still an infant, received from Athene a gift –

SLAVE: Yes – what? Why do you hesitate?

CREUSA: Two drops of blood from the dead Gorgon, which have miraculous power upon the human body: the one kills, the other heals.

SLAVE: Yes, I have heard: the drops were in a phial which she hung round the child's neck by a golden chain.

CREUSA: Erichthonius gave that phial to my father; when he died it passed to me; and I wear it here on my wrist. [*She shows it.*]

SLAVE: And how are those two opposite effects brought about? How must the drops be used?

CREUSA: The drop which fell from the hollow vein repels disease and nourishes life. The other –

SLAVE: Yes?

CREUSA: – is the poison of the Gorgon snakes. It kills.

SLAVE: And the two are not mixed? You have them separate?

CREUSA: Nothing could mingle them. They are good and evil.

SLAVE: My dear child, you have everything you need!

CREUSA: He shall die by the poison; and you shall be the poisoner.

SLAVE: Only tell me how and where: I'll do it.

CREUSA: Do it – in Athens, as soon as he reaches my house.

SLAVE: You disliked my plan: I think yours is unwise.

CREUSA: Why? You see a risk? – Ah, yes!

SLAVE: You will be called the murderer, even if you're innocent.

CREUSA: Of course: the jealous stepmother.

SLAVE: Kill him here, where you can deny any hand in it.

CREUSA: Yes. The sooner it comes, the sweeter.

SLAVE: And you'll cheat your husband just where he means to cheat you.

CREUSA: Now listen carefully. Here is the gold bracelet from my wrist, the same piece of work that Athene gave us many years past: go with it to these furtive celebrations of my husband's; and when the feast is over, and they are going to make libation to the gods, take it from under your cloak and pour this drop [*she points to one of the phials*] into the young man's cup. Make no mistake; keep his cup separate. This is for the would-be lord of my palace – and for no one else! This once down his throat, he will never reach glorious Athens; he will stay in Delphi, dead!

SLAVE: Now you go back to your lodging; I'll carry out my orders. I'm not so young as I was; but when work's to be done I'm young enough, I can laugh at old age. You want to kill him, to rid your palace of him – then I'm your man! – Ha! murder, is it? Those who have no troubles may well keep their hands clean; but there's no law that can stand between a man and his enemy.

*Exeunt* CREUSA *and* SLAVE *severally.*

CHORUS:

Hecate, Goddess of darkened ways, [*Strophe* 1
Queen of wandering ghosts that haunt the night,
Visit this day with deadly power,
Guide the cup that my lady Creusa sends,
Blended with blood
Caught from the Gorgon's gory throat –
Guide the cup to his thirsty lips,
Who comes to usurp Erechtheus' palace!
Let the true royal house,
Free from all alien taint,
Hold for ever the throne and power of Athens!

What if her plans miscarry? [*Antistrophe* 1

If Death aim wide, and the daring moment pass?
If the hope she builds on crumbles?
Then she will die, by the sword or the knotted cord;
Pain will end pain;
She will enter the unfamiliar world.
How could Creusa, proud, a queen,
Live and see in the light of day
A foreign prince rule from her father's throne?


We should be shamed before the God of Songs     [*Strophe* 2
If, in our holy Festival of Spring,
When all night long we sing to Bacchus and watch
The dancing by torchlight on the river-bank,
When the starry sky dances with us, and the moon dances,
And the fifty Nereid nymphs come from the sea
And from the tumbling of eternal streams
To adore the Holy Mother and the Maid of the golden
crown –
Would it not shame us all
If then Apollo's foundling stood among us
Sharing the raptures of that holy night –
He who hopes to inherit wealth
Won by the toil of Kings of Athens?
                    [*They turn to the audience.*]
Look now, you who with changeless songs     [*Antistrophe* 2
Slander us women as unchaste,
Breaking man's law and God's to taste
Forbidden joys: to you belongs
This censure! See how the uncounted wrongs
Man's lust commits debase him far beneath
Our innocence. Truth sings
Another tune, and flings
Men's taunts of lustfulness back in their teeth.
See, here, this man; who, childless, will not share
My lady's grief, but bids his pleasure rove,

Enjoys another, secret love,
And rears a bastard child to be his heir!

*Enter a* MESSENGER, *another slave of* CREUSA.

MESSENGER: Women, where shall I find the Queen, my
mistress? I have looked everywhere in the town without
finding her.

CHORUS: What is the matter, friend? Why are you in such a
hurry: what have you to tell her?

MESSENGER: They are after us. The authorities are looking
for Creusa, to stone her to death.

CHORUS: What? O gods! Is it found out, then – the plot we
laid to kill the young man?

MESSENGER: You knew? Then you're in as much danger as
anyone.

CHORUS: How was the plot discovered?

MESSENGER: Apollo contrived it – to avoid pollution.

CHORUS: What happened? For the gods' sake tell us every-
thing. Even if we lose our lives it would be better not to die
in ignorance.

MESSENGER: As soon as Xuthus left the temple with his new
son for the feast he was preparing, he went off to the moun-
tain where they perform the torchlight dance of Bacchus, to
offer a sacrifice of blood at the Twin Peaks, in place of the
ritual he neglected when the boy was born. He told Ion to
stay behind and get workmen to erect a huge tent. 'Make
your sacrifice,' he said, 'to the gods of birth; and if I am
away long, let your friends who have come begin the
banquet.' So Xuthus took victims and went.

Ion rose to the occasion. He stretched a great awning on
upright poles, taking care to avoid the full fire of the sun
either at noon or in the dying blaze of evening. He measured
it out as a square of a hundred feet each way, large enough
to entertain the whole town. Then he took woven tapes-
tries from the temple storehouse, of marvellous workman-
ship, and hung them from the awning. First, spread across

the roof like a great wing, was a curtain which Heracles
took as spoil from the Amazons and brought as an offering
to Apollo. And there was a design woven in the cloth –
Heaven marshalling the stars in the round sky: the Sun in
his chariot, driving down to his last blaze, drawing after
him the evening star; Night in her black cloak driving a
single pair; with the stars following behind, the Pleiads in
mid-course, and Orion the swordsman, while above went
Arcturus waving his golden tail; there was the round full
moon darting upwards when the month divides; the
Hyades, whose warning every sailor trusts, and Dawn
with his torch chasing the stars away. Round the walls Ion
hung different tapestries, from the East, showing Persian
and Greek ships in battle; creatures half-beast, half-man,
men chasing deer on horseback, or stalking lions in the
desert. Then again, right at the entrance was Cecrops in the
form of a coiled serpent, and his daughters by him, – the
gift of some Athenian.

In the middle of the tent, ready for the banquet, Ion had
placed wine-bowls of gold; and now a herald made a pro-
clamation, raising himself on tip-toe, inviting any Del-
phian who wished to come to the feast. As soon as the
place was full they put garlands on their heads and enjoyed
the lavish meal that was provided. When they had eaten to
their heart's content, into the space in the middle came my
lady's old attendant, bustling about and making the guests
laugh. He brought jugs and poured out water for washing
hands, he burnt resin to scent the air, he set the wine-cups
going round, taking all the work upon himself. When the
time came for music and general drinking, he cried, 'Take
away those little cups! Bring big ones, to make the company
jolly more quickly!' So we were handing round gold cups
and silver cups among the crowd; and he chose a special
cup, as a compliment to the new prince, filled it, and put in
the wine a deadly poison which they say Creusa gave him

to kill the lad. Ion and all the rest were standing with the cups in their hands, when one of the slaves spoke an unlucky word. Ion, of course, brought up by priests in a temple, recognized a bad omen and told them to fill the cups again with fresh wine; then he poured out the first cupful on the ground and told everyone else to do the same. There was a silence, and we filled the cups again with Byblian wine and water.

While we were doing so, a flock of doves – they live tame about the temple – flew into the tent. They dipped their beaks eagerly into the pools of poured-out wine, and tipped it down their pretty throats. They all drank the holy liquor unharmed, except one, which had flown down where the new prince emptied his cup. The bird sipped; at once its whole body shook; it was convulsed; then it uttered an extraordinary scream of agony. The whole company in amazement watched the bird writhing; it struggled; then lay dead; its purple claws dropped.

Ion threw off his cloak, leapt over the table, and shouted, 'Who was trying to murder me? Out with it, old man! It was you who were so eager to hand me the cup.' Then he seized him by the arm and began searching him for proofs of his guilt; and proof was found. Only under torture did he confess how he had plotted with Creusa to kill by poison. Thereupon Ion, followed by his guests, ran straight from the tent to the high court of Delphi and laid his charge before them. 'Lords of the holy city,' he cried, 'this Athenian woman, the daughter of Erechtheus, has attempted my life with poison!' The Delphian lords by a large majority sentenced my mistress to death by flinging from a rock for murder attempted within the precincts against a consecrated person. All Delphi is looking for her. Poor lady! She came to this temple out of her longing for children; now, through resolving on this pitiful course, she has thrown away both the hope of children and her own life.

*Exit the* MESSENGER.

CHORUS:
    Oh, there is no escape for us,
    No escape from a cruel death!
    Guilt is proved, proof is certain –
    There was the murderous wine, mingled
    With the swift snake's venomous drops.
    Death is certain too – our lives
    Are already marked for the doom of blood,
    Our mistress' flesh for the shattering rock!
    How to escape? Through the soaring air,
    Through pitchy crannies deep in the earth?
    Clatter of hooves and wheels like wind,
    Or a plunging prow? Away, away
    From the rocky death and avenging blood!

Nothing can be secret but what God keeps secret.
O my mistress, what suffering now awaits you?
What shall *we* suffer, who plotted malice against our neigh-
    bour?
Will not Justice repay us?
             *Enter* CREUSA.

CREUSA: Women, they are after me to kill me! Apollo's
    court demanded my life; I'm in their hands.
CHORUS: We have heard what happened – what danger you
    are in.
CREUSA: Where can I go? I barely got out of the house in
    time; then I slipped along without being seen – and here I
    am.
CHORUS: Why – the altar, of course!
CREUSA: How will that help?
CHORUS: Kneel there, and they dare not touch you.
CREUSA: But the law condemns me to death.
CHORUS: Not until they lay hands on you. [*Shouts are heard
    approaching.*]
CREUSA: Here they come, with swords, raging and relentless.

CHORUS: Crouch at the altar. If they kill you there they are
blood-guilty.

*Enter* ION, *followed by an infuriated crowd.*

ION: Father Cephisus, river of Athens! What viper is this you
have spawned? A flaming serpent that murders with a look!
What utter audacity – as venomous as the Gorgon poison
she tried to kill me with! Seize her! Throw her from
Parnassus, send her bounding down the cliff-ledges, let the
crags comb out her dainty hair! The gods were kind, and
saved me from going to Athens to put myself in a step-
mother's power. Instead I have taken your measure here,
among friends, and discovered the depth of your criminal
malice. You would have made short work of me, once you
had me trapped in your house. – No, the altar shall not save
you, nor Apollo's temple. My claim for protection is
stronger than yours – to say nothing of my mother; for if I
have no mother in the flesh I still have one in name. – See
how she weaves wickedness with cunning to serve her ends:
to escape the penalty of her crime she kneels at the very
altar of God!

CREUSA: I forbid you to kill me – forbid you in my own right
and in Apollo's, whose temple this is.

ION: You and Apollo! What can you have in common?

CREUSA: I here dedicate my body to him.

ION: Yet you were trying to poison his servant!

CREUSA: His? You were no longer his. You belong to your
father.

ION: Xuthus begot me; but my real father is Apollo.

CREUSA: You *were* Apollo's; but you have ceased to belong
to him. I have taken your place.

ION: How can you? You are guilty, I was innocent!

CREUSA: I guilty? You are an enemy of my house.

ION: I never took arms against Athens.

CREUSA: You did. You were setting Erechtheus' palace on
fire.

ION: Fire! What fire? What do you mean?

CREUSA: You were coming to install yourself forcibly in my place.

ION: My father has a right to give me what he won.

CREUSA: What right had the son of Aeolus in Athens?

ION: He saved Athens; and by arms, not arguments.

CREUSA: He was an ally; does that make him a citizen?

ION: If you ask that, why kill *me* for fear of my hopes?

CREUSA: To save my own life I had to strike first.

ION: Because you are childless you grudge me to my father.

CREUSA: Because I am childless must you snatch my home from me?

ION: Surely I had some right there as a son!

CREUSA: Your right there is – his sword and shield, no more!

ION: Get up! Leave that holy altar!

CREUSA: Keep your advice for your mother, wherever she is!

ION: Do you hope to escape the punishment of murder?

CREUSA: Yes, unless you mean to shed blood in the sanctuary.

ION: Why do you choose to die at an altar?

CREUSA: At least it will hurt Apollo who has hurt me.

ION: Ha! The laws gods make for men – what strange error, what folly! Criminals should not take refuge at an altar, they should be driven away! No tainted hand should touch anything sacred. Sanctuary should be for the innocent when they are wronged. As it is, good and bad come with the same claim, and the gods give both the same privilege!

*Enter from the temple the Delphian* PRIESTESS.

PRIESTESS: Stop, my son! I have come from the prophetic tripod, past the temple wall, to speak to you. [*To* CHORUS.] I am the priestess of Apollo, chosen from all Delphi to preserve the tradition of this ancient oracle.

ION: My dearest mother! – although only in name.

PRIESTESS: So I am called. So I like to be called.

ION: Have you heard? She plotted to murder me!

PRIESTESS: I have heard . . . Your cruel rage is a sin.

ION: A sin? To take a life for a life?

PRIESTESS: A wife always dislikes a stepson.

ION: Dislikes! My stepmother hates me to death!

PRIESTESS: Hush! You are leaving the temple and going to your home –

ION: Then why must I still take advice?

PRIESTESS: You must come as a blessing to Athens; you must come with clean hands.

ION: A man who kills his enemy is clean.

PRIESTESS: No, my son. I have something to tell you.

ION: Tell me; I know you will speak from a kind heart.

PRIESTESS: You see what I am carrying?

ION: I see an old cradle trimmed like something consecrated.

PRIESTESS: It was in this that I first found you as a new-born baby. I have kept it hidden; now you may see it.

ION: What? This is a new detail in my history. Why have you kept it secret so long?

PRIESTESS: Apollo wished you to serve in his temple.

ION: Does he wish that no longer? How am I to know?

PRIESTESS: He has declared whose son you are; in doing so he dismisses you from Delphi.

ION: Were you told to keep this? Why did you?

PRIESTESS: Apollo put it in my mind at the time –

ION: Yes? Go on!

PRIESTESS: To keep it until – today.

ION: And what good or what harm does it hold for me?

PRIESTESS: In this cradle are your infant clothes. Look!

ION: They will help me to find my mother!

PRIESTESS: Yes; it is Heaven's will now. Before it was not.

ION: I am so glad you have shown me these things.

PRIESTESS: Take them. Search for your mother and find her.

ION: Search? . . . All over Asia and Europe?

PRIESTESS: You must decide where. I reared you, my son, for Apollo. By his will – though not his command – I received these tokens and kept them; now I give them back to you. Why Apollo wished it I cannot say; no other human being knew that I had these things or where they were hidden ... Good-bye; I kiss you as if you were really my son. Think first where you should begin the search for your mother. Was it a Delphian girl who laid you here at the temple door? Was she a Greek? There is no more that I can tell you, nor even Apollo, who has had his part in your story.

*The* PRIESTESS *retires and stands by the temple door.*

ION: My poor mother! I cannot keep back tears as I think of that day when she put away from her the fruit of her secret shame, withheld her breast from me, left me to be reared as a nameless temple slave. Apollo was kind, but Fate cruel. All the years when I should have lived happy in the comfort of her arms, I was denied the sweetness of a mother's care. She, too, lost all the joy of motherhood, and suffered the same bitter loneliness. − There may be things I would not want to discover: I will dedicate this cradle to Apollo, and know nothing! If my mother was a slave it would be better to leave her unfound. − Apollo, I dedicate to you this ... What am I doing? Apollo kept these tokens for me, and I am opposing his purpose! I must open it and take the risk. Nothing that I do can stop the course of Fate. − What secret have you for me under these holy knots? You have treasured here the love that I owe − to whom? [*He opens the cradle.*] Look! These wrappings are not stained with age, there is no mould on the basket-work − this is the hand of God! And it has been treasured so many years!

CREUSA: What? Let me look! I cannot believe my eyes!

ION: Be silent! I have already had enough of your −

CREUSA: Silent − not I! Don't tell me what to do! That is the cradle I left you in − yes, you, my child! You were my little baby then! I will leave the altar, though I die for it!

ION: Take her, hold her! Apollo has driven her mad, she has left the altar. Bind her arms!

CREUSA: Go on, kill me, kill me! I have this cradle and what it holds; I have you, and I will not let you go!

ION: This is outrageous! With one word she takes possession.

CREUSA: But I have found you – your mother! You are my dear son!

ION: Your dear son! And you were plotting to murder me!

CREUSA: Should you not be dear to your mother?

ION: Stop play-acting! [He wraps up the cradle again.] I'll soon trap you.

CREUSA: Try! Test me! That's all I ask, my son.

ION: Is this cradle empty or not?

CREUSA: It contains the clothes I left you in.

ION: Can you tell me what they are, before you look?

CREUSA: Yes. If I fail, I accept my death.

ION: Tell me, then. You are very confident.

CREUSA: You will find there a thing I wove when I was a girl.

ION: That might be anything. What was it like?

CREUSA: It was unfinished. You could see it was done by someone just learning to weave.

ION: You shall not catch me like that. What was the pattern?

CREUSA: In the middle of the cloth, a Gorgon –

ION: O Zeus! Is Fate tracking me down?

CREUSA: And it has a fringe of snakes, like Athene's aegis.

ION: Look: here is the cloth. It is as you describe it.

CREUSA: My own weaving! How long since!

ION: Is there anything else, or is that your one lucky guess?

CREUSA: Yes! The golden serpents – they were Athene's gift long ago; by her command every child has them. They are copies of those she gave to Erichthonius.

ION: Tell me, how is this ornament put on, used?

CREUSA: It is hung from the neck of a new-born child.

ION: The golden serpents are here! ... Tell me what the third thing is!

CREUSA: I put on you that day a wreath of leaves from the olive-tree which Athene first brought to the Rock of Athens. If it is there, it can never lose its freshness, it comes from the virgin olive-tree, it will be green still!

*The* PRIESTESS *goes in.*

ION: Mother, my dearest Mother! At last I can kiss you! What happiness, what happiness!

CREUSA: My child! Dearer to me than the sun's own light – God will forgive me! – I thought I should never see you, I thought you had made your home below the earth, among the dead, with Persephone; and now I have you in my arms!

ION: Dear Mother, I was dead, and am alive again; and your arms are round me.

CREUSA:      Bright enfolding arch of sky,
                  Where are words to voice my heart?
             Can a moment change despair to ecstasy,
                  Fill my world with pleasures?

ION: Mother, there is nothing I could have less expected to happen, than that I should prove to be your son.

CREUSA: Still I tremble, still I fear –

ION: Why fear? You have me safe.

CREUSA: Till this moment, so complete was my despair.
                  Priestess! Tell me,
             Whose hand brought my darling to this temple?
                  From whose arms
                  Did your arms receive him?

ION: It was a miracle. But let us hope that future happiness will repay us for all we have suffered in the past.

CREUSA:      My son, with tears I bore you;
                  With sobs I put you from me.
             Now your cheek is resting close beside my own;
                  My joy is more than mortal!

ION: Your words speak my own happiness, Mother.

CREUSA:     No more childless, no more barren!
Now my empty palace is my home!
The royalty of Athens flowers again!
   Erechtheus lives, his youth restored!
    No longer darkness lowers
Over the Earth-born race: the sun has risen!

ION: Mother, my father should be here to share in this joy that I have brought to you both.

CREUSA: O son, my son, what have you said? The truth is out now – and what a truth!

ION: What do you mean?

CREUSA: You have another father; not Xuthus.

ION: Oh! . . . I was a love-child before your marriage?

CREUSA: There were no torches and no dances at your begetting, my son, nor at your birth.

ION: Then the worst is true: I am of common blood! Who was my father?

CREUSA: I swear to you by Athene who killed the Gorgon –

ION: Why are you saying this?

CREUSA: – who has her temple on the Acropolis at home, where she planted the sacred olive –

ION: What is this mystery? Are you deceiving me?

CREUSA: There, by a rock where nightingales sang, Apollo stole upon me –

ION: Apollo?

CREUSA: – and lay with me.

ION: Mother! But . . . your news is good!

CREUSA: When the time came I bore Apollo a son – you!

ION: What joy this is, if . . . if it is true.

CREUSA: This shawl was all I had, girl as I was, to wrap you in – a thing I made playing with my loom. I gave you no milk from my breast, I neither fed nor washed you as a mother should; but left you in the lonely cave to die, a feast for the cruel birds.

ION: Mother, how could you do it?

CREUSA: I was in the grip of terror ... I did not want to kill you.

ION: And just now I was trying to murder you – how horrible!

CREUSA: Yes. Then, long ago, in the cave; today, here, at the altar: both horrible! How our lives are tossed about this way and that with the shifting gales of fortune and misfortune! Now for a steady wind! We have suffered enough, my son; now we have a clear voyage forward out of all our troubles!

CHORUS: After today, nothing can ever again seem strange or unexpected.

ION: Goddess of change, blind Chance, disposing countless human lives to misery or fortune, how narrowly I have escaped this horror of taking my own mother's life, and she mine! [*A deep sigh.*] Is it, after all, possible to understand everything that is involved here, to see it clearly in the searching light of the sun? ... Mother: to have found you is a dear happiness; and to be Apollo's son is beyond all my hopes; but there is something I want to say to you alone. [*Draws her aside.*] Come; this is a private matter between us two – anything you tell me shall be as secret as the grave. Are you certain that you did not – as many a girl does – they cannot help it – become infatuated and yield to a secret love, and then lay responsibility on the god, and to avoid bringing disgrace on me, say that Apollo was my father when he was not?

CREUSA: I swear to you by the victorious Athene, who fought in her chariot at the side of Zeus against the Giants, – no mortal man is your father, my son, but Apollo who reared you.

ION: Then, how came Apollo to give his own son to be son to another man, and say that Xuthus was my father?

CREUSA: Not your real father. You are Apollo's son, and he gave you to Xuthus, as any man might give his own son to a friend to provide him with an heir.

ION: Are Apollo's oracles truth or lies? This troubles me, Mother, as well it may.

CREUSA: This is how I see it, my son: it is out of kindness that Apollo is establishing you in a royal house. Suppose we openly claimed Apollo as your father: you would never have inherited our royal house, nor would his fatherhood be acknowledged. How could it be, when I myself concealed my union with him, and secretly left you to die? No; Apollo gives you to Xuthus for your own good.

ION: That is mere trifling. I am looking for a better answer. I will go into the temple and ask Apollo himself whose son I am.

ATHENE *appears above.*

– Ah! What god is this, rising above the temple with her face towards the East? Come away, Mother, we must not look on the face of a god, unless – unless perhaps it is timely that we should.

ATHENE: Stay! Why should you fly from me as from an enemy? I am your friend here as in Athens, the city whose name I bear – I am Athene! I have come in haste from Apollo. He thought it right not to appear to you himself, lest there should be reproaches openly uttered for what is past; so he sends me with this message to you. Ion, this is your mother, and Apollo is your father. Xuthus did not beget you, but Apollo gave you to him so that you might become the recognized heir of an illustrious house. When Apollo's purpose in this matter was disclosed [*she looks disapprovingly at the* CHORUS] he contrived a way to save each of you from death at the other's hands. His intention had been to keep the truth secret for a while, and then in Athens to reveal Creusa as your mother, and you as her son by Apollo. However, to complete the business for which I harnessed my chariot to come here, listen now to Apollo's prophecies.

Creusa: take your son home with you to Athens, and give

him the place and power of royalty; he is descended from
Erechtheus, and it is his right to rule my land. He shall be
famous throughout Greece; he shall have four sons, who
shall give their names to the four tribes and regions of my
mountain country, the Geleontes, Hopletes, Argades, and
one tribe named after my aegis the Aegicores. They in their
turn shall have sons who in the appointed course of time
shall found cities on the islands of the Cyclades and on the
mainland coasts, to lend their strength to my city. They
shall colonize the lowlands on either side of the strait that
divides Europe from Asia; called after this prince, they shall
bear the glorious name of Ionians. Moreover, you and
Xuthus too shall have sons: first Dorus, from whom shall
spring the celebrated Dorian State; then Achaeus, who shall
be king of the sea-coast by Rhium in Peloponnese, and set
the seal of his name upon a nation.

So, Apollo has done all things well: first, he gave you a
healthy labour and so enabled you to conceal the birth of
your son; then when he was born and you abandoned him
in his cradle, Apollo instructed Hermes to take the infant in
his arms and transport him to Delphi; here he preserved his
life and brought him up.

Now, tell no one that Ion is your true son; so that Xuthus
may enjoy his delusion, and you may enjoy the happiness
that you know to be yours. So, joy be with you all! Your
troubles are over; from this day your good fortune begins.

ION: Athene, daughter of Almighty Zeus, we accept your
words and shall not refuse belief. I believe that I am the son
of Creusa and of Apollo. Even before you came that was
not incredible.

CREUSA: Now I will make my confession! Before, I blamed
Apollo: now I bless him because, though for so long he did
nothing, now he gives my son back to me. Before, I hated
this holy temple: now its porch smiles upon me, I caress
this dear doorway, and touch every stone with delight.

ATHENE: You have changed your curses into blessings: you do well. The ways of gods are slow; but in the end their power is shown.

CREUSA: Come, my son, let us set out for home.

ATHENE: Go, and I will follow.

CREUSA: Worthy guardian of our journey, and our city's friend!

ATHENE [*to* ION]: Take the throne of your fathers!

ION: It is for me a fitting possession.

      ATHENE *disappears. Exeunt* CREUSA *and* ION.

CHORUS: Farewell, Apollo, Son of Zeus and Leto! [*The* CHORUS *begin to leave the stage, while the leader speaks.*] Let any man whose life is pursued by misfortune reverence the gods and take courage. For in the end good men receive the reward they deserve; but evil natures beget evil fortune; and to them happiness can never come.

            *Exeunt.*

# THE WOMEN OF TROY

*

### Characters:

POSEIDON, *God of the Sea*
ATHENE, *a goddess*
HECABE, *widow of Priam King of Troy*
CHORUS *of captive Trojan women*
TALTHYBIUS, *a Greek herald*
CASSANDRA, *daughter of Hecabe*
ANDROMACHE, *daughter-in-law of Hecabe*
MENELAUS, *a general of the Greek army*
HELEN, *his wife*

*

Scene: *The ruins of Troy, two days after the city's capture, before dawn. First are seen only silhouettes of shattered buildings against a red glow and rising smoke; then light falls on the god* POSEIDON.

POSEIDON:
I come from the salt depths of the Aegean Sea,
Where the white feet of Nereids tread their circling dance:
I am Poseidon. Troy and its people were my city.
That ring of walls and towers I and Apollo built –
Squared every stone in it; and my affection has not faded.
Now Troy lies dead under the conquering Argive spear,
Stripped, sacked and smouldering.

       Epeius, a Phocian from Parnassus, made
To Athene's plan that horse pregnant with armed men,
Called by all future ages the Wooden Horse, and sent it
To glide, weighty with hidden death, through the Trojan
   walls.
The sacred groves are deserted; the temples run with blood;

On Zeus the Protector's altar-steps Priam lies dead.
Measureless gold and all the loot of Troy goes down
To the Greek ships; and now they wait for a following wind
To make glad, after ten long years, with the sight of their
    wives and children
The men who sailed from Greece to attack and destroy this
    town.

Athene, and Hera of Argos, the gods who joined in league
To achieve this end, have worsted me: now I must leave
Ilion the famous, leave my altars. When desolation
Falls like a blight, the day for the worship of gods is
    past.

Scamandros echoes with endless cries of captured women
Assigned by lottery as slaves to various Greeks – Arcadians,
Thessalians, or Athenians. Those not yet allotted
Are in this house, reserved for the chiefs of the Greek army;
With them, justly held as a prisoner, is Tyndareus' daughter,
Spartan Helen. Here by the door, you may contemplate,
If you wish, this pitiable, prostrate figure, drowned in tears
For a world of sorrows. It is Hecabe. She does not know
That her daughter Polyxena died just now most pitiably,
An offering slaughtered at Achilles' grave. Her husband,
    Priam,
Is dead, so are her sons. Her daughter the prophetess,
Cassandra, whom Apollo himself left virgin – she
Will be taken by force, in contempt of the god and all pious
    feeling
By King Agamemnon as his concubine.
               Farewell, then, city!
Superb masonry, farewell! You had your day of glory.
You would stand firm yet, were it not for Athene, daughter
    of Zeus.

               *Enter* ATHENE.

ATHENE:

> You are a great god honoured by gods – and my father's
>> brother:
>
> May our old feud be buried? I have something to say to you.

POSEIDON:

> Welcome, Athene. Family love has a magic power.

ATHENE:

> You are generous, and I thank you. The matter I wish to
>> discuss
>
> Equally concerns us both.

POSEIDON:              I suppose you bring some word

> From Zeus, or from some other god, greater or less.

ATHENE:

> No. I come to entreat your powerful aid and alliance
>
> On behalf of Troy – yes, of this place!

POSEIDON:                           Have you renounced

> Your hatred? Now she is blackened with fire, do you pity
>> Troy?

ATHENE:

> First answer: will you support me, and join your will with
>> mine?

POSEIDON:

> Of course. Tell me your mind: is it Greece or Troy you are
>> helping?

ATHENE:

> I am disposed to favour the Trojans, whom I hated;
>
> And to make this homeward voyage disastrous for the
>> Greeks.

POSEIDON:

> But why? Surely your change of affection is somewhat casual?
>
> Why this leaping at random between hate and love?

ATHENE:

> You know of the insult offered my temple – offered to me?

POSEIDON:

> When Aias dragged Cassandra from sanctuary? I know.

ATHENE:

  No punishment from the Greeks, not even a reprimand.

POSEIDON:

  After the decisive help you gave them in winning the war!

ATHENE:

  Therefore I look to you to help me make them suffer.

POSEIDON:

  My powers await your wishes, Athene. What is your plan?

ATHENE:

  I mean to make their homeward journey – unfortunate.

POSEIDON:

  Before they embark, or on the open sea?

ATHENE:                                              At sea!

  When they are under sail from Troy, nearing their homes!
  Zeus will himself send rain in floods with incessant hail
  And black tornadoes – give me his lightning-fire to blast
  And burn the Achaean ships. Then do your part: infuriate
  The Aegean with waves and whirlpools; let floating corpses
      jostle
  Thick down the Euboean Gulf; so that Greeks may learn in
      future
  To respect my altars and show humility before the gods.

POSEIDON:

  Athene, the help you need shall be given without more
      words.
  I will uproar the whole Aegean; the shores of Myconos,
  The Delian reefs, Scyros, Lemnos, the Capherian capes,
  Shall gather the drowned by thousands. Now go back to
      Olympus;
  Receive the lightning-shafts from your father's hand; and
      watch
  For the Argive ships of war to spread their sails for home.
      When a man who takes a city includes in the general
      destruction
  Temples of the high gods and tombs that honour the dead,

He is a fool: his own destruction follows him close.

ATHENE *and* POSEIDON *depart in different directions. The*
*recumbent figure of* HECABE *stirs: she rises on one arm.*

HECABE:

    Lift your neck from the dust;        [*Strophe* 1
    Up with your head!
    This is not Troy; the kings of Troy are dead:
    Bear what you must.
    The tide has turned at length:
    Ebb with the tide, drift helpless down.
    Useless to struggle on,
    Breasting the storm when Fate prevails.
    I mourn for my dead world, my burning town,
    My sons, my husband, gone, all gone!
    What pride of race, what strength
    Once swelled our royal sails!
    Now shrunk to nothing, sunk in mean oblivion!

    How must I deal with grief?        [*Antistrophe* 1
    Hold, or give rein?
    See where my outcast limbs have lain!
    Stones for a bed bring sorrow small relief.
    My heart would burst,
    My sick head beats and burns,
    Till passion pleads to ease its pain
    In restless rocking, like a boat
    That sways and turns,
    Keeping sad time to my funereal song.
    For those whom Fate has cursed
    Music itself sings but one note –
    Unending miseries, torment and wrong!

When the swift-winged Hellene ships    [*Strophe* 2
Sailing from their land-locked ports
Through the salt sea's purple glow
Swooped on sacred Ilion,

Shrill, triumphant from a thousand flutes and pipes
    Rose their martial music.
    In the gulf of Troas
      (Ah, poor Troas!)
They made fast their hawsers of Egyptian twine,
   Sworn to bring back hated Helen,
   The cursed wife of Menelaus,
Sparta's shame and Castor's ruin, her whose sin
Struck down Priam, patriarch of fifty sons,
    Wrecked my life, and left me
    Stranded and despairing.


Here near Agamemnon's tent,          [Antistrophe 2
Prisoner and slave, I sit,
    An unpitied exile,
    Old, my grey hair ravaged
    With the knife of mourning.
Come, you widowed brides of Trojan fighting-men,
   Weeping mothers, trembling daughters,
Come, weep with me while the smoke goes up from
   Troy!
   Once with cheerful Phrygian music,
   Solemn hymns and sacred dances,
I, Queen Hecabe, Priam's sceptre in my hand,
    Led your steps and voices:
    Now the song is saddened
To the seagull's crying round her helpless young.
   *The first half of the* CHORUS *has begun to enter: they*
        *group themselves round* HECABE.

CHORUS I:
   We heard your voice, Hecabe; why did you call? [Strophe 3
   What did you say? As we sat there indoors
   Thinking of slavery with bitter tears,
   Your cry of agony came to us, and we all
   Shuddered with nameless fears.

HECABE:

　The Argive crews muster and grip their oars.

CHORUS:

　Will they take us now? What have you heard?

　Is this our last breath of our native air?

HECABE:

　Who knows? I guess the worst.

CHORUS:

　Soon we shall hear the final, dreaded word:

　'Out of the house, you Trojan slaves! On board!

　The Argive fleet sets sail for home!'

HECABE:

　Cassandra – no! That must not be!

　Keep my frenzied child Cassandra there!

　Hold her – she must not come!

　It would crown my grief to see

　Her go dishonoured to her captor's bed.

　Troy, Troy! This is your ultimate agony –

　Robbed of your living remnant, deserted by your dead!

　　　*The second half of the* CHORUS *now enter.*

CHORUS 2: I came to ask for news;　　　　[*Antistrophe* 3

　　　　　Speak to me, Hecabe! Terrors come crowding

　　　　　　thick –

　　　　　Have they resolved to kill us? Are the crews

　　　　　Taking their places at the oars?

　　　　　Is there no word yet of our fate?

HECABE:　　My child, I do not know.

　　　　　I came out here because, maddened and sick

　　　　　With horror, I could not sleep.

CHORUS:　　Oh! To what pitiless master shall I go?

HECABE:　　You have not long to wait.

CHORUS:　　But long to weep.

　　　　　A slave? Where will my new home be?

　　　　　Some island? Famous Argos, or Thessaly?

　　　　　Far, far from Troy!

HECABE: A queen – to fall so low!
On what strange, distant shore
Shall I, to whom my country gave
Honour, authority, imperial sway,
Be set by some Greek lord
To tend his children, or to keep
Watch at his door –
An aged, useless ghost, unknown, ignored,
A shadow of death – a slave!

CHORUS:
What words of yours can release          [*Strophe* 4
Pity to match your pain?
And I – never again
Shall I sway to the shuttle's song,
Weaving wool spun from a home-bred fleece!
Instead, one last, last look at the faces of my dead sons,
Then go to meet yet worse –
Forced, maybe, to the bed of some lustful Greek –
Listen, gods, to my curse
On the night that hides such wrong!
By day, servile and meek,
Carrying water from the well –
Perhaps, holy Peirene! – This is my first prayer,
To go to famous Athens, where
The streets are golden, so they tell;
But not to Sparta, where the wild Eurotas runs,
Not to hated Helen's cruel employ –
Menial to Menelaus, murderer of Troy!

I have heard it told          [*Antistrophe* 4
That, above broad Peneius, enchanting fields,
The green plinth of Olympus, hold
Rich fruits and heavy harvest; there,
After King Theseus' sacred earth,
My second choice would lie.

They say, the land of Aetna, where
Hephaestus' forge clangs underground,
And eastward, fronting the Phoenician Sound,
The Mother of Sicily's mountains towers high –
Far-reaching fame has crowned
This land for people of heroic worth.
There is a valley, yet again,
Lying nearest to the Ionian Sea,
Where the most lovely of all rivers runs,
Crathis, whose waters, fed by fertile dews,
The gift of Heaven, supply
Wealth and good living to its hardy sons:
There is a home that I would choose!

Look! The herald from the Achaean camp,
Hurrying here with urgent orders!
What has been decided? What will be his message?
Now our slavery begins:
We are chattels of the Dorian State!

*Enter* TALTHYBIUS. HECABE, *who did not turn when the*
CHORUS *announced his approach, still stands without looking
at him.*

TALTHYBIUS:
Hecabe, my frequent journeys here to Troy as herald
Of the Achaean army have made me known to you.
I am Talthybius, lady; and I come with news.

HECABE:
Dear friends, it has come. Women of Troy,
The moment we have dreaded is now here.

TALTHYBIUS:
You have all now been allotted – if this was what you
feared.

HECABE:
What is our fate? Are we for Thessaly?
Or Phthia? Or for the land of Cadmus?

TALTHYBIUS:

  Each is assigned to a different man, not all to one.

HECABE:

    Tell each of us her fortune.

    Which of Troy's women has a golden future?

TALTHYBIUS:

  I know; but you must ask one question at a time.

HECABE:

    Then tell me about my daughter, poor Cassandra.

    Whose share is she?

TALTHYBIUS:

  King Agamemnon chose her as his special prize.

HECABE:

    A slave for his Spartan wife?

    O miserable fate!

TALTHYBIUS:

  No, for his own bed. She is to be his concubine.

HECABE:

    But she belongs to the bright-haired Apollo –

    A consecrated virgin, set aside

    By him to live in single purity!

TALTHYBIUS:

  She is god-possessed; but she has captured the king's heart.

HECABE:

    Cassandra, fling your temple-keys away,

    Strip off your vestments, tear your holy wreath!

TALTHYBIUS:

  Is it not good fortune that she is chosen for the king's bed?

HECABE:

    What of my other daughter, whom you took

    From me last night?

TALTHYBIUS:

  Is it Polyxena you are speaking of?

HECABE:                                        It is.

    Has she been drawn for? Whose yoke does she bear?

TALTHYBIUS:
She has been made attendant at Achilles' tomb.

HECABE:
Attendant at a tomb! My child! Talthybius,
Is this some Greek tradition?

TALTHYBIUS:
Be happy for your daughter; all is well with her.

HECABE:
What do you mean? At least she is alive?

TALTHYBIUS:
Her fate is settled. She is free from suffering.

HECABE:
What is decided for my daughter-in-law,
Iron-hearted Hector's wife, Andromache?

TALTHYBIUS:
She too was specially chosen, by Achilles' son.

HECABE:
And I, whose shaking hand leans on a stick,
Whose slave am I, grey-headed Hecabe?

TALTHYBIUS:
You were assigned to Odysseus, king of Ithaca.

HECABE:
Odysseus? Oh! Odysseus! Now
Shear the head, tear the cheek,
Beat the brow!
Cruellest fate of all! Now I belong
To a perjured impious outcast, who defies
Man's law and God's; monster of wickedness
Whose tongue twists straight to crooked, truth to lies,
Friendship to hate, mocks right and honours wrong!
Now my fated life, dear friends,
Sinks and ends.
Weep for me, and veil my head;
Hope is dead; today I know
The last throe of misery!

CHORUS:

Mistress, you know your own fate now; but what of us?
What Greek lord holds our helpless future in his hands?

TALTHYBIUS:

Men, go inside and bring Cassandra out at once.
First I must hand *her* over to the general; next,
Distribute the other women according to the draw.
– Why, look there! Flames, pine-torches burning! Those
women –
Are they now trying to set the place on fire, or what?
Have they resolved to burn themselves to death, rather
Than be brought back to Argos? Strange how intolerable
The indignity of slavery is to those born free.
Open the door, there! This may suit the prisoners;
But our generals will be annoyed, and they'll blame me.

HECABE:

No, no; there is no fire. It is my poor daughter
Cassandra – here she comes, possessed with prophecy.

CASSANDRA *comes in with a flaming torch in each hand. One she
places in a sconce on the pediment of a broken statue, and to this
she turns when she addresses Hymen; the other she holds in one
hand as she moves about the stage.*

CASSANDRA:

Raise the torch and fling the flame!
Flood the walls with holy light!
　Worship the Almighty
　Hymen, God of Marriage!
Agamemnon, master of my maiden flesh,
　King of Argos, take me!
Heaven's blessing falls on me and falls on you.
　Hear our cry of worship,
　Hymen, God of Marriage!

Mother, since *you* crouch and cry
Weak with tears and loud with grief

For my dear dead city
And my murdered father,
*I* have brought them – torches for my wedding-night,
Leaping light and dancing flame,
In your honour, Hymen, God of hot desire!
Queen of Darkness, send the gleam you love to lend
To the ritual blessing
Of the wedded virgin!

Dancers, come!
Loose your leaping feet,
Wild with wine of ecstasy!
Glorify my father's happy fate!
God Apollo, lead this holy ritual dance!
In your temple-court,
Under your immortal laurel-tree,
I your priestess call on you!
Hymen, mighty god,
Hymen, hear!

Come and dance,
Mother, dance with me;
Charm the Powers with lucky words,
Loudly chant your daughter's wedding-song!
Wildly whirl and turn in purest ecstasy!
Maids of Troy,
Wear your brightest gowns:
Come, and sing my wedding-song,
Hail the lover Love and Fate appoint for me!

CHORUS:
Queen Hecabe, she is out of her mind. Oh, can you not
Control her? – or she'll go dancing down to the Greek
camp!

HECABE:
Hephaestus! In our weddings you are torch-bearer;

But this torch-bearing is a hideous mockery
Of all that I once hoped for. O my child, my child!
I little thought your marriage would be thus – a slave
Taken in war, the plunder of a conquering Greek! –
Give me that torch; to carry it is sacrilege,
When you are raving. You are unchanged; all that we
Have suffered brings no healing to your distracted mind.
Women of Troy, take in these torches. Let your tears
Offer the only answer to her wedding-songs.

CASSANDRA:

Mother, wreathe a triumphal garland round my head;
I'm to be married to a king; rejoice at it!
If you find me unwilling, take me, make me go.
As sure as Apollo is a prophet, Agamemnon,
This famous king, shall find me a more fatal bride
Than Helen. I shall kill him and destroy his house
In vengeance for my brothers' and my father's death.
But let that go; my song shall not tell of the axe
Which is to fall on my neck – and not only mine;
Nor of the agonies my marriage will beget
When son shall murder mother; nor of the overthrow
Of the whole house of Atreus. Yes, there is a god
Possesses me; but this at least is truth untouched
With madness: I will show you that this Troy of ours
Was more to be envied than those Greeks. They, for the
　　sake
Of one woman and her unlawful love, unleashed
The hunt for Helen and sent ten thousand men to death.
Their sage leader, to win what he most loathed, destroyed
What most he cherished; sacrificed the joys of home,
And his own child's life, to his brother – for a woman
Who was not plundered from him, but went willingly.
　　And when they reached the shore where the Scamander
　　　　flows,
What did they die for? To thrust invasion from their borders

Or siege from their town walls? No! When a man was
      killed,
He was not wrapped and laid to rest by his wife's hands,
He had forgotten his children's faces; now he lies
In alien earth. At home, things were as bad; women
Died in widowhood; fathers sank to childless age,
Missing the sons they brought up – who will not be there
To pour loving libation on their graves. Hellas
Has much, in truth, to thank this expedition for!
And there were worse things still, horrors too shameful for
A tongue tuned to the holy muse of prophecy.

   How different for the men of Troy, whose glory it was
To die defending their own country! Those who fell
Were carried back by comrades to their homes, prepared
For burial by the hands they loved, and laid to rest
In the land that bore them; those who survived the field
      returned
Each evening to their wives and children – joys denied
To the invaders. Even in Hector's death, mother,
I can see more than sorrow; for he did not die
Till he had made himself a hero's name; and this
Came through the Greek invasion – had they stayed at home
Where would be Hector's glory? Paris too received
For his bride no nameless stranger, but the daughter
      of Zeus.

   Indeed to avoid war is a wise man's duty; yet
If war comes, then a hero's death confers as much
Fame on his city as a coward's brings infamy.
Therefore, dear Mother, you must not bewail our land,
Nor weep for my lost maidenhood. My bridal-bed
Promises death to my worst enemy and to yours.

CHORUS:
You speak of the extinction of your family
With a bland smile! And as for your prophetic muse,
You've little truth to show for all this eloquence.

TALTHYBIUS:

Were it not that Apollo has unhinged your mind,
Your ill-conceived words, aimed at our commander just
As he sets sail, would meet their proper punishment.

And yet – how strange that reputation and high place
Can prove itself no wiser than a common clown!
Here's Agamemnon, son of Atreus, supreme head
Of a great Hellenic army, picks out this mad girl
To fall in love with! Well, I'm a poor man, but I
Would not accept her as a wife on any terms.
So [to Cassandra] your insults to Argos, and your praise of
    Troy,
May go to the winds, seeing you're not in your right mind.
Follow me to the ship – our general's lovely bride!
– You too, Hecabe, when Odysseus sends for you,
Go at once. You will be servant to Penelope,
Whom all the Greeks here speak of as a virtuous woman.

CASSANDRA:

'Servant'! You hear this servant? He's a herald. What
Are heralds, then, but creatures universally loathed –
Lackeys and menials to governments and kings?
You say my mother is destined for Odysseus' home:
What then of Apollo's oracles, spelt out to me,
That she shall die here? There are other things, and worse,
Which I will not tell. Poor Odysseus! If he knew
What miseries are in store for him, my fate and Troy's
Would seem the bliss of paradise! When he has added
To these ten years at Troy another ten, at last
He shall reach home alone. (In his long wandering
He shall pass the rocky gorge where dread Charybdis lives;
The mountains haunted by the cannibal Cyclopes;
Meet with Ligurian Circe, who turns men to swine;
Be shipwrecked; tested by the lotus-food; appalled
By the sacred oxen of the Sun, whose flesh shall speak
In human tones; he shall go down alive to hell;

Escape the dark mere, and win home to Ithaca

To find his palace plagued with ills innumerable.)

  Why lament Odysseus' troubles with these flights of
    prophecy?

Lead on quickly! At the porch of death my bridegroom
    waits for me.

Great chief of the Hellenes, fleeting shadow of magnificence,

Your accursed life shall sink in darkness to an accursed
    grave;

Me too they'll fling out beside you naked, where the wild
    ravine

Roars in flood – Apollo's priestess; and the beasts will pick
    my bones.

Garlands of a god belov'd, dear ritual vestments, now
    farewell!

Go, his gifts, with the lost joys of holy feasts, my glory once;

From my still untainted body I tear you, thus! – for the
    swift winds

To receive and carry back to Apollo, lord of prophecy.

Where's the commander's ship? Which way? Come, lose
    no time, take me on board;

Watch for a wind to stir the sails. The prisoner you will
    bring to Greece

Comes as one of three Avengers. – Mother, no more tears;
    farewell!

O my brothers, deep in this dear earth of Troy; my father
    too,

Priam, you whose blood we all inherit! You will not be
    long

Waiting for me. I will come triumphant to the house of
    Death,

When I have brought to ruin the sons of Atreus, who
    destroyed us all.

  CASSANDRA *goes out with* TALTHYBIUS. HECABE
*collapses to the ground.*

CHORUS:

Look, friends! Our mistress has collapsed without a word.
We should look after her, not leave her lying there
Stretched out. She is old and weak; come, help her, lift her
      up.

HECABE:

Let me lie. There's no comfort in your comforting.
Here in the dust pain such as mine belongs – today's,
Yesterday's, and tomorrow's pain. O gods! – The gods,
I know, are treacherous allies; yet, when misery
Drives to despair, it seems in some way suitable
To call on gods. First, then, I'll sing past happiness;
This tale will edge the piteousness of present grief.

   I was a princess born; my husband was a king.
The sons I bore were heroes to a man, not cast
In the common mould, but manliest of the Phrygian race;
No mother in Troy, in Hellas, or in all Asia,
Could ever boast such sons. I saw them one by one
Fall to Greek spears. I cut locks of my hair to lay
On their still graves. The father of them all, Priam,
Is gone. No message taught me to weep seemly tears;
Myself, with these same eyes, I saw him hacked to death
At his own altar, and his city laid in dust.
My virgin daughters, whom I cherished as choice gifts
For husbands worthy of them, were torn from my arms,
Given to our enemies. There is no hope that they
Ever again will see their mother, nor I them.
Now comes the last, the crowning agony; that I
In my old age shall go to Hellas as a slave.
They will lay on me tasks to humble my grey head –
Answering the door, or keeping keys, or cooking food –
I, who bore Hector! I shall lay my shrivelled sides
To rest, not in a royal bed, but on the floor;
And wear thin, faded rags to match my skin and mock
My royalty. O misery! Through one woman's love,

What pains have racked me, what despair still waits for me!
  Dear child, Cassandra, you who shared the mysteries
Of gods, what outrage cancels your virginity!
And you, Polyxena, child of sorrow, where are you?
Of all my children, not one daughter, not one son
Is left to help me. Then why lift me up? What hope
Is there? The soft proud days of Troy are past; lead me
To find my hard slave's pallet and my pillow of stones,
And die under the lash of tears. Good fortune means
Nothing; call no man happy till the day he dies.

CHORUS:
Come, Muse, in tears begin,
And sing strange dirges over Ilion's grave.
Now loud and clear the story shall be told
Of that wheeled horse that brought the Argives in,
Made Troy a ruin, me a slave.

On towering legs, bridled with gold,
Stuffed with swords that rang to the sky,
They left it near our city's gate.
Up to the Trojan Rock we rushed, and stood
Shouting, 'The war is over! Come,
Bring in the wooden horse for an offering
To the Daughter of Zeus, Pallas, Lady of Troy!'
Then what girl would stay behind?
When even the old men left their chairs,
And with laughing and singing all laid hold
Of that hidden death that had marked them down.

The nation of Troy streamed from the town,
And Priam himself went with them,
To honour the Virgin Pallas,
Driver of Heaven's immortal horses, and offer to her
This gleaming monster of mountain pine
That hid the waiting swords of Greece.
Hauling on cables of flaxen twine

Like a ship's dark hulk they drew it along
And up the hill to the Temple rising white;
And placed their gift on the holy floor of Pallas,
Where the slaughter of Troy began.

Over their happy weariness fell the shadow of night.
Then Libyan flutes rang out,
And the old tunes were played,
And our hearts were joined in singing
And in music of dancing feet;
Until through the darkened palace
One flare still left alight
Flickered on sleeping faces its dim gleam of fire.
I was at home that night,
Joining in songs and dances
To honour the Maiden Goddess,
Artemis of the Mountains;
When – over the streets of the central city
A shriek of death rose like a grip at the throat;
And trembling children clutched at their mothers' skirts;
And War went forth from his secret lair;
And the work of the virgin Pallas was accomplished.

Men sank in blood while their dead hands clasped the altar;
The head half-raised from the pillow
Defenceless rolled from the severed neck;
And beside the dead the victor's lust
Planted the seed of a son for Hellas,
Watered with tears of Troy's despair.

ANDROMACHE *approaches, drawn in a chariot by Greek
soldiers. She holds* ASTYANAX *on her lap.*

CHORUS:
Hecabe, see! Andromache is coming,
Drawn in a Greek chariot, beating her breast;
And Hector's son Astyanax is with her.
Where are they taking you, sad Andromache,

And beside you Hector's sword and armour of bronze,
And other spoils of Troy, which Achilles' son
Shall dedicate in distant temples of Thessaly?

ANDROMACHE: The Achaeans are carrying home their
property.

HECABE: O Zeus, have pity!

ANDROMACHE:           That prayer is mine by right –

HECABE: O Zeus!

ANDROMACHE: – bought with my husband's blood, my tears.

HECABE: Children! –

ANDROMACHE: No more your children: all that is ended.

HECABE: Once we were happy, and Troy – all that is ended.

ANDROMACHE: Ended.

HECABE:           My noble children!

ANDROMACHE:                     They are gone.

HECABE: Gone; and my home, my lovely city –

ANDROMACHE:                     Gone!

HECABE: Now smoke and ashes!

ANDROMACHE:           Hector, my own husband –

HECABE: Hector is with the dead. Hector, my son!
          My daughter!

ANDROMACHE: Hector, when will you come to help me?

HECABE: Priam, aged king of my princely sons,
          Priam, fallen a sport for your enemies,
          Soothe my head on the pillow of death!

ANDROMACHE: All the love we have lost!

HECABE:                     The grief we have gained!

ANDROMACHE: All that we knew, destroyed!

HECABE:                     All anguish doubled!

ANDROMACHE:
The gods have hated us, since the day when Paris
Was spared at his birth, to live and destroy his country
For the sake of accursed Helen. Now vultures wheel,
Waiting to tear the dead stretched at the feet
Of Pallas, while we – are slaves and must look on.

HECABE:

O city, dead, deserted, I weep for you.
Home where my babes were born, this is your end:
Who would not weep? City lost, children lost,
All lost! Was there ever heard such chorus of pain?
When were such tears shed for a murdered house?
Can even the dead see this, and forget to weep?

CHORUS:

In times of sorrow it is a comfort to lament,
To shed tears, and find music that will voice our grief.

ANDROMACHE:

Do you see this armour? It is your son Hector's. He
With this spear killed more Greeks than any other
    man.

HECABE:

I see how the high gods dispose this world; I see
The mean exalted to the sky, the great brought low.

ANDROMACHE:

I and my son are carried off as spoils of war;
Royalty is enslaved, the world turned upside down.

HECABE:

It's a strange thing to meet the irresistible.
Just now I saw Cassandra dragged away by force.

ANDROMACHE:

Poor child, poor girl! – to meet a second Aias like
The first. But listen: there's more bitterness for you.

HECABE:

There is always more; my suffering has no limit, none;
And each new misery outdoes what went before.

ANDROMACHE:

Polyxena is dead. They sacrificed her at
Achilles' tomb – an offering to a lifeless corpse.

HECABE:

Oh, no! Oh, horror! That was what Talthybius meant
By his evasive answers. It was plain enough.

ANDROMACHE:

I saw her there myself. I left the chariot,
Wrapped a robe round her body, and paid my due of
   tears.

HECABE:

What sacrilegious murder! Oh, my child, my child
Polyxena! How terrible to die like this!

ANDROMACHE:

It is over now. Yes, it was terrible; and yet,
Being dead, she is more fortunate than I who live.

HECABE:

Not so, my daughter; death and life are not the same.
Death is extinction; but in life there is still hope.

ANDROMACHE:

Hecabe! – you are my mother, as you are hers – let me
Comfort your heart with welcome truth. I believe this:
To be dead is the same as never to have been born,
And better far than living on in wretchedness.
The dead feel nothing; evil then can cause no pain.
But one who falls from happiness to unhappiness
Wanders bewildered in a strange and hostile world.
For Polyxena it is as though she had not been born;
In death she recalls none of her past sufferings.
For me it is different. I made high repute my aim,
Achieved it, and now forfeit all that I achieved.
As Hector's wife I strictly set myself to attain
All womanly perfections, every sober grace.
First, since a woman, however high her reputation,
Draws slander on herself by being seen abroad,
I renounced restlessness and stayed in my own house;
Refused to open my door to the fashionable chat
Of other wives. Having by nature a sound mind
To school me, I was sufficient to myself. I kept
Before my husband a quiet tongue, a modest eye.
I knew in what matters it was for me to rule,

And where in turn I should yield him authority.

　　It seems report of me reached the Greek camp; and this
Was my undoing. When I was taken, Achilles' son
Asked for me as his wife. So I shall live a slave
In the house of the very man who struck my husband dead.
If I put from me my dear Hector's memory,
And accept my new husband with an open heart,
I prove a traitor to the dead; but if I hate
This man, I shall be hateful to my own master.
And yet they say one night dispels antipathy
To any man's embrace! How I despise the woman
Who in a strange bed turns against the man she knew
And loves another! Even a horse, when separated
From its stable-companion, will not pull its weight;
And beasts are in their nature far inferior
To man, wanting both voice and rational discourse.

　　Dear Hector, you had all I looked for in a man,
All in abundance – wisdom, birth, wealth, manliness!
You took me untouched from my father's house to be
Your wife; my maiden flesh was first and only yours.
Now you are dead; and I, a prize of war, must sail
To slavery in Hellas. Hecabe, you weep
For dead Polyxena: is not her fate less hard
Than what I have to bear? For me there is not even
The common refuge, hope. I cannot cheat myself
With sweet delusions of some future happiness.

CHORUS:
　Your suffering is the same as ours; your bitter words
　Teach us to sound the depths of our own misery.

HECABE:
　At sea, when sailors meet rough weather, the whole crew
　Works with good heart to outlive danger. One man stands
　By the helm, another trims the sail, while a third keeps
　The hull from filling; though I was never in a ship,
　I have seen pictures and heard many talk of it.

But when the sea boils with an overwhelming surge,
Then they give in to Fate, and let the racing waves
Hurl them along at will. So I am vanquished by
This storm the gods have sent; my troubles multiply
And leave me speechless with despair. But, O my dear
Daughter, cease mourning now for Hector; all your tears
Cannot help him. And honour your new master; win
His love as a husband by your own sweetness and worth.
The favour so gained will bring joy to all your friends,
And – who knows? – you may yet bring up our Hector's
      son
To light new hope for Troy; your sons, one day, may yet
Found a new Ilion, and our city live again.

    But look – I see the Achaean herald coming back.
Word grows from word; why is he here? He has instructions
To tell us something new that they've decided on.

*Enter* TALTHYBIUS.

TALTHYBIUS:
Andromache, now widow of Troy's once greatest man,
Do not hate me. I speak these words reluctantly.
The Greeks and their two generals sent me to convey –

ANDROMACHE: Your words sound heavy with foreboding.
What is it?

TALTHYBIUS: Their joint decision, that your son – how can
I say it?

ANDROMACHE: We are assigned to different masters – is it
this?

TALTHYBIUS: No; no Achaean will ever be your son's
master.

ANDROMACHE: What? Must he stay here, the sole remnant
of our city?

TALTHYBIUS: My news is bad. I don't know how to find
the words.

ANDROMACHE: At least you show some scruple, if you bring
no joy.

TALTHYBIUS: Then know the worst: the Greeks are going
to kill your son.

ANDROMACHE: Oh, no, no! This is worse than what they
do to me.

TALTHYBIUS: Odysseus in a full assembly made his point –

ANDROMACHE: But this is horrible beyond all measure! Oh!

TALTHYBIUS: That such a great man's son must not be
allowed to live –

ANDROMACHE: By such a sentence may his own son be
condemned!

TALTHYBIUS:
But should be thrown down from the battlements of Troy.
Now accept this decision, and be sensible.
Don't cling to him, or tell yourself you have some strength,
When you have none; but bear what must be like a queen.
You have no possible source of help. See for yourself:
Your city is destroyed, your husband dead; you are
A prisoner. Shall we match our strength against one woman?
We can. I hope, therefore, you will not feel inclined
To struggle, or attempt anything unseemly, or
Likely to cause resentment. This too: don't call down
Curses upon the Greeks. If you say anything
To make the army angry, this child will receive
No mourning rites, no burial. If you are quiet,
And in a proper spirit accept what comes to you,
You will not have to leave his body unburied, and
You'll find the Achaeans more considerate to yourself.

ANDROMACHE:
O darling child, prized at too great a worth to live!
You die, at enemy hands, and leave me desolate.
Your noble father's greatness, which to other men
Brought hope and life and victory, will cost you your death.
For you his courage proved a fatal heritage.
O marriage-bed, which welcomed me as Hector's bride –
Ill-fated happiness! I thought then my son would be

King over Asia's teeming multitudes; not die
By a Greek ritual of murder. – Little one,
You are crying. Do you understand? You tug my dress,
Cling to my fingers, nestling like a bird under
It's mother's wing. No Hector will come now to save
Your life, rise from the grave gripping his famous spear;
No army of your father's family, no charge
Of Phrygian fighters. You must leap from that sickening
Height, and fall, and break your neck, and yield your
    breath,
With none to pity you. Dear child, so young in my arms,
So precious! O the sweet smell of your skin! When you
Were newly born I wrapped you up, gave you my breast,
Tended you day and night, worn out with weariness –
For nothing, all for nothing! Say good-bye to me
Once more, for the last time of all. Come close to me,
Wind your arms round my neck, and put your lips to mine.
    Hellenes! Inventors of barbaric cruelties!
What has he done? Why will you kill this child? – Helen,
Tyndareos' daughter! You were never daughter of Zeus!
You had many fathers; the Avenging Curse was one,
Hate was the next, then Murder, Death, and every plague
That this earth breeds. I'll swear Zeus never fathered you
To fasten death on tens of thousands east and west!
My curse on you! The beauty of your glance has brought
This rich and noble country to a shameful end.
Take him, you robbers, throw him, carry out your decree!
Feast on his flesh! The great gods are destroying us;
I am powerless to save my son from death. Hide me,
Fling my miserable body into your ship! I go
To my princely marriage, and leave behind me my dead
    child.
CHORUS:
O miserable Troy, you have lost ten thousand dead
All for one woman's sake and her accursed love!

TALTHYBIUS:

　　Come, child; I pity your mother, but time is up.
　　　　No more embracing now.
　　You must climb to the topmost fringe of your father's
　　　　towers,
　　Where the sentence says you must leave your life behind.
　　　　Take him. – A job like this
　　Is fit for a man without feeling or decency;
　　　　I'm not half brutal enough.

TALTHYBIUS *and his men go out with* ASTYANAX,
*followed by* ANDROMACHE.


HECABE:

　　O little child, son of my dear lost son,
　　Your life is ravished from us by murderers.
　　What will become of us? What can I do for you?
　　Only to beat the head and bruise the breast –
　　　　This we can give; no more.
　　Lost city, lost child: what climax of suffering
　　　　Lacks now? Have we not reached
　　　　In a headlong plunge the abyss of pain?


CHORUS:

　　Far off in the island of Salamis, whose　　　　[*Strophe* 1
　　　　bee-haunted slopes
　　Look out over the circling surf to that holy rock
　　Where Athene first displayed the dark-green shoot of an
　　　　olive
　　To anoint and bless with a heavenly crown the city of
　　　　Athens, –
　　　　In Salamis lived King Telamon,
　　Who once, as ally and friend of the mighty archer Heracles,
　　　　Came with an army to Ilion,
　　Came long ago to plunder and burn our city of Ilion.

That was the former time, when Heracles,    [*Antistrophe* 1
   enraged
For loss of the just reward our king refused him, landed
The flower of Grecian youth on the lovely banks of Simois,
Eased his oars from the sea, and fastened his stern-cables.
   Then from the ship he brought his bow,
Shaped for the skill of his hand, bent for Laomedon's blood;
And he split with fire's red blast the stones that Apollo squared,
   And laid in the dust our city's life.
So twice the reeking sword has pierced the heart of Troy,
   Twice her towers have crashed in thunder.

Why, then, Ganymede, son of Laomedon,    [*Strophe* 2
You who walk delicately among golden wine-cups
Pouring out wine for Zeus, your exalted office
Brought little help to your boyhood's home!
Look! The land of your birth is a blazing heap!
Listen! What cry comes from the shore?
Seagulls robbed of their young?
No! Wives for their husbands, mothers for sons,
Daughters for aged mothers weep and howl!

   The sandy course you ran and wrestled on,
   The dewy fountains where you bathed, are gone.
   Still near the heavenly throne the same fresh grace
   Lights the untroubled beauty of your face;
     But Troy, where you began,
     Greeks have stamped out to the last man.

Love once came to the house of Laomedon,    [*Antistrophe* 2
Beguiling gods to favour the royal family,
Linking Troy with Olympus in marriage-bonds,
Exalting Troy to the height of Heaven.
Had Zeus, for Ganymede's sake – No! no reproach!
But how could Dawn, of the gleaming wing,

Dawn, that the whole world loves,
How could *she* smile down on us dying, dying,
Rise on our devastated streets, and smile?


For this land gave her what she held most dear,
Our royal prince, Tithonus, who begot
Her sons, whom in her golden chariot
She bore off heavenward through the starry sphere.
He was Troy's hope; but he
And all Troy's hopes from Heaven were vanity.
*Enter* MENELAUS, *with soldiers.*

MENELAUS:
How gloriously the sun shines on this happy day!
Today I shall lay hands on Helen my wife. I am
Menelaus, the man who has endured this ten years' toil –
With the help of the Greek army. Yes, I came to Troy
Not so much for her sake as people think; but rather
To find the man who entered my house as a guest,
Deceived me, and stole my wife. That man – the gods be
    praised –
Has paid for it; so has his country, laid in ruin
By the Greek army. And I am here now to fetch home
The Spartan woman, once my wife – even to speak
Her name I find distasteful. She is in this building,
Held prisoner with all the women taken in Troy.
The men whose years of fighting captured her at last
Gave her to me to kill, or not kill, if I chose
Instead to take her back to Argive territory.
And I've decided not to carry out sentence here
But take her back to Hellas, and there see that she
Pays with her blood for all my friends who died at Troy.
[*To the soldiers*] What are you waiting for? Get in and fetch
    her here,
Drag her out by the hair – bloodthirsty murderess!
Then all we need is a fair wind, and we'll have her home.

HECABE:

O thou, this earth's upholder, throned above the earth,
Great Zeus, whoever thou art, mysterious and unknown,
Be thou human intelligence, or natural law,
I praise thee! For thou movest on a noiseless path
And guidest all the affairs of men to their just end.

MENELAUS:

That's a new kind of prayer to heaven. What does it mean?

HECABE:

I applaud you, Menelaus, if you will kill your wife;
But avoid seeing her, or she will take prisoner
Your tender heart. She captures men's eyes, destroys cities,
Burns houses to the ground, so potent are her spells.
I know her, so do you, and all who have suffered know.

HELEN *enters, the soldiers following her.*

HELEN:

Menelaus, is this beginning meant to frighten me?
Your men seized me and hurried me out here by force.
I think I know you hate me; but I wish to ask,
What sentence have the Greeks, and you, passed on my life?

MENELAUS:

There was no question in your case. The whole army
Of Greece gave you to me, whom you had wronged, to
   kill.

HELEN:

Have I permission to reply to that sentence
And plead that it would be unjust to take my life?

MENELAUS:

I've come to kill you, not to bandy arguments.

HECABE:

Let her speak, Menelaus; she must not die without
A hearing. And let *me* undertake in turn to speak
Against her. Of the mischief that she made in Troy
You know nothing. The whole indictment, once complete,
Will ensure her death; there can be no chance of escape.

MENELAUS:

It is a favour, and will take time; but if she wants
To defend herself, she may. I grant this, let her note,
For your sake, not from any indulgence towards her.

HELEN:

Perhaps, since you regard me as your enemy,
You will not answer, whether I speak well or ill.
But I will guess what charges you would level at me,
And, since I too have things I would accuse you of,
I will reply by weighing the one against the other.

　　Hecabe here produced the first cause of our troubles
When she bore Paris. Secondly, this city, and I,
Were doomed by Priam, when he ignored the warning
　　　given
By a dream of firebrands, and refused to kill his child.
What followed then? Listen, I'll tell you. Paris was
Made judge between three goddesses. Athene's bribe
Was this: that he should lead the Phrygians to war
And destroy Hellas. Hera promised him a throne
Bestriding Asia and Europe, if he placed her first.
Aphrodite, with extravagant praise of my beauty,
Promised him that, if he judged her the loveliest,
I should be his. What next? See how the story goes.
Aphrodite won; and from my marriage Hellas gained
This benefit: you today are neither overwhelmed
By Asian armies, nor ruled by an Asian king.
The gain for Hellas was for me disastrous loss;
Sold for my beauty, I endure vile calumny
From those who should have placed a crown upon my
　　　head.
　　You will say that I have not yet answered the main
　　　point –
How I came to set forth in secret from your house.
It was a goddess of invincible power who came
With Hecabe's evil genius, Paris (call him by

That name, or Alexander, as you please); and you,
To your shame, sailed off to Crete and left him in your
    house.
    My next question I ask myself rather than you.
What happened in my heart, to make me leave my home
And my own land, to follow where a stranger led?
Rail at the goddess; be more resolute than Zeus,
Who holds power over all other divinities
But is himself the slave of love. Show Aphrodite
Your indignation; me, pardon and sympathy.
    There is a further charge you may feel justified
In urging against me. When Paris was in his grave,
And no god was concerned to find me a husband – then,
You will say, I ought to have left Troy and made my way
To the Argive ships. I tried to do this. The gate-warders,
The sentries on the city walls, could testify
That more than once they found me slipping secretly
Down from the battlements by a rope. Then Deiphobus,
Defying the whole city's wish, took me by force
And kept me as his wife. Can you still think it just
To kill me? Would it not be more just to comfort me?
Not only was this marriage forced upon me, but
What ought to have been my crown of glory, my own
    person,
Condemned my life to this harsh bondage. Do you aspire
To govern gods? To wish this is mere foolishness.

CHORUS:
Now, Queen, speak for your children and your
    fatherland.
Demolish this persuasiveness. Plausible speech
Combined with such immorality is sinister.

HECABE:
To begin, then, I will vindicate the goddesses,
And show how she has slandered them. I don't believe
Gods to be capable of such folly, as that Hera

Should bargain away Argos to barbarians,
Or virgin Pallas see her Athens subjected
To Troy. Why should they indulge in such frivolity
As travelling to Mount Ida for a beauty-match?
What reason could the goddess Hera have for being
So anxious about beauty? Did she want to get
A husband of higher rank than Zeus? Or was Athene,
Who begged her father for perpetual maidenhood,
Disdaining love – now husband-hunting among the gods?
To cloak your own guilt, you dress up the gods as fools;
But only fools would listen to you. And Aphrodite,
You say – what could be more absurd? – went with my
    son
To Menelaus' palace! Could she not have brought
You, and your town of Amyclae, from Peloponnese
To Ilion, without stirring from her seat in heaven?

    No; Paris was an extremely handsome man – one look,
And your appetite became your Aphrodite. Why,
Men's lawless lusts are all called love – it's a confusion
Easily made. You saw him in his gorgeous robes
Glittering with oriental gold; and you went mad.
At home your style was cramped by insufficient means;
Once clear of Sparta – Troy would be a perpetual
Fountain flowing with gold, you hoped, for you to spend.
The palace of Menelaus was too confined a sphere
To give full scope to your luxurious insolence.

    Well now, you say my son abducted you by force.
What Spartan noble heard you call for help? What sort
Of outcry did you raise? Both Castor and his twin
Were there – they had not yet been placed among the
    stars.
Then, when you came to Troy, the Argives on your track,
And spears and shields were locked in battle, when you
    heard
Of a Greek victory, at once you praised Menelaus,

To remind my son of his great rival and gall his heart;
When Troy gained ground, you had no use for Menelaus.
You watched events; became a practised follower
Of fortune; duty and loyalty were not your concern.
    And then – this tale of slipping away by ropes let down
From the battlements, of being kept here against your
        will!
I'd like to ask, when were you found fitting a noose
To your neck, or sharpening a dagger? That was the
        obvious course
For a woman of breeding, if she pined for her first
        husband.
In fact I urged you constantly to get out of Troy;
My sons, I told you, could find other women to love.
'Go on,' I said, 'I'll help you escape to the Greek ships,
And end the war for them as well as for us.' But no;
The proposal did not please you; for in Paris's house
You could queen it haughtily; you liked to see Phrygians
Kneeling before you; this flattered your pride. And now,
To crown all, you have come out here beautifully
        dressed,
You have the loathsome impudence to lift your eyes
To the same sky as your husband! If you felt some sense
Of what you have been guilty of in the past, you would
Have come crawling and shivering, your dress in rags,
Your hair clipped to the scalp, to show some penitence.
    Menelaus, this is my last word: be worthy of
Yourself, and set the crown on Hellas' victory.
Kill Helen, and establish in all lands this law,
That every wife unfaithful to her husband dies.

CHORUS:
    Punish your wife, Menelaus, in a manner worthy
    Both of the house of Atreus, and of your ancestors;
    Make Greece, which calls you womanish, keep silence; be
    A pattern of noble vengeance on your enemies.

MENELAUS:

Your verdict tallies with my own exactly: she
Left my house willingly for a lover's bed. Her talk
Of Aphrodite is mere invention and pretence. –
Get out of my sight! Death by stoning is too short
A penance for the long-drawn sufferings of the Greeks;
But it will teach you not to bring disgrace on me.

HELEN [*kneeling*]:

No, no, I beg of you! The gods sent this on me;
Don't take my life for their misdoing, but forgive!

HECABE [*also kneeling*]:

Think of your fellow-soldiers whom this woman killed.
I beg you not to fail them, and their children, now.

MENELAUS:

Say no more, Hecabe; I pay no heed to her.
She shall sail back to Sparta. Men, put her on board.

HECABE: Menelaus, let her not sail on the same ship with you!

MENELAUS: And why not? Is she heavier than she used to be?

HECABE: A lover once, a lover always!

MENELAUS:                                That depends
On the ensuing attitude of the person loved.
However, since you wish it, she shall not set foot
On my own ship; there may be truth in what you say.
Once back in Sparta, shameful death will fittingly
Reward her shameful life, and thus commend all women
To chastity – no easy matter; but at least
Her end will inspire terror in their lecherous hearts,
Even if their hatred burns more deadly than before.

MENELAUS *goes, the soldiers leading* HELEN *before him*.

CHORUS:

So, Zeus, our God, you have forsaken us;          [*Strophe* 1
Given to Troy's enemies temple and ritual,
Smoke of rich spices, altar and incense-flame,
The holy Rock of Pergamus,
And Ida – dear remembered name –

Where steep snow-swollen rivers foam and fall
Through ivied forest-glades, past that bare height,
Earth's frontier, hushed with breath of gods, that glows
With dawn's first shaft of light.

Zeus, God, farewell! Now with your going　　　[*Antistrophe* 1
　goes
Music of prayer, sweet singing, mystic nights
Of darkness and of vision, the dear forms
Of golden gods we knew,
The Trojan Twelve, the full-moon festal rites.
Therefore we ask, Monarch of all that lives,
Firm in your heavenly throne,
While the destroying Fury gives
Our homes to ashes and our flesh to worms –
We ask, and ask: What does this mean to You?

Dearest husband, dear lost ghost,　　　　　　[*Strophe* 2
　Seas and worlds divide our ways:
　　You, unwashed, unburied,
　　Roam the shadowy spaces,
I to Argos wing the sea with restless oars,
　To the Cyclops' walls of stone
Rising heaven-high from green turf where horses graze.
　　At Troy's gates our children
　　Cling and cry by hundreds,
Calling, wailing, 'Mother, they are taking me
　　From you! See their dark ships,
　　Oars and rowers ready!
　Will our home be holy Salamis,
　Or the peak between two seas
　　Where the gate of Isthmus
　　Guards the Spartan stronghold?'

And when Menelaus' ship　　　　　　　　[*Antistrophe* 2
In mid-ocean rides and runs

May there fall a furious
Thunderbolt from heaven,
Blaze amidships, burn his oars and break his keel!
Fall while I, poor prisoner, sail,
Lost in weeping, farther every hour from home;
Fall while Helen gazes
In her golden mirror
Aping girlhood! May she never come safe home
To the streets of Sparta
And the Brazen Temple!
She whose lightness shamed the pride of Greece,
Fouled with blood and tears of Troy
The once pure and lovely
Waters of Simois!


Look, oh, look, you weeping wives of Troy!
Stroke on stroke
Scars our bleeding land!
See, the dead Astyanax,
Whom the Greeks
Murdered without mercy,
Flung from Troy's high towers!

*Enter* TALTHYBIUS *with the body of* ASTYANAX *carried on*
HECTOR'S *shield.*

TALTHYBIUS:
Hecabe, one ship of Neoptolemus still rides
At anchor, ready to set sail for Thessaly
With the remainder of the spoils assigned to him.
Neoptolemus himself has gone; disturbing news
Reached him that Peleus, his grandfather, had been driven
Out of the country by Acastus, Peleas' son.
He had no wish to linger; and on hearing this
He at once set sail, and took with him Andromache.
She, as the ship left harbour, wailed aloud for Troy
And called on Hector's grave. She brought tears to my eyes.

She implored Neoptolemus that this child, your grandson,
Who was flung from the city walls and gave up his life,
Might receive burial; asking that this bronze-ribbed
    shield,
The terror of the Achaeans, which his father carried
To fence his body in battle, be not sent away
To Peleus' palace, to hang in that same chamber where
Andromache his mother, now her captor's bride,
Would see it to her sorrow; but that it should serve
This child in place of a coffin of cedar-wood or stone.
She wished him to be given into your care, to dress
And adorn his body, as time and your constraint allows;
Since she herself is far away, and her master's haste
Prevented her from staying to give him burial.

So now, as soon as you have made him ready, we
Will wrap him in a mound of earth, and then hoist sail;
But do what you have been asked as quickly as possible.
One sad task I have saved you: as we came along
By the Scamander, I bathed him in the running stream
And cleaned his wounds. I am going now to break the
    ground
For a grave. If only you and I both do our best
To waste no time, we'll soon be under way for home.

TALTHYBIUS *goes. The soldiers bearing* ASTYANAX *obey*
  HECABE'S *direction to lay the shield on the ground; then*
                    *follow him out.*

HECABE:
Bring the great rounded shield of Hector; lay it here –
A sight which should be welcome, but now stabs my eyes.
  You Achaeans are fine fighters; but where is your
    pride?
Did you so dread this young boy that you must invent
A new death for him? Were you afraid that he one day
Would raise Troy from the dust? When Hector held the
    field,

With thousands fighting at his side, even then we fell
Before your swords; today, with Troy a ruined heap,
And every Trojan dead, did you so shake with fear
Before this babe? Are you not cowards? Fear is bad;
But fear lacking all ground or reason is far worse.

   O dearest child, there is deep bitterness in your death.
If you had fallen in battle for your city, knowing
Your manhood's strength, love's sweetness, and the
    godlike pride
Of royalty, then – if blessing can be in this world –
You would be blessed. But, though you saw and
    recognized
This wealth of life which was your heritage, my son,
You had no use of it; and now you know it not.

   Poor little head, your soft curls were a garden where
Your mother planted kisses; oh, how cruelly they
Were shorn by your own city's god-built bastions!
Now through the shattered skull the blood smiles,
    tempting me
To unseemly words. Your little hands – how like your
    father's!
But when I lift them they hang limp. Dear, lifeless lips,
You made me a promise once, nestled against my dress:
'Grandmother, when you die,' you said, 'I will cut off
A long curl of my hair for you, and bring my friends
With me to grace your tomb with gifts and holy words.'
You broke your promise, son; instead, I bury you;
I, an old, homeless, childless woman, bury you.
All my fond kisses, anxious care, and wakeful nights –
All end in this. What would a poet write for you
As epitaph? 'This child the Argives killed because
They feared him.' An inscription to make Hellas blush.

   Now, though you lose your father's heritage, you shall
    have
His broad, bronze-fronted shield to make your earthy bed.

Dear shield! You guarded Hector's splendid arm, as he
Courageously kept you; but you have lost him now.
Here on your handgrip is the dear print of his palm;
Here, where his beard pressed on your round rim, ran
    the sweat
Which in the heat of battle flowed from Hector's brow.
[*To the* CHORUS] Come, bring whatever robes our
    poverty can find
To drape his body. Rigorous Fate does not allow
The handsome gift; from what I have, these shall be
    yours.
  The man who finds his own wealth and security
A cause for pleasure, is a fool. Those forces which
Control our fortunes are as unpredictable
As capering idiots. Happiness does not exist.

CHORUS:
See, we have brought robes taken from our Trojan dead;
Wrap him in these, to dignify his burial.

HECABE:
Dear child, your father's mother lays on you these gifts;
Not as a prize for chariot-race or archery –
In honouring such things Phrygians use due restraint;
But these gifts are the remnant of what once was yours,
Now robbed from you by Helen, whom the gods abhor,
Who took your life, and laid your father's house in dust.

CHORUS:   Yesterday so great a prince;
          Now a sight to break my heart!

HECABE:
I fasten on you the Phrygian splendour of this robe
You should have put on for your wedding, to lead home
The royalest bride in Asia. And you, Hector's shield,
Triumphant once, mother of many victories,
Receive your crown – an honour far more richly earned
Than any the cunning coward Odysseus' arms could win.
Earth shall receive you, the undying, with the dead.

CHORUS:
  Earth shall receive you, child, with anguish and tears.
  Mother, intone the dirge for the dead.
HECABE:                                    Farewell!
CHORUS: Farewell, dead by the curse of heaven!
HECABE:                                    Farewell!
  Here's linen to close up your wounds. This wound I'll
      heal,
  And this, and this. Pitiful healer, having skill,
  But not the effect of healing! All your other hurts
  Your father's hands shall care for in the home of death.
CHORUS:   Beat the breast and bruise the head,
              Let the hand be merciless!
HECABE: O dearest friends, I see the cold abyss of truth.
CHORUS:      Take courage, Hecabe, speak;
              What will you say to us?
HECABE:
  All through these years the gods had but one end in
      mind,
  No other destiny than this for me, and Troy –
  The one city they chose for their especial hate.
  Our sacrifices and our prayers have all been vain.
  Yet, had not heaven cast down our greatness and
      engulfed
  All in the earth's depth, Troy would be a name
      unknown,
  Our agony unrecorded, and those songs unsung
  Which we shall give to poets of a future age.
[*Two* SOLDIERS *of* TALTHYBIUS *appear;* HECABE *turns to
    them.*] Go now and lay him in his pitiful grave. He has
His burial robe and garland; they are all he needs.
A costly funeral proclaims the self-conceit
Of the living; I think the dead care little for such things.
              *The* SOLDIERS *carry* ASTYANAX *away.*

CHORUS:
  Weep for Andromache – all her strong hopes broken
  With this broken body! And weep for him
  Whose royal birth the world envied and honoured,
  Whose death will be told with terror. –

                              Look! Who are they,
  There on the city heights, waving their arms
  With torches ablaze? What is to happen now?

                    *Enter* TALTHYBIUS, *attended.*

TALTHYBIUS [*shouting*]:
  You officers appointed to burn Priam's town,
  Why are those torches idle in your hands? Use them!
  Let flame swallow this rubble that was Ilion;
  Our work's over; so good-bye Troy, and hoist for home!
  [*To the* CHORUS] The same order concerns you too; as
        soon as you hear
  A fanfare on the trumpets from the generals' tents,
  Get straight down to the ships, ready to sail. – Hecabe,
  I am sorry for you; but you must go with these men.
  They've come for you from Odysseus, who is your
        master now.

HECABE:
  My hour has come. The gods have pity on me! This is
  My last ordeal, to sail away and see Troy fall
  In flames. Up, aged feet; if you can climb so far,
  I will stand here and bid farewell to my poor city.

                  [*She climbs on to a step.*]

  Troy! You who once among the Asian cities drew
  The breath of pride, your glorious name shall vanish
        now.
  They are burning you. They are carrying me away, a
        slave.
  Gods! Gods! Where are you? – Why should I clamour
        to the gods?
  We called on them before, and not one heard us call.

Now! Into the fire! There is a royal way to die –
Wrapped in the flame that swallows my beloved city!
[*She makes towards the flames, but is seized by the soldiers.*]

TALTHYBIUS:

Poor creature! You are out of your mind with suffering.
– You men, take her to the ships; be watchful. She belongs
To Odysseus; she's his prize, and he must have her safe.

HECABE [*sobbing violently*]:

Zeus, our maker, begetter, Lord of our land!
We are Dardanus' children! See: is our torment just?

CHORUS:

He sees, and the flames burn on. The Mother of Cities
Is now no city; Troy is no longer Troy.

HECABE:

Troy is a beacon – look! On the hill every house is
    blazing;
Along the crest of the ramparts, over the roofs,
The fire rushes and roars in the wake of the spear!

CHORUS:

Troy in her fearful fall has faded, vanished
At the breath of War, as smoke at the beating of wings!

HECABE [*kneeling and gazing at the ground*]:

Listen, Phrygian earth that nursed my children!    [*Strophe*
Listen, my sons! You know your mother's voice.

CHORUS:

No more prayers to the gods:
Call the dead in a ghostly chant!

HECABE:

I call the dead, I who am near to death,
Stretched on the soil, my hands beating the ground.

CHORUS [*kneeling with her*]:

            We will kneel at your side,
            Call on our dear lost dead below.

HECABE:    Listen, souls of the dead!

CHORUS:                            Tell them our torment!

HECABE: We are driven like cattle far from home,
         Away to a house of slavery!
            Dead Priam, do you hear,
            Unburied and unwept?
         No, your ghost knows nothing of my agony.
CHORUS:            Though he died
            By unholy murder,
               Holy Death
            Darkly closed his eyes.

HECABE:
   Listen, temples of gods, beloved city,        [Antistrophe
   Ravaged with flame, flowing with guiltless blood!
CHORUS:
      Soon you will fall, and lie
      With the earth you loved, and none shall name you!
HECABE:
   Dust mingled with smoke spreads wings to the sky,
   I can see nothing, the world is blotted out!
CHORUS: Earth and her name are nothing;
            All has vanished, and Troy is nothing!
               *A distant crash is heard.*
HECABE: Listen, friends – did you hear?
CHORUS:                      Pergamus fell!
HECABE:  Reverberations rock the walls,
            Each ruin reels and sinks engulfed!
               *A fanfare of trumpets.*
            Come, trembling aged feet,
            You must not fail me now.
      There your way lies: forward into slavery!
CHORUS:         Farewell, Troy!
            Now the lifted oar
               Waits for us:
            Ships of Greece, we come!
                  *Exeunt.*

# HELEN

\*

## Characters:

HELEN, *daughter of Zeus and Leda*
TEUCER, *a Greek*
CHORUS *of captive Spartan women*
MENELAUS, *husband of Helen and King of Sparta*
OLD WOMAN, *portress at the palace*
MESSENGER, *one of Menelaus' crew*
THEONOE, *sister of Theoclymenus*
THEOCLYMENUS, *King of Egypt*
MESSENGER, *servant of Theoclymenus*
THE DIOSCORI, *sons of Zeus and Leda, now deified*

\*

*The scene is Egypt, before the royal palace, not far from the shore. On one side of the stage is a monument enshrining a stone sarcophagus, at which* HELEN *has taken sanctuary.*

HELEN: This is Egypt; here flows the virgin river, the lovely Nile, who brings down melted snow to slake the soil of the Egyptian plain with the moisture heaven denies. Proteus, while he lived, was King here, ruling the whole of Egypt from his palace on the island of Pharos. Now Proteus married Psamathe, one of the sea-nymphs, and formerly the wife of Aeacus. She bore Proteus two children: a son, Theoclymenus (a name contradicted by his impious life) and a daughter, the apple of her mother's eye, called Eido when she was a child; when she grew up and was ripe for marriage they called her Theonoe, for she had divine knowledge of all things present and to come – a gift inherited from her grandfather Nereus.

But I am not an Egyptian; my home country is a place of some note – Sparta; and my father was Tyndareus. There is – you know – a legend which says that Zeus took the feathered form of a swan, and that being pursued by an eagle, and flying for refuge to the bosom of my mother, Leda, he used this deceit to accomplish his desire upon her. That is the story of my origin – if it is true. My name is Helen. Now let me tell you of my misfortunes.

The three goddesses, Hera, Aphrodite, and Athene, daughter of Zeus, came as rivals to the glen of Mount Ida, where Paris lived, each one eager to be judged the first in beauty. And *my* beauty – if so great a misfortune can be so named – was used by Aphrodite as the bribe by which she won the prize, promising Paris that he should marry me. So Paris left his dairy-farm on Mount Ida and came to Sparta to win me as his bride.

But Hera, baulked of her victory over the other goddesses, in her resentment turned the substance of Aphrodite's promise into air. She gave the royal son of Priam for his bride – not me, but a living image compounded of the ether in my likeness. Paris believes that he possesses me: what he holds is nothing but an airy delusion.

And Zeus by his subsequent arrangements has added to my misfortune. He brought war upon Hellas and the unhappy Phrygians, to ease the swarming earth of her measureless burden of men and make Achilles famous among the fighters of Greece. The Helen who went to Phrygia as a prize for Troy to defend and the Greeks to fight for – that Helen was not I, only my name. Zeus did not forget me: I was taken by Hermes, wrapped in a cloud, borne through the secret places of the upper air, and set down here in the palace of Proteus, whom Zeus picked out as the most honourable of all men, so that I might preserve my chastity inviolate for Menelaus. So here I have lived, while my poor husband gathered an army and in pursuit of his stolen wife sailed to the fortress of Troy. Many souls of men perished for my sake by the river Scamander; and I, the centre of these tragic events, am named with curses, as the betrayer of my husband, who brought upon Greece the pestilence of war.

Why do I still live? Because Hermes told me this: once my husband learns that I did not go to Troy to accept the embraces of a lover, I shall once again live with him in the famous land of Sparta. As long as Proteus lived my marriage was not threatened; now he is in his dark grave, and his son Theoclymenus is pestering me to marry him. So in loyalty to my true husband I have come here as a suppliant to the tomb of Proteus, praying him to preserve me for Menelaus; so that even if my name is reviled in Hellas, here in Egypt I may keep my body free from reproach.

*Enter* TEUCER.

TEUCER: Who is master of this imposing palace? These royal precincts, that magnificent pediment, suggest the very house of Plutus, the temple of Wealth. [*With a sudden cry he catches sight of* HELEN.] Ye gods! What do I see? It is the accursed woman – her very image! The murderess who blasted my life and ruined Greece! May the gods abhor you as the perfect copy of Helen! If I were not standing on foreign soil, with this good arrow I would take your life in payment for your likeness to the daughter of Zeus!

HELEN: What do you say? Poor soul, who are you? Why do you shrink from me? You say I am like Helen: why blame me for that? Why hate me because of what happened to her?

TEUCER: I was wrong; I let anger get the better of me. The daughter of Zeus is hated all over Hellas. Forgive what I said.

HELEN: But who are you? Where have you come from?

TEUCER: I am one of those ruined Greeks.

HELEN: No wonder, then, that you hate Helen. But who are you? Of what country, what family?

TEUCER: My name is Teucer; my father is Telamon, and I was born and brought up in Salamis.

HELEN: Then what brings you here to the valley of the Nile?

TEUCER: I have been driven out of my father's land. I am an exile.

HELEN: That is hard. Who drove you out?

TEUCER: The man who should have loved me most: my own father, Telamon.

HELEN: Exiled you! There must have been some serious reason. What had happened?

TEUCER: I had a brother, Aias; his death at Troy was the cause of it.

HELEN: How? You did not kill him yourself?

TEUCER: No. He died by his own hand, his own sword.

HELEN: Was he mad? Surely no man in his right mind could do it?

TEUCER: I will tell you. You have heard of Achilles, son of Peleus?

HELEN: He was one of the suitors of Helen – so I have heard.

TEUCER: At his death he left his armour to be competed for by those who had fought with him.

HELEN: And how did that hurt Aias?

TEUCER: He ended his life because the armour was awarded to another man.

HELEN: And his troubles were the cause of your exile?

TEUCER: Yes, because I did not die at his side.

HELEN: So you too went to the famous city of Ilion?

TEUCER: I was in at the death – and lost my own life for my pains.

HELEN: Is the city now burnt and destroyed?

TEUCER: Utterly. Not even the outline of the walls can be traced.

HELEN: Oh, Helen, Helen! It was for you Troy died!

TEUCER: Troy? Greece too! Untold harm has been done.

HELEN: How long is it since the city was sacked?

TEUCER: Seven harvests have been reaped since Troy lay barren.

HELEN: And before that, how long had you been there?

TEUCER: Months without number – ten interminable years.

HELEN: And did you capture the Spartan queen?

TEUCER: Menelaus took her – dragged her off by the hair.

HELEN: Poor woman! Did you see her? Or are you telling me what you heard?

TEUCER: I saw her as plainly as I see you now.

HELEN: Is it not possible that the gods made you all imagine this?

TEUCER: Talk about something else – that is enough of Helen.

HELEN: Then – you all really believed it was true?

TEUCER: Why, I saw her with my own eyes carried off by Menelaus.

HELEN: And is Menelaus now at home – with his wife?

TEUCER: Not in Argos, certainly; nor in Sparta.

HELEN: That is sad news – for those who hoped for better.

TEUCER: He is said to have vanished, and his wife with him.

HELEN: But surely all the Argives were sailing home together?

TEUCER: They were; but a storm scattered them in all directions.

HELEN: Where were they when the storm fell?

TEUCER: Cresting the rollers of the mid-Aegean.

HELEN: And since then – no one has news of his landing anywhere?

TEUCER: No one. He is generally reported as dead.

HELEN [*aside*]: Dead! What shall I do? [*To* TEUCER] And what of Leda? Is she alive?

TEUCER: No, Leda is dead and gone.

HELEN: Can it be that Helen's disgrace broke her heart?

TEUCER: So they say; she was of royal blood. She hanged herself.

HELEN: And her two sons by Tyndareus – are they alive or dead?

TEUCER: Dead and not dead; of them there are two different accounts.

HELEN: Tell me the truer. [*Aside*] My mother – how can I bear it?

TEUCER: It is said they were deified – in the form of stars.

HELEN: That would be well. What was the other?

TEUCER: That shame for their sister drove them to end their lives with the sword. But enough of tales – I have wept for these things once already.

My reason for coming here to the king's palace was to see the prophetess Theonoe, and ask for divine help in getting a fair wind for Cyprus. Will you take me to her? An oracle of Apollo told me I was to settle in Cyprus, and give to my new home there the name of Salamis, in remembrance of that other island where I was born.

HELEN: From here to Cyprus is plain sailing; but you must get clear of land before Theoclymenus sees you. He is the king of this country, and at present he is away slaughtering wild beasts with the aid of hounds. Every Greek that he captures here he kills. Why? don't ask me – I won't tell you. What good would it do you?

TEUCER: Just as you say, my lady; and thank you for telling me. The gods reward you for your kindness! You are like Helen only in appearance; in heart you are utterly different. I pray she may never reach home, but come to a bad end. But you – good luck be with you always!

*Exit* TEUCER.

HELEN:

Strong griefs ask strong lamenting. Who shall be
Pattern and partner to my crying soul?
    What tearful song can match the toll
Of deep pain paid by silent misery?


Come, Seiren maidens, daughters of Earth,      [*Strophe* 1
Young and light of wing,

Come with Libyan flute, with pipe and string,
Bring music for my despair,
Share your tears to suit my sorrow,
Couple note with note, pain with my pain;
And when songs of death,
Solemn chants dear to departed souls,
Ring through the vaulted shades of death,
Hear and accept them, Queen Persephone,
Echoes of my heart's agony,
Offerings to fill my tears' deficiency.

*The* CHORUS *begin to enter.*

CHORUS:

Where the spring grass grows rank beside          [*Antistrophe* 1
    blue water
I was at work, spreading
Purple clothes on the young reeds to dry
In golden heat of the sun;
When I heard my lady's voice, a pitiful cry,
A joyless clamour of pain,
An anguished wail of loss –
What could it be? –
Like the haunted scream of a woodland nymph
At bay in the echoing depths of a rocky cave,
Caught and spoiled by the lust of Pan.

HELEN:

Women of Greece, victims of piracy!          [*Strophe* 2
Listen: a Grecian sailor has been here
Bringing new tears to flow with those I had.
Great Troy lies dead: fire is her monument.
And I – my hated name – must bear the guilt
Of countless agonies and countless dead.
Leda is dead; for her, my name's disgrace
Fastened the noose. My husband's lost from sight,
His endless voyage ended in death. My brothers,
Their country's glory and pride, are seen no more

Riding like thunder through the reedy marsh,
Or wrestling with their fellows by the stream.

CHORUS:

Weep for Helen, victim of Destiny!            [*Antistrophe* 2
Mocked cruelly with the gift of life, when Zeus
Swan-winged like snow swooping thro' dazzled air
Touched Leda's womb! Your single life has known
All sorrow, knows it still. Leda is dead;
Twin sons of Zeus, your brothers are no more;
Your eyes can never see your native land;
Rumour through every state and street in Greece
Gives you as paramour to a foreign prince;
Your husband's life is lost in the salt sea;
And you will no more gladden your dear home
Or thank Athene in her brazen temple.

HELEN:

Whose was the Trojan hand that felled            [*Strophe* 3
The fateful pine whose timbers held
Tears for the Trojans, tears for Greece?
Thence the accursed ship was built
That brought to Sparta Priam's son
(A dark-skinned slave at each oar-hilt)
To seek my beauty, break my peace,
And tempt my heart with love and guilt.
With Paris, till his prize was won,
Came murderous Aphrodite, mistress of deceit –
    Goddess, what have you done? –
To prostrate Greece and Troy in slaughter at her feet.


Then Hera, loved of Zeus, who shares            [*Antistrophe* 3
His golden throne and soothes his cares,
Sent the swift-footed Hermes down.
He found me gathering in a glade
Fresh roses folded in my gown,
An offering for the Holy Maid;

Carried me swiftly through the sky
Into this land of little joy,
To live accursed and know that I
Sent my own race to bloody war with Ilion.
  Now by the shores of Troy
My fair name is reviled for wrong I have not done.

CHORUS: You have cause for sorrow, I know; but it is best to bear what burdens life lays upon us as cheerfully as we can.

HELEN: Burdens! Look, what a millstone life has hung round my neck! From the moment my mother bore me I was pointed at for a freak. It's not usual in Hellas or anywhere else for a woman to produce her young enclosed in a white shell – which is the way Leda is said to have borne me, with Zeus for my father! Since then every fresh misfortune – in fact my whole life has been a freak; partly through Hera's fault, partly because my very beauty led to my taking on an untrue and hideous appearance in the eyes of the world. Oh, if the picture could have been wiped out and painted over again, to give me my true beauty, so that the Greeks could forget the blemishes I now possess, and remember the good instead of the bad!

When a man broods on a single misfortune and feels the gods are against him, though his suffering is real, it can be borne; but I am crushed by innumerable blows at once. In the first place, though I am innocent, my name is a byword of reproach; and if there is any worse fate than suffering for real crimes, it is suffering for crimes that were never committed. Then, the gods have uprooted me from my home, and planted me among an outlandish race, where I am friendless, and degraded from nobility to slavery; for in a country like this all are slaves except one man. The sole anchor of hope that I cling to, that some day my husband would come and rescue me – that hope has gone, if he is dead. And my mother is dead, and men say I killed her –

say it unjustly, but it is an injustice I must bear. My daughter, the pride of her home, and of her mother, grows grey in virginity; and my two brothers, whom they call the sons of Zeus, are gone. Meanwhile, surrounded by so many disasters, in this makebelieve situation I too am dead, though in fact I am alive. To crown all, even if I were to reach my home, Sparta would shut the door on me as a foreigner; for they all think the sea swallowed me together with Menelaus. For if he were alive, we would recognize each other by certain secrets known to us alone. But he is not alive; I shall never see him again.

Then why should I go on living? What is left to me now? To save my life I can choose to marry Theoclymenus, to live as an Egyptian wife, the lady of a great house. But an odious husband makes even wealth odious. The wisest course is – to die.

How can I do it well? A rope? No. I will not be seen dangling in a noose. Even slaves think it beneath them. To strike with a knife has a certain touch of royalty, of heroism. But that way of escape hurts, and I shrink from it. What a depth of desperation! Beauty is a blessing to other women: it reduces *me* to this!

CHORUS: Helen, you should not assume that this Greek, whoever he may be, told you nothing but the truth.

HELEN: He told me clearly enough that Menelaus was dead.

CHORUS: Many tales might be clear, and yet not true.

HELEN: Truth itself is often bewildering.

CHORUS: You dwell on the worst that may happen, instead of the best.

HELEN: Fear grips me and drives me to the thought that I dread.

CHORUS: Tell me – how much good-will have you in the palace?

HELEN: They are all my friends, except the man who is bent on marrying me.

CHORUS: Then listen: this is what you must do: leave your
   sanctuary here and –
HELEN: Leave sanctuary? What are you suggesting?
CHORUS: Go to the house of Theonoe, daughter of the sea.
   She possesses all knowledge: inquire of her whether your
   husband is alive or dead; and when you have a clear answer
   you may rejoice or weep accordingly. Before you know for
   certain, what do you gain by grieving? Do as I suggest:
   leave this tomb, go to Theonoe, and you will know every-
   thing. When you have here in the palace one who can tell
   you the truth and is also your friend, why look further? I
   will willingly go myself and join with you in asking for a
   divine revelation. Women ought to help each other.

HELEN:      Friends, I will do as you say.
            Into the palace, quickly in,
            To learn what I must lose or win!

CHORUS:    We are ready now, at your word.

HELEN:      I tremble! This is a day
            Of fear: what answer waits to be heard?
            What doom of tears?

CHORUS:                          But why
            Be sure of the worst, and weep too soon?

HELEN:      What bitter fate has my husband found?
            Does he live to see the sun
            Charioting the sky,
            And the journeys of stars and moon?
            Or has his soul begun
            Its endless, lifeless exile under ground?

CHORUS:    Whatever is to come,
            Helen, accept and use for the best.

HELEN:      Eurotas, river of home,
            With reedy banks of green,
            If report of him is true,
            If death holds him at rest,
            Hear what I swear to do –!

CHORUS: This is folly! What do you mean?

HELEN: To die! I will swing high,
My throat in a choking rope,
Or the hand shall war on the wincing skin
And eager iron shall grope
And blood leap forth where the deadly blade passed in;
My death a sacrifice
To the three goddesses, and to Priam's son,
The shepherd whose heart was won,
The judge whose word was bought
For Aphrodite's price.

CHORUS:
Hold to this happier thought,
That the clouds of fear may pass unshed.

HELEN:
Weep for the tears of Troy!
For Troy, deeds without name have bred
Pain without end. Aphrodite, goddess of joy,
Gave, and I was her gift; thence without respite sprang
Anguish of blood and tears and deep despair;
Mothers of Troy wailed for their vanished sons;
Sisters knelt by Scamander's brims to hang
On new-made tombs locks of their virgin hair.

But listen! Loud and full
Through Hellas too the same river of weeping runs,
And hands are clasped over the stricken head,
And nerveless fingers clutch and pull
The unfeeling flesh till the nails are red.

Happy Arcadian girl, who long ago
Lay in the bed of Zeus! For you, once fair,
Still in the rough pelt of a shambling bear
Made your shape gentle with your eyes' soft glow.
Beauty, that tortures me, to you was kind:

With it, you left the pangs of grief behind.

And Merops' daughter, happy too was she,
The Titan maid whom for her beauty's flower
Artemis drove out from her company
And turned her to a hind with horns of gold;
But my curs'd beauty damned with deadly power
Trojan and wandering Greek to sufferings untold.

    HELEN *and* CHORUS *exeunt into the palace. Enter*
        MENELAUS.

MENELAUS: O Pelops my grandfather, winner of your famous chariot-race against Oenomaus at Pisa! How I wish that on the same day when you were prepared as a banquet for the gods, you had ended your life forthwith between immortal teeth! Then you could never have begotten my father Atreus; who in his turn was father, by his wife Aerope, to Agamemnon and myself, a celebrated pair of sons. In fact, my opinion is – I say this without any wish to boast – that, of the two of us, I took the larger part in the transporting of our armament by sea to Troy; a monarch owing his authority not to superior force, but to the willing obedience of the fighting men of Hellas.

Many of those men are dead; many others – the exact figure is ascertainable – rejoice in a happy escape from the perils of the sea, and have returned home bringing with them tokens and keepsakes of those who died. But I, through all the years since I overthrew the towers of Troy, have been an unhappy wanderer upon the stormy wastes of the grey ocean. I long to reach my own country; but the gods have not thought me worthy. I have sailed into every desolate landing-place, every hostile port, on the Libyan coast. Every time I near the shores of my own country a storm drives me back; no favouring wind ever fills my sail to bring me home.

And now here I am on this coast, a wretched castaway,

all my friends lost; our ship broken in a thousand pieces against the rocks. But a curiously-fitted keel remained intact, and on this, with much difficulty, and much to my surprise, I was able to get ashore, and with me Helen whom I dragged off from Troy. What country this is, what nation inhabits it I have no idea. I could have inquired; but I preferred not to meet people in my present embarrassing costume, which decency demands should be kept out of sight. A man accustomed to high position feels misfortune more than one who is inured to it. I am, in fact, exhausted: no food, no clothes – these rags I have on are what I could save from the wreck, as anyone can see. My usual clothes – rich cloaks, soft gowns – the sea has taken them all. But I have my wife – the source of all my sufferings; and before coming up here I hid her in a cave together with the survivors of my company, and ordered them to guard her for me. I have come alone to procure any supplies I can find for them. As soon as I saw this palace I approached it; the high surrounding wall, the imposing entrance, indicate a man of wealth. Sailors in need may hope for something from a well-stocked house; otherwise we shall die; for a whole ship's crew, if they can get no supplies, can give no help, however willing. [*He shouts*] Hallo, there! Porter! Come to the door, and take a message in for me. I need help.

*An* OLD WOMAN *answers from inside.*

OLD WOMAN: Who's that at the door? Go away, will you? Don't stand there in the porch disturbing my master! Or you'll get killed: you're a Greek, and we have no dealings with Greeks.

MENELAUS: Old woman, these are empty threats. I may speak bluntly, for I've no time to spare. Come on, undo the bolt!

*She opens the door and appears.*

OLD WOMAN: Go away! My orders are that no Greek shall come near the house.

MENELAUS: Look here, don't shake your finger at me or push me about.

OLD WOMAN: It's your fault; you won't do what I tell you.

MENELAUS: Go and tell your master I'm here.

OLD WOMAN: I wouldn't take the risk of delivering your message.

MENELAUS: I'm a shipwrecked man; he would not dare to harm me.

OLD WOMAN: Now you go away from here to some other house.

MENELAUS: I won't. I'm coming in. Do as I tell you.

OLD WOMAN: I tell you you're troublesome. Before long you'll be thrown out.

MENELAUS: Ah! If only I had my army here!

OLD WOMAN: No doubt you were a great man in your army; here you're not.

MENELAUS: Gods! that I should suffer such indignity!

OLD WOMAN: Ha! Tears in your eyes! Who do you think is sorry for you?

MENELAUS: The gods were once kind to me.

OLD WOMAN: Then go away and bestow your tears on your friends.

MENELAUS: What country is this? Whose is this palace?

OLD WOMAN: This is Proteus' palace; and the country is Egypt.

MENELAUS: Egypt! Could anything be worse? What a place to have reached!

OLD WOMAN: Why do you speak ill of the jewel of the Nile?

MENELAUS: I did not. I was groaning at my own misfortune.

OLD WOMAN: Many are unfortunate; you are not the only one.

MENELAUS: Is this king – whatever you called him – at home?

OLD WOMAN: This is his tomb. His son reigns now.

MENELAUS: Then where is his son, at home or away?

OLD WOMAN: He is not at home. And he is a bitter enemy of all Greeks.

MENELAUS: Why does he hate Greeks – so unhappily for me?

OLD WOMAN: Helen is in this palace, the daughter of Zeus.

MENELAUS: What? What did you say? Say that again.

OLD WOMAN: The daughter of Tyndareus, who used to live in Sparta.

MENELAUS: But where did she come from? What can this mean?

OLD WOMAN: Why, she came here from Lacedaemon.

MENELAUS: When? [*Aside*] Surely my wife can't have been kidnapped out of the cave.

OLD WOMAN: Before the Greeks went to Troy, my friend. But get away from this house. There's an extraordinary trouble that's upsetting us just now; you have come at a most unfortunate time. If my master catches you, your welcome will be death. I'm a friend to you Greeks, in spite of what I said; I spoke harshly for fear of my master.

*Exit.*

MENELAUS: What does it mean? What can I think? This story of hers seems to alter the whole situation. Is it possible that I should capture my wife in Troy, bring her here and put her in a cave for safety, and now find another woman, with the same name as my wife, living in this palace? But she called this woman the daughter of Zeus! Can there be a *man* by the name of Zeus living on the banks of the Nile? There's only one Zeus, the one in heaven. And where in the world is there a Sparta, except on the reedy banks of the lovely Eurotas? Are there two men called Tyndareus? Is there another Lacedaemon, another Troy? I don't know what to say.

Well, after all, the world's a big place: no doubt many women have the same names – many towns too. There's really nothing to wonder at. Nor is there anything to run away from in a slave's threats. No man could be so un-civilized as to refuse me food – once he heard my name. The fire of Troy is famous; so is the man who lit it – known all over the world: Menelaus!

I will wait for the master of the house. That means two things to look out for: if the man's a savage, I must first hide, then get back to the wreck; if he shows any softness, I must be sure to ask for the provisions we need. – This, then, was the final humiliation in store for me, that I should beseech a fellow-king for bread to keep me alive! Well, I must. *Nothing is stronger than necessity* – I did not invent that proverb, but it's true none the less, and very well known.

*Re-enter* CHORUS.

CHORUS:     When in her need my lady Helen
            Went to the royal palace to inquire,
            I heard the virgin prophetess say
            That King Menelaus has not vanished
            To the land of shadows under the earth
            Where light is dark, but lives, the sport
            Of the stormy seas, and never yet
            Has moored in the harbour of his own city;
            But sick with travel, stripped of friends,
            Has grounded keel, in his voyage from Troy,
            On every shore between East and West.

*Re-enter* HELEN.

HELEN: Now, back to my place of sanctuary – but Theonoe's answer has warmed my heart! She knows everything, and it is true! She says openly that my husband is alive, alive! that he wanders endlessly from sea to sea, this way and that; but at last, when he is exhausted with travel, and reaches the appointed end of his sufferings, he will come! – One thing she did not tell me, whether after coming he will get safely away; but I was so overjoyed at hearing he was alive that I refrained from pressing her further. She says that he's some-where near at hand, that he has been wrecked, and has landed with only a few companions. Oh, Menelaus, when will you come? How I long to see you! [*She sees him.*]

Oh! Who is that? He is lying in wait for me – this is some sacrilegious plot of Theoclymenus! Quick, to the tomb, fast as the wind, fast as frenzy! He means to capture me! What a wild look he has!

MENELAUS: Listen to me! Stop clutching so desperately at that tomb – those altar pillars – wait! Why run away? ... Ah! now that you show me your face, you strike me speechless with astonishment.

HELEN: Friends, this is a cruel wrong! He is keeping me away from sanctuary! He is going to seize me, and give me as wife to the king, whom I hate!

MENELAUS: I'm not a criminal, nor has anyone sent me to commit any crime.

HELEN: Are you not? But you're dressed in rags!

MENELAUS [*returning from the tomb*]: Don't run away; there's nothing to be afraid of.

HELEN: Now that I can cling to the tomb, I'll stay.

MENELAUS: Who are you? Whose face am I looking at?

HELEN: But who are *you*? We are both in the same perplexity.

MENELAUS: I never saw anyone more exactly like –

HELEN: O gods! Yes, there is something godlike in recognition!

MENELAUS: Are you a Greek, or a native here?

HELEN: A Greek. I want to know your country too.

MENELAUS: To me you appear to be exactly like Helen!

HELEN: To me you look like Menelaus! I don't know what to think.

MENELAUS: You are right! I am Menelaus – to my sorrow.

HELEN [*stretching out her arms*]: Come to me – I am your wife! I have waited so long for you! [*She kneels, clasps his rags, and kisses them.*]

MENELAUS: Wife? What do you mean? Leave my clothes alone!

HELEN: I am! My father Tyndareus gave me to you!

MENELAUS: Hecate, bringer of light, send me good dreams!

HELEN: I am not a dream, Hecate has not sent me!

MENELAUS: But neither am I the husband of two women!

HELEN: What other woman's husband are you?

MENELAUS: I left her hidden in the cave – I was bringing her back from Troy.

HELEN: You have no wife other than me.

MENELAUS: I am not mad – can there be something wrong with my sight?

HELEN: There is nothing wrong! When you look at me do you not know that I am your wife?

MENELAUS: In appearance you are the same; but the mystery of it baffles me.

HELEN: Look at me! What plainer proof do you want?

MENELAUS: You are like her; that I don't deny.

HELEN: Then what evidence should you trust, if not your eyes?

MENELAUS: My difficulty is this: I have another wife!

HELEN: I did not go to Troy. That was a phantom.

MENELAUS: And who can make a phantom that lives and breathes?

HELEN: Air! It was the gods' work. That wife of yours is made – of air!

MENELAUS: Which of the gods made her? I never heard of such a thing!

HELEN: Hera made her as a substitute for me, so that Paris should not have me.

MENELAUS: What? Then you were here and in Troy at the same time?

HELEN: A name can be in any number of places: a person can only be in one place. [*She clasps his hand.*]

MENELAUS: Let go! I had enough to plague me before I came.

HELEN: Will you leave me, and go away with your phantom wife?

MENELAUS: Yes! You are too much like Helen; so good-bye!

HELEN: You kill me to say so. I have found you, my husband, and now I cannot keep you!

MENELAUS: The memory of what I went through at Troy is more convincing than you are.

HELEN [*weeping*]: Oh, oh! was anyone ever so miserable? My husband is leaving me once more; I shall never live in my own country or see my own home again!

*Enter a* MESSENGER, *one of* MENELAUS' *men.*

MESSENGER: Menelaus, here you are at last! I have been wandering all over this outlandish place, trying to find you. The others that you left behind sent me.

MENELAUS: What's the matter? you are not being robbed by natives, I hope?

MESSENGER: Something extraordinary – but the word doesn't describe it.

MENELAUS: Tell me. It's something strange, to judge by the state you're in.

MESSENGER: All your endless hardships – all suffered for nothing!

MENELAUS: That's no news to me. What has happened?

MESSENGER: Your wife has gone, vanished into the air! She just went up and disappeared! Now she's out of sight, in the sky, and the cave where we were guarding her is empty! But before she went she said this: 'You poor pitiful Trojans and suffering Greeks, it was a trick of Hera's that sent you to your deaths on the banks of the Scamander. Paris did not possess Helen, as you thought. Now that I have stayed as long as I had to stay, I return, as Fate ordains, to the sky that formed me. The curses that men heap on the unhappy Helen are mistaken: she has done nothing wrong.' [*He sees* HELEN.] Oh! *there* you are, daughter of Leda! So you were here all the time! I have just been reporting you as departed to the regions of the stars, being unaware that you possessed wings. Now I'm not letting you play tricks on us a second

time: you gave quite enough trouble to your husband and
his friends when you were in Troy.

MENELAUS: It's true – this proves it! All she said is con-
firmed! Helen! [*He holds out his arms and* HELEN *runs to him;*
*they embrace.*] How I have longed for this day, longed to take
you in my arms! Now you are mine!

HELEN: O dearest love! year after endless year
  Crept by: now joy has come, for you are here!
   Women, I laugh for joy:
   My husband is mine once more,
   And my arms are round his neck.
   He comes like a flare of flame
   Lighting my dark despair.

MENELAUS:
 And you are mine. So much, since then, has passed –
 What should I tell – what ask you – first or last?

HELEN: My hair wings wild in the wind for joy;
  My eyes are brimming, while my hands
   Feel your dear form, and taste
   Pleasure so long denied!

MENELAUS:
 No dearer sight than this! All grief forgotten!
 Daughter of Zeus, you are mine to have and hold.
 I claimed you once, when the Heavenly Twins your
  brothers
 Rode their white horses under the torchlit night,
 And their shouts of blessing echoed, echoed again –
  Once, long ago; and then
 Hera stole you away, and my house was empty.

HELEN:
 Now Heaven leads us on from this happy meeting
  To a still happier day.

MENELAUS:
 Good defeats ill once more; we are united.
  Though joy was long on the way,
 Now fortune smiles, and may blessing follow!

CHORUS:
Blessing indeed; we too pray the same prayer,
    For your fate and hers are one:
  You cannot suffer, and she be safe.

HELEN:
Dear friends, pain that is past has lost its sting;
    My husband is mine, is mine!
  He has come, and my long despair is over.

MENELAUS:
We have each other. In truth, I dimly guessed,
As the endless chain of tedious days went on,
    That the Queen of Gods was at work.
    There is more joy in my tears
  Than all the sorrow of all the past.

HELEN:
Bliss beyond words, sweeter than heart could hope –
    I hold you close to my breast.

MENELAUS:
And you to mine – you who we thought were living
    In the shadow of Mount Ida,
  Behind the sad battlements of Troy.
    – Helen, how did you steal from home that day?

HELEN:      The story you seek began in pain,
               Cruel to suffer, cruel to recount again.

MENELAUS: Tell me; for every mortal must
               Accept Heaven's gifts as best he may.

HELEN:      The words will choke me. How can I speak?

MENELAUS: Speak, for my sake.

HELEN:                        I felt no guilty lust;
               I did not fly over the sea to seek
               The unlawful bed of an Eastern prince.

MENELAUS: What god, what fate, then, stole you away?

HELEN:      Hermes the son of Zeus conveyed me here
               To the banks of the Nile.

MENELAUS:               At whose command?
          – The son of Zeus!

HELEN:                              I wept long since,
              And now I weep again for fear –
              My enemy is the Queen of Heaven.
MENELAUS: Hera! and how have *we* incurred her curse?
HELEN:
   The cruel reproaches I have borne
   Flowed from that fountain-source
   Where the three bright immortals came to adorn
   Their beauty on which the famous judgement then was
      given.
MENELAUS: But why must Hera's spite be vented
              On you, for judgement she resented?
HELEN:         To despoil Paris of the bride
              The Cyprian promised him –
MENELAUS:                              Of you!
HELEN:         She sent me to this desert land,
              Weeping –
MENELAUS:            And in your place supplied
              A phantom Helen – all too true!
HELEN:         At home there is more sorrow yet:
              My mother –
MENELAUS:               What of her?
HELEN:                              Is dead.
              She tied the noose with her own hand,
              Believing I had shamed your bed.
MENELAUS: O gods! – What of Hermione?
HELEN:         What joy has she? What hope to get
              Husband or child, when all men point to me?
MENELAUS:
   Paris! You who have murdered my whole house,
   Your deed brought death to your city and to you,
   And to ten thousand bronze-armed men of Greece.
HELEN:
   And I, accursed, unhappy, not untrue,
   Exiled perforce, guiltless of broken vows,
   Was robbed of city, home, my husband, and my peace!

CHORUS: If only you meet with good luck for the future, it will compensate you for all that is past.

MESSENGER: Menelaus, I realize that something has made you happy, though I have not yet fully grasped what it is. Will you let me share your good news?

MENELAUS: Why, of course, you must share it, old fellow.

MESSENGER: Then is not this lady Helen, the prize of all we went through at Troy?

MENELAUS: This lady was never in Troy. We were tricked by the gods. The Helen we captured was a phantom to make fools of us.

MESSENGER: What? All our sweat and blood – spent for a ghost?

MENELAUS: Yes. Hera was in a rage because of the Judgement of Paris.

MESSENGER: Then the one who really is your wife is this lady here?

MENELAUS: She is. You must take my word for it.

MESSENGER [to HELEN]: My daughter! The ways of the gods are involved and mysterious; they send us good and bad fortune in turn, and all is for the best. One man suffers, but soon his suffering is over and he prospers beyond his hopes; another man does not suffer, but when his turn comes the luck he enjoyed so long deserts him, and he perishes miserably. So you and your husband had your share of suffering – you were ill spoken of, he was caught in the storm of battle. As long as he struggled for what he wanted, he gained nothing; now good fortune has come to him of its own accord, and he's a happy man. So, you did not disgrace your old father and your two brothers, as the world says you did.

How well I remember your wedding-day! I can see it all again now – the horses, four in a yoke, with me running beside them holding a torch, and you in the chariot with Menelaus, leaving your lovely home to be married! [He wipes a tear.] Excuse me. To a slave his master's affairs mean a great deal; he shares in joy and sorrow alike; if not, he's no true man. I'm a slave by birth, I know; but there are slaves who are noble, who have the mind of a free man, if not the name: I want to count as one of them. It's the best way; otherwise you've a double misfortune – you take orders from every one all round, and you *feel* like a slave as well.

MENELAUS: You're a good old man; you've borne your full share of hardship in my service on the field; and now that you're here to share in my good fortune, go back to the others and tell them what has happened. Explain the present position; warn them to wait on the shore and be ready in case I have to make a fight for it, as I expect; and if we should find any possible way of getting my wife out of this place, after meeting so miraculously, they must see to it that we aren't caught by the natives.

MESSENGER: I'll do it, my lord. And I'll tell you, this is my experience of prophets: you can expect nothing from them but silliness and lies. Shapes of sacrifices, cries of birds – there's no truth in any of it, never was! Can birds do men any good? The very notion's foolish. Calchas saw his friends dying in battle for the sake of a phantom, yet he gave them neither word nor sign; no more did the Trojan Helenus – his city was sacked for nothing. You may say it was because the god did not wish them to speak. Then why do we consult prophets? Better ask the gods for blessing, after due offerings; and leave prophets alone. Prophecy was invented to entrap men with the promise of success; no one ever got wealth without labour by studying sacrifices. The best oracle is care and common sense.

CHORUS: I entirely agree with the old man about oracles. To make friends with the gods is better than all the skill of prophets.

*Exit* MESSENGER.

HELEN: So far, then, everything goes well. But tell me about

your adventures on the voyage from Troy. I gain nothing
by knowing it, but because you are dear to me I want to
share in all you have suffered.

MENELAUS: You have asked me a hundred questions in one.
There were shipwrecks in the Aegean; the false beacons
that Nauplius lit on Euboea; cities in Crete and Libya we
visited; the watch-tower of Perseus – why should I tell you
all this? I have endured it once in reality; the distress of
telling you would make me endure it twice.

HELEN: I am sorry if I asked you things too painful to speak
of. Leave the rest and tell me one thing: how long have you
wandered over the ridges of the salt sea?

MENELAUS: We were at Troy ten years; since then I have
been voyaging seven summers and seven winters.

HELEN: Seven years! What a terrible, weary time! And even
now, after finding me, you must not stay. You must get
away from this country as quickly as possible. You have
escaped the war and the sea, but death waits for you here.

MENELAUS: What do you mean? Death? This is bad news.

HELEN: The man who owns this palace will kill you.

MENELAUS: What have I done to deserve that?

HELEN: He wants to marry me; your unexpected arrival
will put a stop to that.

MENELAUS: What? A man was proposing to marry my wife?

HELEN: Yes, and to take me by force, if I had not escaped
from him.

MENELAUS: How could he have the power? Is he a private
person, or – is it the king?

HELEN: He is the king of Egypt, the son of Proteus.

MENELAUS: Oh! I see now what the old woman at the door
meant.

HELEN: What door? Have you called at some house here in
Egypt?

MENELAUS: This door, the king's. I was driven away as a
beggar.

HELEN: You surely were not asking for food? Oh, how dreadful!

MENELAUS: I was in fact begging; but I didn't say so.

HELEN: Then no doubt you know all about his plans for marrying me.

MENELAUS: I do. What I don't know is whether you have managed to evade them.

HELEN: Be reassured: your wife's chastity is untouched.

MENELAUS: What deterred him? I should be most happy to believe you.

HELEN: You see this tomb where you found me sitting in despair?

MENELAUS: I see you have a mattress there; what was that for?

HELEN: I was a suppliant there, praying to escape this marriage.

MENELAUS: Was there no altar? Or do the Egyptians reverence a tomb?

HELEN: This was as strong a protection as any temple.

MENELAUS: Then can I not take you with me and sail for home?

HELEN: You are more likely to be killed than ever to have me for your wife again.

MENELAUS: Gods forbid such a cruel fate!

HELEN: Now, don't be ashamed to seek your own safety, but escape!

MENELAUS: And leave you here? I took Troy for your sake.

HELEN: Better leave me than be killed for my sake.

MENELAUS: You counsel me to be a coward – the man who took Troy!

HELEN: Perhaps you think of killing the king – you could not do it.

MENELAUS: Why not? Is his skin steel-proof?

HELEN: You will see. It is folly to attempt the impossible.

MENELAUS: Why, then, shall I meekly hold out my hands to be manacled?

HELEN: You're in a trap. We must contrive some way out.

MENELAUS: Certainly; I would rather be killed in action.

HELEN: There is one hope, one way of escape; and only one.

MENELAUS: What shall we use? Bribes, boldness, or persuasion?

HELEN: If the king could be prevented from knowing of your arrival –

MENELAUS: Who will tell him? At least he won't know who I am.

HELEN: He has an ally in his palace whose help is worth as much as a god's.

MENELAUS: Do you mean some divine voice that speaks inside his walls?

HELEN: No, I mean his sister; they call her Theonoe.

MENELAUS: Her name is prophetic. What of her actions?

HELEN: She knows everything, and will tell her brother you are here.

MENELAUS: If she does we shall be killed. I've no way of hiding.

HELEN: If we both together appealed to her –

MENELAUS: Yes?

HELEN: Not to tell her brother about you –

MENELAUS: If she agreed, we could escape!

HELEN: Yes, easily, with her help; but no chance without telling her.

MENELAUS: *You* must persuade her; she will listen to a woman.

HELEN: At least she will let me approach her as a suppliant.

MENELAUS: Well; what if she rejects our appeal?

HELEN: You will be killed, and I shall be forced into marriage.

MENELAUS: To consent would prove you false. He could not force you – that is an excuse.

HELEN: I swear solemnly by your life –

MENELAUS: You swear – to die, rather than to belong to another man.

HELEN: By the same sword that kills you. I will lie at your side.

MENELAUS: To seal that promise, take my hand.

HELEN [taking his hand]: I swear, if you die, to die too.

MENELAUS: And I swear that if I lose you I will take my own life.

HELEN: How shall we die so that our death brings us fame and honour?

MENELAUS: Here on this tomb. I will kill you, and afterwards myself. But first I will put up a mighty struggle to win you. Let them all come! I shall not disgrace the name I won at Troy; nor am I going back to Greece to be black-guarded as the man who robbed Thetis of Achilles, saw Ajax fall on his sword, and led Nestor's son to his death, but was not ready to die himself for his own wife's sake. I am ready, with all my heart. If the gods have understanding, the earth of burial lies lightly on a brave man killed by his enemies; but to a coward his grave is a crushing rock.

CHORUS: O gods, let the house of Tantalus find good fortune at last, and be delivered from all their troubles!

*Voices are heard in the palace, and the name of 'Theonoe', and the sound of heavy bolts being moved.*

HELEN: Oh! Gods have pity! What cruel fortune! Menelaus, we are caught. Here comes the priestess Theonoe. I hear them unbolting the door. You must fly! – yet, what is the use? She knows you're here whether she sees you or not. O Menelaus! this is my fate! You escaped the cruelty of Troy only to meet other cruel swords here.

*Enter* THEONOE.

THEONOE: Hold the lamp bright before me and lead on. Sanctify every corner of the air with pure ritual, that I may draw holy breath from heaven. If any man has polluted this place with unhallowed tread, purge my path with flame;

wave the torch before me, that I may pass. Your sacred service done, carry back the fire to the central hearth.

Helen, I have news for you, divinely revealed. Your husband Menelaus has come: there he stands before you! He has lost both his ships and the phantom of yourself. Unhappy Menelaus! What sufferings, what escapes you have known! This was not, after all, your homeward voyage; not, at least, if you loiter here. For among the gods this day there is conference and dispute about you in the court of Zeus. Hera, who once hated you, is now your friend; she wishes to bring you both safely to your home, so that all Hellas may know Paris was deceived in the wife whom Aphrodite gave him. But Aphrodite hopes to frustrate your return, lest she be known to have bargained with Helen's beauty for an unlawful love, and men condemn her. Thus, in the event, it lies in my power either to destroy you, as Aphrodite desires, by telling my brother of your arrival, or to take Hera's part and save your life by deceiving my brother, who has ordered me to inform him immediately upon your appearance here.

I will safeguard my own position. Go, one of you, and tell my brother that Menelaus has come.

HELEN: Maiden, I fall a suppliant at your feet, beseeching you in misery and humility for myself and for Menelaus. After many years I have found him: yet in this moment I must see him die. Now that my beloved husband has come, and I hold him in my arms, do not betray him to your brother, but spare him, I entreat you. Do not purchase the favour of tyranny, the gratitude of a wicked heart, by shaming your own piety. God hates violence, and bids us possess what we possess without robbery. What can only come by crime we must not touch. As the sky is a common grace to all mankind, so is the earth, where each may fill his house with goods but must not hold what is another's, nor take it by force. My coming here was timely, but has turned

to misery. Hermes gave me to your father to keep safe for
my husband; now my husband is here and wants to receive
what is his. How can he, if they kill him? How can the king
pay his just debt by bestowing the living on the dead? That
debt was contracted between the god and your father, and
it is their integrity, their wishes, that you must consider.
Would they not have what belongs to another duly re-
turned? You should not feel more bound to your impious
brother than to your noble father. You are a seer, and believe
in divine providence: if now you pervert your father's
purpose, and take your unjust brother's part, is it not shame-
ful that you who know the secrets of Heaven both now and
to come, should not know right from wrong? Look at my
husband and me, persecuted by misery and misfortune;
pity us and save us. Use your power for this better purpose.
I am Helen, hated by the whole world, infamous throughout
Hellas as the wife who betrayed her husband for the sake of
a wealthy home in Phrygia. But if I return to Hellas and
live again in Sparta, if their own ears and eyes prove to
them that they were cruelly tricked by the goddess, and
that I did not betray my husband, then they will give me
back my good name: I shall see my daughter married,
whom no man will take now; this hateful, homeless life
that I live here will end, and I shall enjoy the comfort and
splendour of my own home. If Menelaus had died across
the sea, I should be weeping at the news, without even
being able to see him; but he is alive, and here: must he
be taken from me?

No, no, Theonoe! I implore you, be like your noble
father, and grant what I ask. A good man's daughter can
have no higher praise, than that her goodness equals his.

CHORUS: Your pleading words, Helen – and still more you
yourself – move my pity. But Menelaus has yet to speak for
his life: I long to hear what he will say.

MENELAUS: You need not expect me to fall at your feet in

tears; such weakness now would make Troy blush for her conqueror. Certainly weeping is held no disgrace to a king when Fate is hard; though even if tears be a credit, I prefer courage.

If you intend to help, as in duty bound, a man who rightfully asks to receive back his own wife, give her to me, and further, ensure my escape. If not, I am already familiar with misfortune; and your reward will be infamy. But I will make my appeal for that just treatment which I claim to deserve, my appeal for the sympathy of your inmost heart, as a suppliant here before the tomb of your father. [MENELAUS *moves to the tomb*.]

Aged Proteus, guardian spirit of this marble tomb! Restore to me my wife, whom Zeus sent here to you in trust for me. Death, I know, forbids that I should receive her from your own hands; but surely your daughter will not allow that men should call you from the dead to curse your once noble name. We are in her hands. [*He turns from the tomb and addresses the earth*.]

Lord of the lower world, you too I call upon for help. You have received countless bodies of men that fell by my sword: you have your payment. Either restore now those dead to life, or bid Theonoe prove herself more righteous than this impious king, by giving me my wife. [*He turns to* THEONOE *again*.]

But if you and the king steal my wife from me – I will tell you now what she has left unsaid. You must know, Theonoe, that I have bound myself by solemn oaths, first, to engage your brother in combat, till one of us kills the other: that is final. But if he will not meet me sword to sword, but besieges us with hunger here in our sanctuary, then I am resolved, first to kill Helen, afterwards to drive this two-edged sword into my own heart, here upon the slab of this monument, that our blood may stream down upon Proteus' grave; we shall lie both dead together upon this polished stone, to wring your heart and soil your father's name for ever. Neither your brother nor any other man shall have Helen: I shall take her myself, to my own home, if possible; if not, to the dead. [*His voice breaks, and he brushes a tear.*]

What is this – *tears*? Because my eyes are womanish you perhaps think me readier to sue than to do. Kill me, if that is your mind: the crime will brand you. But make the better choice; do what is just and right: let me have my wife.

CHORUS: You must judge, Theonoe, what each has said; make a decision that will satisfy everyone.

THEONOE: Both nature and inclination prompt me to piety. I love myself; I am anxious not to cloud my father's good name; while to my brother I must refuse any service that would turn to his dishonour. There is in my soul a great temple of righteousness, a gift that I have from my father Nereus. So I will try to save Menelaus; and since Hera wishes to help him, I will cast my vote with hers. For Aphrodite – may she forgive me; but I have had no dealings with her in the past, and I will grow old a virgin as I am now. Your appeal to my father to vindicate his honour is one which I myself echo. To refuse to deliver you your wife would be to wrong him; for if he were living he would certainly restore you to each other. Right and wrong are rewarded in every country on earth, and not less among the dead. The mind of one departed may not have life; but it has become one with immortal spirit, and therefore has immortal understanding.

So, to be brief, I will, as you have asked, keep silence, and be no accomplice to my brother's wickedness. Indeed, what I do is a true service to him, turning his impious intent to righteousness.

Now I will leave you to yourselves and say nothing; you must discover some way of escape. Let your first thought be of the gods: pray that Aphrodite may allow you a safe voyage home; and that Hera, who now intends the welfare of you both, may not change her mind.

*She turns to the tomb.*

Father, I make this promise to your departed soul: no deed of mine shall ever profane your pious memory.

*Exit.*

CHORUS: Wickedness never prospers; but goodness may hope for its reward.

HELEN: Menelaus, as far as she is concerned we are safe. For the rest – make some suggestion; together we must plot our escape.

MENELAUS: Listen then: you have lived in the palace a long time; you are intimate with the servants?

HELEN: Why do you ask? Yes, there might be a hope there. Tell me your plan.

MENELAUS: Could you persuade one of the stable-men to get us a four-horse chariot?

HELEN: I could; but how should we escape by land – over these endless plains, and with Egyptians all round us?

MENELAUS: No, it's impossible. Well, what if I hid in the palace – I have my sword – and killed the king?

HELEN: Theonoe would never allow her brother to be killed; she would warn him.

MENELAUS: Even if we reach the shore, there is no ship to escape in; mine is at the bottom of the sea.

HELEN: Listen, Menelaus – a woman's plan might succeed: will you let me invent a story that you are dead?

MENELAUS: It may invite ill-luck; but if there's something solid to be gained, I'm willing to die – in fiction.

HELEN: Good; then I will appear before this pagan king in mourning for you, and weeping –

MENELAUS: How will that help our escape? This plan of yours seems a bit old-fashioned.

HELEN: I will tell him you were drowned at sea, and ask his permission to make a cenotaph for you.

MENELAUS: Suppose he agrees; giving me a cenotaph won't save our lives without a ship.

HELEN: I will ask him to provide us a ship, from which we may drop your burial-offerings into the lap of the sea.

MENELAUS: It's a good plan, except for this: if he tells you to perform the rites on land your story will be no use.

HELEN: But I'll tell him it's against Greek custom to bury on land those drowned at sea.

MENELAUS: Yes, that will do; then I'll go on board with you to help in the ritual.

HELEN: Yes, you, of course, chiefly; and all your sailors too who survived the wreck.

MENELAUS: Once I get hold of a ship at anchor, my men will be there, armed and disciplined.

HELEN: You must see to that; I only pray for favouring winds and a fair voyage.

MENELAUS: We shall have them; the gods are going to be kind! – By the way, who will you say told you I was dead?

HELEN: You. Say that you are the sole survivor of Menelaus's crew, and that you saw him drown.

MENELAUS: Yes! And this strip of sail I've tied round me will confirm your story of the wreck.

HELEN: It was luckily found, though you at that moment were almost lost. You're a pitiful sight; and that is going to save us.

MENELAUS: Had I better come indoors with you, or shall I sit quietly here by the tomb?

HELEN: Stay here; if he tries violence with you, the tomb gives you sanctuary – and you have your sword. I will go in now, change this white dress for mourning black, cut my hair short and tear my face with my nails till the blood runs. [MENELAUS *begins to protest.*] I must indeed; everything is at stake – my safe home-coming and your life. There is no third way; if we fail, if the king discovers my deception, I must die.

We pray to you, Queen Hera, who lie in the bed of Zeus, stretching our hands towards heaven, where you live in the star-embroidered heights: have pity upon us both and deliver us!

We pray to you, child of Dione, Aphrodite, for whom the prize of beauty was won by the promise of my hand: do not destroy me! Did I not suffer enough before, when you gave my name to dishonour among my own people? Will you now give my body to death in a foreign land? If you wish for my death, let me die in the city of my fathers. Why are you never sated with mortal suffering?

You traffic in lust and falsehood, crooked intrigue and secret drugs are your instruments of death. Were there but measure in your power, no other gives gifts so sweet as yours. That is all I can say.

HELEN *goes into the palace;* MENELAUS *remains.*

CHORUS:

Shy nightingale, mistress of woodland music,    [*Strophe* 1
Rapt votress, sweetening with each anguished note
The green leaf-curtained chambers of the forest,
Come to my call, and share my sorrow's burden
With shrill grief rippling from your russet throat.

Sharp was the pain of Helen, hot the tears
Troy's women shed, cursing the Hellene spears,
Since Trojan oars raced the rough Malean water,
And Paris, doomed in love, brought home from Sparta,
With mocking Aphrodite as his guide,
The phantom Helen for his fatal bride.

The sword played and the slung stone    [*Antistrophe* 1
    flew; and breath
Failed, and ten thousand Hellenes dwell with death,
Leaving heart-broken wives to mourn shorn-headed
In empty chambers. The lone sailor Nauplius

Lit his false fire on the Capherian Cape –
A star turned liar, that lured ten thousand more
To ram the sunk rocks like fierce jaws agape;
And watched men die amidst the Aegean's roar.

Menelaus, wandering storm-swept leagues from Sparta,
From Malea's bare cliff, to this foreign water,
Clutched the sham prize of many a gory blade –
The phantom Helen, that mocking Hera made.

You who in earnest ignorance          [*Strophe* 2
Would check the deeds of lawless men,
And in the clash of spear on spear
Gain honour – you are all stark mad!
If men, to settle each dispute,
Must needs compete in bloodshed, when
Shall violence vanish, hate be soothed,
Or men and cities live in peace?

  Why have the sons of Priam
Received each his portion in chambers of quiet earth,
When reasonable words could have solved the quarrel for
    Helen?
Now they lie deep in the lap of Death;
And flames leaping like Zeus's thunderbolt
Have levelled their walls with dust;
Helen, your heart bears grief on grief;
And brave Menelaus wrings tears from every eye.

You who with learned patience plod          [*Antistrophe* 2
Remotest realms of toilsome thought,
Can you by searching find out God,
Or bound his nature? Look at man!
From want to wealth, now forth, now back,
Now tossed from fame to infamy
By unforeseen, ambiguous chance!

Zeus was your father, Helen;
Winged like a swan he swooped to plant you in Leda's
    womb;
Yet, your name was shouted with execration
Through cities of Hellas, East to West:
Breaker of man's law and God's, breaker of faith!
So now I cannot tell
What mortal utterance may be called sure;
But truth is found in the mouth of God.

*Enter* THEOCLYMENUS *from hunting, with attendants. He does
not at first see* MENELAUS, *but turns to pay respect to the tomb.*

THEOCLYMENUS: Proteus, my father, I salute your monu-
ment, which I placed here that I might greet you at my
doorway. Always, going or coming, your son Theocly-
menus thus pays you worship.

Men, take the hounds and all your hunting gear into the
palace.

*Attendants go in;* THEOCLYMENUS *turns to the* CHORUS.

I've just been calling myself a fool. The trouble is, I don't
punish slackness in servants with death. And now I discover
that some Greek has landed here in broad daylight, and
slipped past my scouts; come to reconnoitre for Helen, or
even hoping to steal her away. Well, if we only catch him,
he shall die.

*He notices* HELEN'S *absence.*

Why! By the gods, I'm too late; he seems to have done
it. There's no one here. Helen's gone – she has been carried
off, taken out of the country! Ho, there, open the doors!
The woman I mean to marry shall not get clear of our shores
if I can prevent it.

*The doors open revealing* HELEN; *she is dressed in mourning.*

Wait, wait! I see what I was looking for. She is here in
the palace. She has not escaped.

Why, Helen! You have changed your white dress for
mourning black; you have laid the shears to your proud

head, and mown off your hair; your cheek is wet; you are weeping! Why is this? Is it some vivid dream that has made you sad? Or some rumour you have heard from Hellas, that has so changed your looks?

HELEN: My lord – now I may indeed call you 'my lord' – I am in deep distress; all my hopes are lost; my life is over.

THEOCLYMENUS: But what is your trouble? What has happened?

HELEN: Menelaus – oh, how can I say it? – Menelaus is dead.

THEOCLYMENUS: Then I do not grudge you your tears, if my good fortune is so great. But how do you know? Did you hear this from Theonoe?

HELEN: Yes, from her; and from a man who witnessed his death.

THEOCLYMENUS: What? Has someone come who can vouch for this?

HELEN: Yes, he has come; and may he go where I would have him go!

THEOCLYMENUS: Who is he? Where is he? I want to hear more details.

HELEN: There he sits, crouching by the tomb.

THEOCLYMENUS: By Apollo, what a sight! The man's in rags.

HELEN [weeping]: Oh! My poor husband suffered as he does!

THEOCLYMENUS: What is his country? Where was he sailing from?

HELEN: He is a Greek; one of those who were sailing with Menelaus.

THEOCLYMENUS: How does he say Menelaus died?

HELEN: The most piteous of deaths: drowned in the salt sea.

THEOCLYMENUS: Where was he sailing at the time?

HELEN: He was wrecked on the steep rocks of the Libyan coast.

THEOCLYMENUS: If this man was on the same ship, how did he escape?

HELEN: A slave is sometimes luckier than a king.

THEOCLYMENUS: Where has he left his wrecked ship?

HELEN: At the bottom of the sea – my curse on it! If only Menelaus had escaped!

THEOCLYMENUS [*with a satisfaction he cannot resist*]: But Menelaus was drowned. What vessel brought this man here?

HELEN: Sailors found him and picked him up, so he says.

THEOCLYMENUS: And what of the phantom that was sent in your place to curse Troy?

HELEN: It has vanished into air.

THEOCLYMENUS: Then Priam and his people perished for nothing.

HELEN: And I was involved in their disaster – for nothing.

THEOCLYMENUS: Did he leave your husband's body un-buried, or –

HELEN: Yes, unburied, unburied. [*She weeps.*]

THEOCLYMENUS: So this is why you have cut your golden locks.

HELEN: I loved him long ago when he was with me; I love him still.

THEOCLYMENUS: It is true, then? This is really what you are weeping for?

HELEN: Would it be easy for me to deceive your sister?

THEOCLYMENUS: It would not. Well: are you going to remain clinging to this tomb?

HELEN: I shrink from you – out of loyalty to my husband.

THEOCLYMENUS: Why tantalize me? Must you still re-member him?

HELEN: I will not any more. Now you may begin preparing for our marriage.

THEOCLYMENUS: Your consent has been long in coming; but it makes me happy.

HELEN: You know what must be done. Let us forget the past.

THEOCLYMENUS: I must be gracious in return. What shall I do?

HELEN: Let us call a truce, and be friends.

THEOCLYMENUS: All my anger – I renounce it, fling it to the winds.

HELEN: Then, since you are my friend, I fall at your feet and beg you, I cling to you as a suppliant –

THEOCLYMENUS: What do you desire?

HELEN: I want to bury my husband who has died.

THEOCLYMENUS: Bury him? What, a grave without a body? Do you want to bury his ghost?

HELEN: It is the custom in Hellas, when a man is lost at sea, to prepare an empty winding-sheet and perform the rites of burial.

THEOCLYMENUS: True, the sons of Pelops are skilled in these matters. Perform what is due; build a tomb for him anywhere you wish.

HELEN: We do not build tombs for men who go down with their ships.

THEOCLYMENUS: What, then? I know nothing of your customs.

HELEN: We lower into the sea the gifts that are due to the dead.

THEOCLYMENUS: What would you like me to provide for him?

HELEN: This man knows. I have no experience – such a loss is new to me.

THEOCLYMENUS [to MENELAUS]: Fellow, you have brought me happy news.

MENELAUS: Not happy for me; nor for the dead.

THEOCLYMENUS: How do you bury those who are drowned at sea?

MENELAUS: It varies according to the dead man's means.

THEOCLYMENUS: I will spare no expense, for Helen's sake. Tell me everything that should be done.

MENELAUS: First, an offering of blood to the powers of the earth.

THEOCLYMENUS: What beast should we offer? I will do as you say.

MENELAUS: You yourself must decide; whatever you give will be suitable.

THEOCLYMENUS: Our custom here is to kill a horse or a bull.

MENELAUS: But see that the beast you offer is without blemish.

THEOCLYMENUS: My herds are large; we have perfect beasts in plenty.

MENELAUS: Next we bring rugs and coverlets, as it were for a bed.

THEOCLYMENUS: You shall have them. What else?

MENELAUS: Armour and weapons of bronze: he was a soldier.

THEOCLYMENUS: The arms I give you shall be fit for a son of Pelops.

MENELAUS: And last, an offering of fine fruit, of every sort your soil produces.

THEOCLYMENUS: Good. Then how do you lower these gifts into the sea?

MENELAUS: There must be a ship manned with rowers.

THEOCLYMENUS: And how far must the ship go from shore?

MENELAUS: Till her white wake is hardly visible.

THEOCLYMENUS: But why? What do you achieve with this observance?

MENELAUS: That the tide may not cast up our offerings again on land.

THEOCLYMENUS: You shall have a Phoenician barque, which will prove swift enough.

MENELAUS: That is well; you are generous to Menelaus.

THEOCLYMENUS: Cannot you perform these rites alone, without Helen?

MENELAUS: The dead must be buried by mother, or wife, or child.

THEOCLYMENUS: You mean, this observance is Helen's duty.

MENELAUS: Those who fear God do not scant the service of the dead.

THEOCLYMENUS: Let her go; I would wish my wife to be a god-fearing woman. Go indoors, choose what gifts you need, make all arrangements; and if Helen is pleased with your work, I shall not send you away empty-handed. Pitiable figure as you are, you have brought me welcome news; then you shall have clothes for your nakedness, and food, and a happy return to your own country. And you, Helen – do not wear yourself out with useless weeping. I am sorry for you; but Menelaus has met his fate, and the dead cannot come back to life.

MENELAUS: It is your duty to obey, my lady. You must accept the husband who stands before you, and forget the one whose claim is ended. In your present position this will be best for you. And if I come safely home to Hellas, I will put an end to evil tales about you; only be the wife you should be to your husband.

HELEN: I will; and you shall be there to witness that my husband will have no cause to blame me.

But now go indoors and have a bath, poor man, and change your clothes. I will give you your reward at once; after all, you are more likely to show real devotion in performing what is due to my beloved Menelaus, if you have found me properly grateful.

*Exeunt into the palace* THEOCLYMENUS *and* HELEN, *followed by Guards escorting* MENELAUS.

CHORUS:
There was a time, they say, when the Great     [*Strophe* 1
    Mother
Ran to and fro frantic over the mountains,
Through green glades of the forest,
Scanning the swirl of every river,

Scouring the deep-voiced swell of the salt ocean,
Searching in anguish for her lost Persephone,
Maiden of mysteries.

Then with a shrill shout
Sang out the ecstatic cymbals,
The Phrygian lions were yoked,
And in her gorgeous chariot the goddess rode
To seek Persephone, stolen from the dancing ring of girls.
Beside her swept like whirlwinds the virgin goddesses,
Artemis armed with invincible arrows,
Athene with spear and Gorgon shield.
But Zeus from the throne of heaven saw their purpose,
And the will of Zeus went a different way.

Now when, weary and bewildered, the        [*Antistrophe* 1
    Great Mother
Ceased her swift searching over the mountains,
In despair for her stolen daughter
She climbed the dazzling snow-bound summits
Sacred to nymphs of Ida; and at her command
The swollen torrents that leap down the mountain gorges
Were swallowed in the sink of the sea.

And cattle starved on the brown plains;
The sapless earth could bear no fruit;
The child died in the womb;
No lusty bud or curling tendril-spray
Burst from the vine; and on cities a deathly silence fell;
No pious thanksgiving thronged the temples,
No altar flamed with holy oil;
Even the shining springs the goddess forbade to flow,
In frenzy of grief for her lost child.

So when the Phrygian Mother had compelled     [*Strophe* 2
Mortals and gods to cease from banqueting,

To soothe her, Zeus the King
Spoke to the Graces, those dread deities:
'Go to the goddess of Earth, who is angry still
For her stolen virgin child;
Charm her resentful heart with melodies,
And let the Muses lend their skill,
Dancing and singing.' First of the immortals came
Glorious Aphrodite, and she held
High the bronze cymbals, voiced like subterranean flame,
And the leathern tabors rattling wild.
And the goddess-mother smiled,
And her hands received the flute of sonorous tone
Which filled her heart with music like its own.

But the maid had sinned, in childish          [*Antistrophe* 2
    innocence
Breaking her fast in the dark rooms of earth.
The Mother of all birth
Saw her law slighted, and her anger rose.

A fearful power fills the bright dappled folds
Of a fawnskin cloak, fills the young ivy-shoot
Wreathed round a sacred fennel-wand;
Godhead itself is seen
In flash of an ecstatic hand that holds
High in the wind the whirling tambourine;
The toss of loose hair live with Bacchus' power;
Rapt vigil in the holy midnight hour.
And this dread deity who goes
Blazoned with glory on every hand –
She pardons none who taste the forbidden fruit.

HELEN *enters from the palace.*

HELEN: My dears, all goes well for us in the palace. The King
questioned Theonoe; but she is on our side and told him
nothing about my husband's arrival. Out of pure kindness

to me she told him that Menelaus was dead. As for the
equipment my husband needs, it was his own master-stroke
that procured it. He asked for bronze weapons to throw
into the sea: now he's bringing them himself, with his left
hand firm on the grip of the shield, and his right holding
the spear – all this by way of partaking in the ceremonies
due to the dead. So he's ready armed for the fight; and once
we're on board and under way, he'll settle accounts with
any number of Egyptians. I have provided him with clothes
instead of those rags from the wreck, and at last, after all
these years, he has had a proper bath in fresh water. – I must
be silent; here comes the man who thinks that marriage
with me is in his grasp. I beg of you, be my friends; guard
your tongues. It may be, if we escape, some day we could
help you to escape too.

*Enter* THEOCLYMENUS, *attended.*

THEOCLYMENUS: Now, men, take these gifts consecrated
to the sea, and pass on in due order, following this man's in-
structions. Helen: if I may suggest it, take my advice and
stay here. You will honour your husband equally whether
present at the ceremony or not. I am afraid some frenzy of
grief or devotion may drive you to throw yourself into the
sea. You are giving way to sorrow too much; especially
since his body is not even here.

HELEN: My husband – to be, duty insists that I honour my
first husband, and the memory of our marriage; and for
love of him I would even die with him. But what pleasure
could it give him, that I should share his death? No; let me
go myself, and give my gifts to the dead; and may the gods
grant to you everything that I wish; and to this man too,
for his help in what I am doing. You shall find in me such a
wife as your goodness to us both deserves; for all this leads
to a happy end. Now, complete your generosity by com-
manding a ship to be given us, to carry these gifts.

THEOCLYMENUS [*to an attendant*]: Go; give them a fifty-
oared Sidonian ship fully manned.

HELEN: As this man is arranging the burial, had he not better command the ship?

THEOCLYMENUS: Certainly; my men must take his orders.

HELEN: Repeat that command, to make sure your men understand you.

THEOCLYMENUS [to the attendants]: I repeat it: you take his orders. [To HELEN] I will say it a third time, if you wish.

HELEN: Blessings on you – and on my undertaking.

THEOCLYMENUS: Now, you must not spoil your beauty with too many tears.

HELEN: Today will show how grateful I am to you.

THEOCLYMENUS: This is wasted labour: the dead are nothing.

HELEN: I remember both the dead and the living.

THEOCLYMENUS: You will find in me as good a husband as Menelaus.

HELEN: You have been wonderful. All I pray for is good fortune.

THEOCLYMENUS: That lies with you. Only give me your heart.

HELEN: My heart knows now where its love belongs.

THEOCLYMENUS: Would you like my help? Shall I escort you myself?

HELEN: By no means; my lord must not serve his own servants.

THEOCLYMENUS: Away, then; your Greek ritual is nothing to me. My house is clean – it was not here that Menelaus died. Go, someone, tell my nobles to bring their wedding-gifts to the palace. Let the land ring aloud with music and songs of blessing, to celebrate the joy of my marriage with Helen.

[To MENELAUS] You, stranger, go and deliver these gifts into the arms of the sea, to honour him who was once her husband. When you have done it, bring my wife back with all speed to my palace. Then you shall share my table at our wedding-feast; and afterwards either sail for Hellas or live happily here.

*Exit* THEOCLYMENUS *to the palace.*

MENELAUS: O Zeus, named the Father of men, the com-
passionate, look upon us in our peril and save us. As we drag
our hopeful fortunes up the steep hill, stretch out your hand
and help us. One touch of your finger, and we shall reach
the deliverance we long for. Are my past sufferings not
enough for me to bear? Gods, I have blamed you foolishly,
and I repent. I have not deserved perpetual misery; now my
path should be straight. You have shown me one favour:
grant me now a lasting joy.

> MENELAUS, HELEN *and attendants move off*
> *towards the shore.*

CHORUS:

  Oars of the East,       [*Strophe* 1
 Winged Sidonian galley,
  Flash through the foam-spray!
 Darling of Nereus, dance,
 While the dancing dolphins follow!
 Now in the soft season,
 The sea smoothed with the wind's caress,
When the voice of Calm, the grey-blue daughter of Ocean,
  Quietly sings,
  Now spread sails to the breeze,
  Good-bye to the sheltering port,
 Grip and pull on the pinewood sweep,
 Crew of Menelaus, and carry in triumph
Helen to the harbours of home and the city that Perseus
 built.

  What will she see?     [*Antistrophe* 1
 Perhaps the daughters of Leucippus
  By the rough Eurotas
 Or before the temple of Pallas,
 If she comes at the season of dances,
 Or on the enchanted night
When the Spartans revel for Hyacinthus,

Whom Apollo killed by chance with his discus-rim
  In the game of throws;
    For whose sake the son of Zeus
    Appointed a holy day,
  Slaughter of bulls and banqueting.
  Perhaps she will see in the dancing ring
  The child she left, long ago, at home –
Hermione, waiting still for the bridal torches' flame.

  O for wings to tread the air　　　　　　[*Strophe* 2
    Where the cranes in ordered flight
      Shun the wintry rain-storm,
      Seek their southern homeland;
  Swift, obedient to their eldest leader's cry
      Rising shrill, triumphant,
      As they near the frontiers
Of this land, where rainless valleys teem with corn.

  Turn, you long-necked travellers,
  Who run winged races with the dancing clouds,
  And while the Pleiads still are in mid-course
  And Orion rides the darkened sky, swoop down,
  Alight on Eurotas and proclaim your news
  That the taker of Troy, Menelaus, is coming home.

  Speed along your airy path,　　　　　　[*Antistrophe* 2
  Riding sons of Tyndareus,
    You whose home is heaven
    And the stars' bright orbits!
  Helen's brothers, Helen's rescuers, ride on,
    Skim the green and foam-white ridges
    On the dark face of the ocean,
  Bring soft breath of welcome winds, the gift of Zeus.

  Cleanse your sister's fame,
  Slandered as paramour of a foreign prince.

Dearly she paid for that hot feud begun
When on Mount Ida goddesses came to trial;
Though never did Helen sail to the land of Troy
Or see the towers that Apollo built.

*Enter* THEOCLYMENUS, *unannounced, from the palace; before he
can speak, the* MESSENGER, *one of the attendants sent by*
THEOCLYMENUS *to accompany the procession, arrives from
the shore.*

MESSENGER: My lord! We know you were never one to
harbour suspicion; and now listen to the terrible news I have
to tell.

THEOCLYMENUS: What has happened?

MESSENGER: You must begin looking for another bride.
Helen has gone – fled the country.

THEOCLYMENUS: Gone! Has she escaped on foot or taken
wings?

MESSENGER: Menelaus has sailed clean away with her. It
was Menelaus who came and told you the tale of his own
death.

THEOCLYMENUS: Terrible news indeed; it is incredible!
How could they get away by sea?

MESSENGER: In the ship you gave to that Greek. Briefly, he
cleared your crew out, and sailed off with your ship.

THEOCLYMENUS: How? I want to know how! Was I to
suppose he could overpower a whole crew single-handed?
You were one of them!

MESSENGER: I will tell you all that took place after we left
the palace. As soon as the daughter of Zeus reached the
shore, with gestures and cries she made an accomplished
pretence of mourning for her husband – who, so far from
being dead, was there at her side. We entered the royal
dock, and launched a Sidonian ship of the first line, with a
full complement of fifty rowers. Everything was done in
order: one man was setting the mast, another placing the
oars, others knitting the line of them in a clean row, furling

the white sails, dropping the rudders into position by the cords.

While we were busy, some Greek sailors, who had come with Menelaus and must have been watching for the right moment, came towards us on the shore. They were fine-looking men, but wild and unkempt and dressed in rags like castaways. As soon as Menelaus saw them, with a fine show of grief in his voice and face he spoke to them. 'O you un-lucky Greeks, what was your ship? How were you wrecked? We are going to pay funeral honours to Menelaus, son of Atreus; his body is lost, but this lady, his wife Helen, will perform the ceremonies. Will you come and join us?' So they, with pretended tears, and solemnly bringing their own sea-offerings, came on board. To us that seemed suspicious; and some of us remarked that they were too many for the ship. However, we kept your instructions and held our tongues; it was putting that Greek in command that caused the whole disaster.

Now most of the gear, being light, we hoisted on board easily enough; but the bull for sacrifice stuck in his heels and refused to set foot on the gangway. He bellowed, rolled his eyes, humped his back, looked down his horn and would not let anyone touch him. Then Helen's husband shouted, 'Come on, you sackers of Troy, pick up that bull Greek-fashion! Get your shoulders under him and heave him on board; we'll offer him to the dead!' At the same time he drew his sword and held it high. The men came at his command, picked up the bull, carried him and set him down on deck. With the horse there was no trouble; Menelaus stroked his neck and forehead, and coaxed him on board.

At last, when everything was stowed, Helen set her lovely foot on the ship's ladder, and there she was, sitting near the stern, and Menelaus – the dead man – at her side. The rest of the Greeks were sitting along the gunwale, left and right, man for man, each with a sword hidden in his clothes; and the hull was full of our voices as we shouted the rowing-song.

When we were some way from shore – not too far, but well out – the helmsman called to Menelaus, 'Tell us, are we to sail on further? You are in command; will this do?' Menelaus replied, 'Far enough.' Then he made his way, sword in hand, to the prow. And as he stood there to slaughter the bull, and as he cut its throat, instead of utter-ing any dead man's name, he prayed, 'Poseidon, Lord of the sea, and you divine Nereids, bring my wife and me safe to the shores of Nauplia, home to a free land!' The blood streamed out in a long jet and fell into the sea – a good omen for the Greek. One of our men said, 'There's treachery afoot; let's get back to shore. Make them pull on the right; put the helm over.' Menelaus left the bull dead and stood and shouted to his men, 'Now is the time! Make Hellas proud of you! Cut these Egyptians to pieces and throw them into the sea!' And our captain in reply shouted to your crew, 'Up men, they are enemies! Get spars for weapons, smash benches, tear out rowlocks; at them and break their heads!'

Every man leapt to his feet. We had poles, they had swords; the ship was a welter of blood. We heard a voice from the stern cheering them on – it was Helen: 'Show these Egyptians the way you fought at Troy!' she cried, and her eager voice whetted their spirits for the battle. Your men were falling, struggling to their feet again; some you could see lying still and dead. Menelaus, in full armour, wherever he saw his friends worsted, went to their help; his sword flashed among his enemies, and their bodies flew hurtling overboard, till he had cleared every one of your rowers from the ship. Then he went over to the steersman and told him to make course for Hellas. The Greeks hoisted sail, and the wind was in their favour.

So they have gone. I escaped being killed and lowered

myself into the sea by the anchor. I was nearly exhausted when a fisherman picked me up and put me ashore to bring you the news. – Well, there is one thing every man has to learn: it is, not to be too trustful.

CHORUS: My lord, I could never have believed that Menelaus could come here, as he did, in person, without being recognized either by yourself or us.

THEOCLYMENUS: Oh! to be so miserably outwitted by a woman! That my chosen wife should slip from my hands! If there were any hope of overtaking them by ship, I would spare no effort to lay hands on them. As things are – it was my sister who betrayed me: she saw Menelaus in the palace and said nothing to me; then I will be revenged on her. She used her prophetic power to cheat me: it shall be the last time!

*He turns to enter the palace; but the* MESSENGER *has stepped between him and the palace door.*

MESSENGER: Now, my lord, where are you going? Do you mean to commit murder?

THEOCLYMENUS: Get out of my way. I am going to commit justice.

MESSENGER: It would be a terrible crime. I will not let you go.

THEOCLYMENUS: Am I to take orders from a slave?

MESSENGER: Yes, because I am right!

THEOCLYMENUS: You are doing me wrong, unless you let me go –

MESSENGER: I will not!

THEOCLYMENUS: My sister deserves death; she is a traitress.

MESSENGER: No, she is a woman who fears the gods; it was just and right to deceive you.

THEOCLYMENUS: She gave my wife to another man.

MESSENGER: She was his by right; her father gave her to Menelaus.

THEOCLYMENUS: Fortune gave her to me. Menelaus had no right to what was mine.

MESSENGER: Fate took her from you: it was to be.

THEOCLYMENUS: I can judge my own affairs.

MESSENGER: But I am a better judge than you.

THEOCLYMENUS: Who is king, you or I?

MESSENGER: It is for the king to do right, not wrong.

THEOCLYMENUS: You are in love with death, I think.

MESSENGER: Kill me! But you shall not kill your sister if I
   can prevent it. The noblest thing a slave can do is to die for
   his master.

   *The* DIOSCORI *suddenly appear above the palace door.*

DIOSCORI:

   Control your sinful fury, Theoclymenus, King of Egypt!
   We are the sons of Zeus and Leda, the Dioscori,
   Brothers of this same Helen who has escaped from your
      palace.
   Despite your rage, know that this marriage was not for you;
   Theonoe your sister, the Nereid's daughter, did not wrong
      you,
   But honoured the will of Heaven and your father's just
      command.
   Destiny ordained that Helen until this present day
   Should live here in your palace; but now that Troy's strong
      walls
   Are breached and blackened, no divine end is further served
   By Helen's borrowed name; it is right that she once more
   Be joined with her true husband and live in her own home.
   Then sheathe that murderous sword drawn for your
      sister's blood;
   Confess her wisdom. We, now raised by Zeus to godhead,
   Would long ago have contrived to rescue her from your land,
   But bowed to Fate, and the divine purpose thus fulfilled.

   So much for you, Theoclymenus; next I speak to Helen:
   Sail on with your true husband; fair winds shall speed you;
      and we

Your brothers, riding the waves, will escort you safely
    home.
And when your course is run, and your mortal term ful-
    filled,
You shall rise divine, and with us receive from the race of
    men
Worship and holy feasts; for such is the will of Zeus.


The island where Hermes first, running the sky from Sparta,
A thief with his spoil, your beauty, to cheat the ardent
    Paris –
Where Hermes hid his treasure, the straggling isle that lines
The Actaean coast, henceforth shall bear your name for
    remembrance.
Menelaus the far-voyager wins by the will of Heaven
A home in the Isle of the Blest. For the noble and brave are
    not
Hated by the gods; but they meet more trouble than com-
    mon men.

THEOCLYMENUS:

Sons of Leda and Zeus! I renounce my bitterness of heart
For my lost bride. Let her go to her home, since Heaven so
    wills.
Theonoe's life I spare. Immortal Twins, the sister
Your almighty Father gave you is perfect in faith and
    chastity.
Women, I wish you joy in the virtuous heart of Helen –
A joy which many women can have no hope to share!

CHORUS:

The gods reveal themselves in many forms,
Bring many matters to surprising ends.
The things we thought would happen do not happen;
The unexpected God makes possible:
And this is what has happened here today.

# THE BACCHAE

*

## Characters:

DIONYSUS
CHORUS *of Oriental women, devotees of Dionysus*
TEIRESIAS, *a blind Seer*
CADMUS, *founder of Thebes, and formerly king*
PENTHEUS, *his grandson, now king of Thebes*
A GUARD *attending Pentheus*
A HERDSMAN
A MESSENGER
AGAUË, *daughter of Cadmus and mother of Pentheus*

*

*Scene: Before the palace of Pentheus in Thebes. At one side of the
stage is the monument of Semele; above it burns a low flame, and
around it are the remains of ruined and blackened masonry.*

DIONYSUS *enters on stage right. He has a crown of ivy, a
thyrsus in his hand, and a fawnskin draped over his body. He
has long flowing hair and a youthful, almost feminine beauty.*

DIONYSUS:
I am Dionysus, son of Zeus. My mother was
Semele, Cadmus' daughter. From her womb the fire
Of a lightning-flash delivered me. I have come here
To Thebes and her two rivers, Dirce and Ismenus,
Veiling my godhead in a mortal shape. I see
Here near the palace my mother's monument, that records
Her death by lightning. Here her house stood; and its
    ruins
Smoulder with the still living flame of Zeus's fire –
The immortal cruelty Hera wreaked upon my mother.
Cadmus does well to keep this ground inviolable,
A precinct consecrated in his daughter's name;

And I have decked it round with sprays of young vine-
    leaves.
  From the fields of Lydia and Phrygia, fertile in gold,
I travelled first to the sun-smitten Persian plains,
The walled cities of Bactria, the harsh Median country,
Wealthy Arabia, and the whole tract of the Asian coast
Where mingled swarms of Greeks and Orientals live
In vast magnificent cities; and before reaching this,
The first city of Hellas I have visited,
I had already, in all those regions of the east,
Performed my dances and set forth my ritual
To make my godhead manifest to mortal men.
  The reason why I have chosen Thebes as the first place
To raise my Bacchic shout, and clothe all who respond
In fawnskin habits, and put my thyrsus in their hands –
The weapon wreathed with ivy-shoots – my reason is
    this:
My mother's sisters said – what they should have been
    the last
To say – that I, Dionysus, was not Zeus's son;
That Semele, being with child – they said – by some
    mortal,
Obeyed her father's prompting, and ascribed to Zeus
The loss of her virginity; and they loudly claimed
That this lie was the sin for which Zeus took her life.
  Therefore I have driven those same sisters mad, turned
    them
All frantic out of doors; their home now is the mountain;
Their wits are gone. I have made them bear the emblem of
My mysteries; the whole female population of Thebes,
To the last woman, I have sent raving from their homes.
Now, side by side with Cadmus' daughters, one and all
Sit roofless on the rocks under the silver pines.
For Thebes, albeit reluctantly, must learn in full
This lesson, that my Bacchic worship is a matter

As yet beyond her knowledge and experience;
And I must vindicate my mother Semele
By manifesting myself before the human race
As the divine son whom she bore to immortal Zeus.

  Now Cadmus has made over his throne and kingly
    honours
To Pentheus, son of his eldest daughter Agaue. He
Is a fighter against gods, defies me, excludes me from
Libations, never names me in prayers. Therefore I will
Demonstrate to him, and to all Thebes, that I am a god.

  When I have set all in order here, I will pass on
To another place, and manifest myself. Meanwhile
If Thebes in anger tries to bring the Bacchants home
By force from the mountain, I myself will join that army
Of women possessed and lead them to battle. That is
    why
I have changed my form and taken the likeness of a man.

  Come, my band of worshippers, women whom I have
    brought
From lands of the east, from Tmolus, bastion of Lydia,
To be with me and share my travels! Raise the music
Of your own country, the Phrygian drums invented by
Rhea the Great Mother and by me. Fill Pentheus' palace
With a noise to make the city of Cadmus turn and look!
– And I will go to the folds of Mount Cithaeron, where
The Bacchants are, and join them in their holy dance.

  DIONYSUS *goes out towards the mountain. The* CHORUS
*enter where Dionysus entered, from the road by which they
have travelled.*

CHORUS:
  From far-off lands of Asia,                    [*Strophe* 1
  From Tmolus the holy mountain,
  We run with the god of laughter;
  Labour is joy and weariness is sweet,
  And our song resounds to Bacchus!

Who stands in our path? [*Antistrophe* 1
Make way, make way!
Who in the house? Close every lip,
Keep holy silence, while we sing
The appointed hymn to Bacchus!

Blest is the happy man [*Strophe* 2
Who knows the mysteries the gods ordain,
And sanctifies his life,
Joins soul with soul in mystic unity,
And, by due ritual made pure,
Enters the ecstasy of mountain solitudes;
Who observes the mystic rites
Made lawful by Cybele the Great Mother;
Who crowns his head with ivy,
And shakes aloft his wand in worship of Dionysus.

On, on! Run, dance, delirious, possessed!
Dionysus comes to his own;
Bring from the Phrygian hills to the broad streets of Hellas
The god, child of a god,
Spirit of revel and rapture, Dionysus!

Once, on the womb that held him [*Antistrophe* 2
The fire-bolt flew from the hand of Zeus;
And pains of child-birth bound his mother fast,
And she cast him forth untimely,
And under the lightning's lash relinquished life;
And Zeus the son of Cronos
Ensconced him instantly in a secret womb
Chambered within his thigh,
And with golden pins closed him from Hera's sight.

So, when the Fates had made him ripe for birth,
Zeus bore the bull-horned god

And wreathed his head with wreaths of writhing snakes;
Which is why the Maenads catch
Wild snakes, nurse them and twine them round their hair.


O Thebes, old nurse that cradled Semele,     [*Strophe* 3
Be ivy-garlanded, burst into flower
With wreaths of lush bright-berried bryony,
Bring sprays of fir, green branches torn from oaks,
Fill soul and flesh with Bacchus' mystic power;
Fringe and bedeck your dappled fawnskin cloaks
With woolly tufts and locks of purest white.
There's a brute wildness in the fennel-wands –
Reverence it well. Soon the whole land will dance
    When the god with ecstatic shout
    Leads his companies out
    To the mountain's mounting height
    Swarming with riotous bands
    Of Theban women leaving
    Their spinning and their weaving
    Stung with the maddening trance
        Of Dionysus!


O secret chamber the Curetes knew!     [*Antistrophe* 3
O holy cavern in the Cretan glade
Where Zeus was cradled, where for our delight
The triple-crested Corybantes drew
Tight the round drum-skin, till its wild beat made
Rapturous rhythm to the breathing sweetness
Of Phrygian flutes! Then divine Rhea found
The drum could give her Bacchic airs completeness;
    From her, the Mother of all,
    The crazy Satyrs soon,
    In their dancing festival
    When the second year comes round,
    Seized on the timbrel's tune

To play the leading part
In feasts that delight the heart
   Of Dionysus.


O what delight is in the mountains!                          [*Epode*
There the celebrant, wrapped in his sacred fawnskin,
Flings himself on the ground surrendered,
While the swift-footed company streams on;
There he hunts for blood, and rapturously
Eats the raw flesh of the slaughtered goat,
Hurrying on to the Phrygian or Lydian mountain heights.
Possessed, ecstatic, he leads their happy cries;
The earth flows with milk, flows with wine,
Flows with nectar of bees;
The air is thick with a scent of Syrian myrrh.
The celebrant runs entranced, whirling the torch
That blazes red from the fennel-wand in his grasp,
And with shouts he rouses the scattered bands,
Sets their feet dancing,
As he shakes his delicate locks to the wild wind.
And amidst the frenzy of song he shouts like thunder:
'On, on! Run, dance, delirious, possessed!
You, the beauty and grace of golden Tmolus,
Sing to the rattle of thunderous drums,
Sing for joy,
Praise Dionysus, god of joy!
Shout like Phrygians, sing out the tunes you know,
While the sacred pure-toned flute
Vibrates the air with holy merriment,
In time with the pulse of the feet that flock
To the mountains, to the mountains!'
And, like a foal with its mother at pasture,
Runs and leaps for joy every daughter of Bacchus.
    *Enter* TEIRESIAS. *Though blind, he makes his way*
         *unaided to the door, and knocks.*

TEIRESIAS:

Who keeps the gate? Call Cadmus out, Agenor's son,
Who came from Sidon here to build these walls of
      Thebes.
Go, someone, say Teiresias is looking for him.
He knows why; I'm an old man, and he's older still –
But we agreed to equip ourselves with Bacchic wands
And fawnskin cloaks, and put on wreaths of ivy-shoots.

*Enter* CADMUS.

CADMUS:

Dear friend, I knew your voice, although I was indoors,
As soon as I heard it – the wise voice of a wise man.
I am ready. See, I have all that the god prescribes.
He is my daughter's son; we must do all we can
To exalt and honour him. Where shall we go to dance
And take our stand with others, tossing our grey heads?
You tell me what to do, Teiresias. We're both old,
But you're the expert.
[*He stumps about, beating his thyrsus on the ground.*]
                              I could drum the ground all night
And all day too, without being tired. What joy it is
To forget one's age!

TEIRESIAS:                I feel exactly the same way,
Bursting with youth! I'll try it – I'll dance with the rest.

CADMUS: You don't think we should go to the mountain in
a coach?

TEIRESIAS: No, no. That would not show the god the
same respect.

CADMUS: I'll take you there myself then – old as we both are.

TEIRESIAS: The god will guide us there, and without weari-
ness.

CADMUS: Are we the only Thebans who will dance to him?

TEIRESIAS: We see things clearly; all the others are perverse.

CADMUS: We're wasting time; come, take my hand.

TEIRESIAS:                              Here, then; hold tight.

CADMUS: I don't despise religion. I'm a mortal man.

TEIRESIAS:
We have no use for theological subtleties.
The beliefs we have inherited, as old as time,
Cannot be overthrown by any argument,
Not by the most inventive ingenuity.
It will be said, I lack the dignity of my age,
To wear this ivy-wreath and set off for the dance.
Not so; the god draws no distinction between young
And old, to tell us which should dance and which should
    not.
He desires equal worship from all men: his claim
To glory is universal; no one is exempt.

CADMUS:
Teiresias, I shall be your prophet, since you are blind.
Pentheus, to whom I have resigned my rule in Thebes,
Is hurrying here towards the palace. He appears
Extremely agitated. What news will he bring?

*Enter* PENTHEUS. *He addresses the audience, without at first
noticing* CADMUS *and* TEIRESIAS, *who stand at the opposite
side of the stage.*

PENTHEUS:
I happen to have been away from Thebes; reports
Of this astounding scandal have just been brought to me.
Our women, it seems, have left their homes on some
    pretence
Of Bacchic worship, and are now gadding about
On the wooded mountain-slopes, dancing in honour of
This upstart god Dionysus, whoever he may be.
Amidst these groups of worshippers, they tell me, stand
Bowls full of wine; and our women go creeping off
This way and that to lonely places and give themselves
To lecherous men. They are Maenad priestesses, if you
    please!
Aphrodite supplants Bacchus in their ritual.

Well, those I've caught, my guards are keeping safe;
    we've tied
Their hands, and lodged them at state expense. Those
    still at large
On the mountain I am going to hunt out; and that
Includes my own mother Agaue and her sisters
Ino and Autonoe. Once they're fast in iron fetters,
I'll put a stop to this outrageous Bacchism.

    They tell me, too, some oriental conjurer
Has come from Lydia, a magician with golden hair
Flowing in scented ringlets, his face flushed with wine,
His eyes lit with the charm of Aphrodite; and he
Entices young girls with his Bacchic mysteries,
Spends days and nights consorting with them. Once let
    me
Get that fellow inside my walls – I'll cut his head
From his shoulders; that will stop him drumming with
    his thyrsus,
Tossing his long hair. *He*'s the one – this foreigner –
Who says Dionysus is a god; who says he was
Sewn up in Zeus's thigh. The truth about Dionysus
Is that he's dead, burnt to a cinder by lightning
Along with his mother, because she said Zeus lay with
    her.
Whoever the man may be, is not his arrogance
An outrage? Has he not earned a rope around his neck?
[PENTHEUS *turns to go, and sees* CADMUS *and* TEIRESIAS.]
Why, look! Another miracle! Here's Teiresias
The prophet – in a fawnskin; and my mother's father –
A Bacchant with a fennel-wand! Well, there's a sight
For laughter! [*But he is raging, not laughing.*]
            Sir, I am ashamed to see two men
Of your age with so little sense of decency.
Come, you're my grandfather: throw down that ivy-
    wreath,

Get rid of that thyrsus! – *You* persuaded him to this,
Teiresias. By introducing a new god, you hope
To advance your augurer's business, to collect more fees
For inspecting sacrifices. Listen: your grey hairs
Are your protection; otherwise you'd be sitting now
In prison with all these crazy females, for promoting
Pernicious practices. As for women, I tell you this:
Wherever the sparkle of sweet wine adorns their feasts,
No good will follow from such Bacchic ceremonies.

CHORUS:

Have you no reverence, Sir, no piety? Do you mock
Cadmus, who sowed the dragon-seed of earth-born men?
Do you, Echion's son, dishonour your own race?

TEIRESIAS:

When a good speaker has a sound case to present,
Then eloquence is no great feat. Your fluent tongue
Promises wisdom; but the content of your speech
Is ignorant. Power and eloquence in a headstrong man
Spell folly; such a man is a peril to the state.

   This new god, whom you ridicule – no words of mine
Could well express the ascendancy he will achieve
In Hellas. There are two powers, young man, which are
    supreme
In human affairs: first, Demeter – the same goddess
Is also Earth; give her which name you please – and she
Supplies mankind with solid food. After her came
Dionysus, Semele's son; the blessing he procured
And gave to men is counterpart to that of bread:
The clear juice of the grape. When mortals drink their fill
Of wine, the sufferings of our unhappy race
Are banished, each day's troubles are forgotten in sleep.
There is no other cure for sorrow. Dionysus,
Himself a god, is thus poured out in offering
To the gods, so that through him come blessings on
    mankind.

And do you scorn this legend, that he was sewn up
In Zeus's thigh? I will explain the truth to you.
When Zeus snatched Dionysus from the lightning-flame
And took the child up to Olympus as a god,
Hera resolved to cast him out of heaven. But Zeus
Found such means to prevent her as a god will find.
He took a fragment of the ether that surrounds
The earth, fashioned it like a child, presented it
To Hera as a pledge to soothe her jealousy,
And saved Dionysus from her. Thus, in time, because
The ancient words for 'pledge' and 'thigh' are similar,
People confused them, and the 'pledge' Zeus gave to
    Hera
Became transformed, as time went on, into the tale
That Dionysus was sewn up in Zeus's thigh.

    And this god is a prophet; the Bacchic ecstasy
And frenzy hold a strong prophetic element.
When he fills irresistibly a human body
He gives those so possessed power to foretell the future.
In Ares' province too Dionysus has his share;
Sometimes an army, weaponed and drawn up for battle,
Has fled in wild panic before a spear was raised.
This too is an insanity sent by Dionysus.

    Ay, and the day will come when, on the very crags
Of Delphi, you shall see him leaping, amidst the blaze
Of torches, over the twin-peaked ridge, waving aloft
And brandishing his Bacchic staff, while all Hellas
Exalts him. Pentheus, pay heed to my words. You rely
On force; but it is not force that governs human affairs.
Do not mistake for wisdom that opinion which
May rise from a sick mind. Welcome this god to Thebes,
Offer libations to him, celebrate his rites,
Put on his garland. Dionysus will not compel
Women to be chaste, since in all matters self-control
Resides in our own natures. You should consider this;

For in the Bacchic ritual, as elsewhere, a woman
Will be safe from corruption if her mind is chaste.
Think of this too: when crowds stand at the city gates
And Thebes extols the name of Pentheus, you rejoice;
So too, I think, the god is glad to receive honour.

  Well, I at least, and Cadmus, whom you mock, will
    wear
The ivy-wreath and join the dancing – we are a pair
Of grey heads, but this is our duty; and no words
Of yours shall lure me into fighting against gods.
For a most cruel insanity has warped your mind;
While drugs may well have caused it, they can bring no
    cure.

CHORUS:

What you have said, Teiresias, shows no disrespect
To Apollo; at the same time you prove your judgement
    sound
In honouring Dionysus as a mighty god.

CADMUS:

My dear son, Teiresias has given you good advice.
Don't stray beyond pious tradition; live with us.
Your wits have flown to the winds, your sense is
    foolishness.
Even if, as you say, Dionysus is no god,
Let him have *your* acknowledgement; lie royally,
That Semele may get honour as having borne a god,
And credit come to us and to all our family.

  Remember, too, Actaeon's miserable fate –
Torn and devoured by hounds which he himself had
    bred,
Because he filled the mountains with the boast that he
Was a more skilful hunter than Artemis herself.
Don't share his fate, my son! Come, let me crown your
    head
With a wreath of ivy; join us in worshipping this god.

PENTHEUS:

Keep your hands off! Go to your Bacchic rites, and don't
Wipe off your crazy folly on me. But I will punish
This man who has been your instructor in lunacy.
Go, someone, quickly to his seat of augury,
Smash it with crowbars, topple the walls, throw all his
    things
In wild confusion, turn the whole place upside down,
Fling out his holy fripperies to the hurricane winds!
This sacrilege will sting him more than anything else.
The rest of you – go, comb the country and track down
That effeminate foreigner, who plagues our women with
This new disease, fouls the whole land with lechery;
And once you catch him, tie him up and bring him here
To me; I'll deal with him. He shall be stoned to death.
He'll wish he'd never brought his Bacchic rites to Thebes.

*Exit* PENTHEUS.

TEIRESIAS:

Foolhardy man! You do not know what you have said.
Before, you were unbalanced; now you are insane.
Come, Cadmus; let us go and pray both for this man,
Brutish as he is, and for our city, and beg the god
To show forbearance. Come, now, take your ivy staff
And let us go. Try to support me; we will help
Each other. It would be scandalous for two old men
To fall; still, we must go, and pay our due service
To Dionysus, son of Zeus. – Cadmus, the name
*Pentheus* means *sorrow*. God grant he may not bring
    sorrow
Upon your house. Do not take that as prophecy;
I judge his acts. Such foolish words bespeak a fool.

*Exeunt* TEIRESIAS *and* CADMUS.

CHORUS:

Holiness, Queen of heaven,                    [*Strophe* 1
Holiness, golden-winged ranging the earth,

Do you hear his blasphemy?
Pentheus dares – do you hear? – to revile the god of joy,
The son of Semele, who when the gay-crowned feast is
    set
Is named among gods the chief;
Whose gifts are joy and union of soul in dancing,
Joy in music of flutes,
Joy when sparkling wine at feasts of the gods
Soothes the sore regret,
Banishes every grief,
When the reveller rests, enfolded deep
In the cool shade of ivy-shoots,
On wine's soft pillow of sleep.

The brash unbridled tongue,                    [*Antistrophe* 1
The lawless folly of fools, will end in pain.
But the life of wise content
Is blest with quietness, escapes the storm
And keeps its house secure.
Though blessed gods dwell in the distant skies,
They watch the ways of men.
To know much is not to be wise.
Pride more than mortal hastens life to its end;
And they who in pride pretend
Beyond man's limit, will lose what lay
Close to their hand and sure.
I count it madness, and know no cure can mend
The evil man and his evil way.

O to set foot on Aphrodite's island,                    [*Strophe* 2
On Cyprus, haunted by the Loves, who enchant
Brief life with sweetness; or in that strange land
Whose fertile river carves a hundred channels
To enrich her rainless sand;
Or where the sacred pastures of Olympus slant

Down to Pieria, where the Muses dwell –
Take me, O Bromius, take me and inspire
Laughter and worship! There our holy spell
And ecstasy are welcome; there the gentle band
Of Graces have their home, and sweet Desire.

Dionysus, son of Zeus, delights in banquets; [*Antistrophe 2*
And his dear love is Peace, giver of wealth,
Saviour of young men's lives – a goddess rare!
In wine, his gift that charms all griefs away,
Alike both rich and poor may have their part.
His enemy is the man who has no care
To pass his years in happiness and health,
His days in quiet and his nights in joy,
Watchful to keep aloof both mind and heart
From men whose pride claims more than mortals may.
The life that wins the poor man's common voice,
His creed, his practice – this shall be my choice.

*Some of the guards whom* PENTHEUS *sent to arrest* DIONYSUS
*now enter with their prisoner.* PENTHEUS *enters from the palace.*

GUARD:

Pentheus, we've brought the prey you sent us out to
        catch;
We hunted him, and here he is. But, Sir, we found
The beast was gentle; made no attempt to run away,
Just held his hands out to be tied; didn't turn pale,
But kept his florid colour, smiling, telling us
To tie him up and run him in; gave us no trouble
At all, just waited for us. Naturally I felt
A bit embarrassed. 'You'll excuse me, Sir,' I said,
'I don't want to arrest you; it's the king's command.'
    Another thing, Sir – those women you rounded up
And put in fetters in the prison, those Bacchants;
Well, they're all gone, turned loose to the glens; and
        there they are,

    Frisking about, calling on Bromius their god.

    The fetters simply opened and fell off their feet;

    The bolts shot back, untouched by mortal hand; the doors

    Flew wide. Master, this man has come here with a load

    Of miracles. Well, what happens next is your concern.

PENTHEUS:

    Untie this man's hands. [*The* GUARD *does so.*] He's
        securely in the trap.

    He's not so nimble-footed as to escape me now.

      Well, friend: your shape is not unhandsome – for the
        pursuit

    Of women, which is the purpose of your presence here.

    You are no wrestler, I can tell from these long curls

    Cascading most seductively over your cheek.

    Your skin, too, shows a whiteness carefully preserved;

    You keep away from the sun's heat, walk in the shade,

    So hunting Aphrodite with your lovely face.

      Ah, well; first tell me who you are. What is your
        birth?

DIONYSUS:

    Your question's easily answered, it is no secret.

    Perhaps you have heard of Tmolus, a mountain decked
        with flowers.

PENTHEUS: A range that curves round Sardis? Yes, I know
    of it.

DIONYSUS: That is my home. I am a Lydian by birth.

PENTHEUS: How comes it that you bring these rituals to
    Hellas?

DIONYSUS: Dionysus, son of Zeus, himself instructed me.

PENTHEUS: Is there a Lydian Zeus, then, who begets new
    gods?

DIONYSUS: I speak of Zeus who wedded Semele here in
    Thebes.

PENTHEUS: Did he possess you in a dream, or visibly?

DIONYSUS: Yes, face to face; he gave these mysteries to me.

PENTHEUS: These mysteries you speak of: what form do they take?

DIONYSUS: To the uninitiated that must not be told.

PENTHEUS: And those who worship – what advantage do they gain?

DIONYSUS: It is not for you to learn; yet it is worth knowing.

PENTHEUS: You bait your answer well, to arouse my eagerness.

DIONYSUS: His rituals abhor a man of impious life.

PENTHEUS: You say you saw him face to face: what was he like?

DIONYSUS: Such as he chose to be. I had no say in that.

PENTHEUS: Still you side-track my question with an empty phrase.

DIONYSUS: Just so. A prudent speech sleeps in a foolish ear.

PENTHEUS: Is Thebes the first place where you have introduced this god?

DIONYSUS: No; every eastern land dances these mysteries.

PENTHEUS: No doubt. Their moral standards fall far below ours.

DIONYSUS: In this they are superior; but their customs differ.

PENTHEUS: Do you perform these mysteries by night or day?

DIONYSUS: Chiefly by night. Darkness promotes religious awe.

PENTHEUS: For women darkness is deceptive and impure.

DIONYSUS: Impurity can be pursued by daylight too.

PENTHEUS: You must be punished for your foul and slippery tongue.

DIONYSUS: And you for blindness and impiety to the god.

PENTHEUS: How bold this Bacchant is! A practised pleader too.

DIONYSUS: Tell me my sentence. What dread pain will you inflict?

PENTHEUS: I'll start by cutting off your delicate long hair.

DIONYSUS: My hair is sacred; I preserve it for the god.

PENTHEUS: And next, that thyrsus in your hand – give it to
  me.

DIONYSUS: Take it from me yourself; it is the god's emblem.

PENTHEUS: I'll lock you up in prison and keep you there.

DIONYSUS:                                          The god
  Himself, whenever I desire, will set me free.

PENTHEUS: Of course – when you, with all your Bacchants,
  call to him!

DIONYSUS: He is close at hand here, and sees what is done
  to me.

PENTHEUS: Indeed? Where is he, then? Not visible to my
  eyes.

DIONYSUS: Beside me. You, being a blasphemer, see noth-
  ing.

PENTHEUS [to the GUARDS]: Get hold of him; he's mocking
  me and the whole city.

DIONYSUS [to the GUARDS]: Don't bind me, I warn you.
  [To PENTHEUS] I am sane, and you are mad.

PENTHEUS: My word overrules yours. [To the GUARDS] I
  tell you, bind him fast.

DIONYSUS: You know not what you are saying, what you
  do, nor who
  You are.

PENTHEUS:         Who? Pentheus, son of Echion and Agauë.

DIONYSUS: Your name points to calamity. It fits you well.

PENTHEUS:
  Take him away and shut him in my stables, where
  He can stay staring at darkness. – You can dance in there!
  As for these women you've brought as your accomplices,
  I'll either send them to the slave-market to be sold,
  Or keep them in my own household to work the looms;
  And that will stop their fingers drumming on
    tambourines!

DIONYSUS:
  I'll go. Nothing can touch me that is not ordained.

But I warn you: Dionysus, who you say is dead,
Will come in swift pursuit to avenge this sacrilege.
You are putting *him* in prison when you lay hands on
    me.

GUARDS *take* DIONYSUS *away to the stables;* PENTHEUS
                                    *follows.*

CHORUS:

    Dirce, sweet and holy maid,                    [*Strophe*
    Acheloüs' Theban daughter,
    Once the child of Zeus was made
    Welcome in your welling water,
    When the lord of earth and sky
    Snatched him from the undying flame,
    Laid him safe within his thigh,
    Calling loud the infant's name:
    'Twice-born Dithyrambus! Come,
    Enter here your father's womb;
    Bacchic child, I now proclaim
    This in Thebes shall be your name.'
Now, divine Dirce, when my head is crowned
And my feet dance in Bacchus' revelry –
Now you reject me from your holy ground.
Why should you fear me? By the purple fruit
That glows in glory on Dionysus' tree,
His dread name yet shall haunt your memory!

    Oh, what anger lies beneath                    [*Antistrophe*
    Pentheus' voice and sullen face –
    Offspring of the dragon's teeth,
    And Echion's earth-born race,
    Brute with bloody jaws agape,
    God-defying, gross and grim,
    Slander of his human shape!
    Soon he'll chain us limb to limb –
    Bacchus' servants! Yes, and more:
    Even now our comrade lies

Deep on his dark prison floor.
   Dionysus! Do your eyes
See us? O son of Zeus, the oppressor's rod
Falls on your worshippers; come, mighty god,
Brandish your golden thyrsus and descend
From great Olympus; touch this murderous man,
And bring his violence to a sudden end!

Where are you, Dionysus? Leading your dancing   [*Epode*
   bands
Over the mountain slopes, past many a wild beast's lair,
Or on Corycian crags, with the thyrsus in their hands?
Or in the wooded coverts, maybe, of Olympus, where
Orpheus once gathered the trees and mountain beasts,
Gathered them with his lyre, and sang an enchanting air.
Happy vale of Pieria! Bacchus delights in you;
He will cross the flood and foam of the Axius river, and
   there
He will bring his whirling Maenads, with dancing and
   with feasts,
Cross the father of waters, Lydias, generous giver
Of wealth and luck, they say, to the land he wanders
   through,
Whose famous horses graze by the rich and lovely river.
   *Suddenly a shout is heard from inside the building –*
      *the voice of* DIONYSUS.

DIONYSUS:
Io, Io! Do you know my voice, do you hear?
Worshippers of Bacchus! Io, Io!

CHORUS:
Who is that? Where is he?
The shout of Dionysus is calling us!

DIONYSUS:
Io, Io! Hear me again:
I am the son of Semele, the son of Zeus!

CHORUS:

Io, Io, our lord, our lord!

Come, then, come to our company, lord of joy!

DIONYSUS: O dreadful earthquake, shake the floor of the
world!

CHORUS [with a scream of terror]:

Pentheus' palace is falling, crumbling in pieces! [They
continue severally]

– Dionysus stands in the palace; bow before him!

– We bow before him. – See how the roof and pillars

Plunge to the ground! – Bromius is with us,

He shouts from prison the shout of victory!

The flame on Semele's tomb grows and brightens.

DIONYSUS:

Fan to a blaze the flame the lightning lit;

Kindle the conflagration of Pentheus' palace!

CHORUS:

Look, look, look!

Do you see, do you see the flame of Semele's tomb,

The flame that lived when she died of the lightning-stroke?

A noise of crashing masonry is heard.

Down, trembling Maenads! Hurl yourselves to the ground.

Your god is wrecking the palace, roof to floor;

He heard our cry – he is coming, the son of Zeus!

The doors open and DIONYSUS appears.

DIONYSUS:

Women of Asia, why do you cower thus, prostrate and
terrified?

Surely you could hear Dionysus shattering Pentheus'
palace? Come,

Lift yourselves up, take good courage, stop this trembling
of your limbs!

CHORUS:

We are saved! Oh, what a joy to hear your Bacchic call
ring out!

We were all alone, deserted; you have come, and we
    rejoice.

DIONYSUS:

Were you comfortless, despondent, when I was escorted
    in,

Helpless, sentenced to be cast in Pentheus' murky prison-
    cell?

CHORUS:

Who could help it? What protector had we, once
    deprived of you?

Tell us now how you escaped the clutches of this wicked
    man.

DIONYSUS: I alone, at once, unaided, effortlessly freed myself.

CHORUS: How could that be? Did not Pentheus bind your
    arms with knotted ropes?

DIONYSUS:

There I made a mockery of him. He thought he was
    binding me;

But he neither held nor touched me, save in his deluded
    mind.

Near the mangers where he meant to tie me up, he
    found a bull;

And he tied his rope round the bull's knees and hooves,
    panting with rage,

Dripping sweat, biting his lips; while I sat quietly by and
    watched.

It was then that Dionysus shook the building, made the
    flame

On his mother's tomb flare up. When Pentheus saw this,
    he supposed

The whole place was burning. He rushed this way, that
    way, calling out

To the servants to bring water; every slave about the
    place

Was engaged upon this futile task. He left it presently,

Thinking I had escaped; snatched up his murderous
    sword, darted indoors.

Thereupon Dionysus – as it seemed to me; I merely
    guess –

Made a phantom hover in the courtyard. Pentheus flew
    at it,

Stabbing at the empty sunlight, thinking he was killing
    *me.*

Yet a further humiliation Bacchus next contrived for
    him:

He destroyed the stable buildings. Pentheus sees my
    prison now

Lying there, a heap of rubble; and the picture grieves his
    heart.

  Now he's dazed and helpless with exhaustion. He has
    dropped his sword.

He, a man, dared to take arms against a god. I quietly
    walked

Out of the palace here to join you, giving Pentheus not
    a thought.

But I hear his heavy tread inside the palace. Soon, I think,

He'll be out here in the forecourt. After what has
    happened now,

What will he have to say? For all his rage, he shall not
    ruffle *me.*

It's a wise man's part to practise a smooth-tempered
    self-control.

*Enter* PENTHEUS.

PENTHEUS:

This is outrageous. He has escaped – that foreigner.

Only just now I had him locked up and in chains.

    *He sees* DIONYSUS *and gives an excited shout.*

He's there! Well, what's going on now? How did you
    get out?

How dare you show your face here at my very door?

DIONYSUS: Stay where you are. You are angry; now control
  yourself.

PENTHEUS: You were tied up inside there. How did you
  escape?

DIONYSUS: I said – did you not hear? – that I should be set
  free –

PENTHEUS: By whom? You're always finding something
  new to say.

DIONYSUS: By him who plants for mortals the rich-
  clustered vine.

PENTHEUS: The god who frees his worshippers from every
  law.*

DIONYSUS: Your insult to Dionysus is a compliment.

PENTHEUS [to attendant GUARDS]: Go round the walls and
  tell them to close every gate.

DIONYSUS: And why? Or cannot gods pass even over walls?

PENTHEUS: Oh, you know everything – save what you
  ought to know.

DIONYSUS:
  The things most needful to be known, those things I
    know.
  But listen first to what this man has to report;
  He comes from the mountain, and he has some news for
    you.
  I will stay here; I promise not to run away.

                   *Enter a* HERDSMAN.

HERDSMAN:
  Pentheus, great king of Thebes! I come from Mount
    Cithaeron,
  Whose slopes are never free from dazzling shafts of snow.

PENTHEUS: And what comes next? What urgent message do
  you bring?

HERDSMAN:
  I have seen the holy Bacchae, who like a flight of spears

  * This is conjecturally supplied in place of a missing line.

Went streaming bare-limbed, frantic, out of the city gate.
I have come with the intention of telling you, my lord,
And the city, of their strange and terrible doings – things
Beyond all wonder. But first I would learn whether
I may speak freely of what is going on there, or
If I should trim my words. I fear your hastiness,
My lord, your anger, your too potent royalty.

PENTHEUS:

From me fear nothing. Say all that you have to say;
Anger should not grow hot against the innocent.
The more dreadful your story of these Bacchic rites,
The heavier punishment I will inflict upon
This man who enticed our women to their evil ways.

HERDSMAN:

At dawn today, when first the sun's rays warmed the
　　earth,
My herd of cattle was slowly climbing up towards
The high pastures; and there I saw three separate
Companies of women. The leader of one company
Was Autonoë; your mother Agauë was at the head
Of the second, Ino of the third; and they all lay
Relaxed and quietly sleeping. Some rested on beds
Of pine-needles, others had pillows of oak-leaves.
They lay just as they had thrown themselves down on
　　the ground,
But modestly, not – as you told us – drunk with wine
Or flute-music, seeking the solitary woods
For the pursuit of love.
　　　　　　　　　When your mother Agauë
Heard the horned cattle bellowing, she stood upright
Among the Bacchae, and called to them to stir themselves
From sleep; and they shook off the strong sleep from
　　their eyes
And leapt to their feet. They were a sight to marvel at
For modest comeliness; women both old and young,

Girls still unmarried. First they let their hair fall free
Over their shoulders; some tied up the fastenings
Of fawnskins they had loosened; round the dappled fur
Curled snakes that licked their cheeks. Some would have
        in their arms
A young gazelle, or wild wolf-cubs, to which they gave
Their own white milk – those of them who had left at
        home
Young children newly born, so that their breasts were
        full.
And they wore wreaths of ivy-leaves, or oak, or flowers
Of bryony. One would strike her thyrsus on a rock,
And from the rock a limpid stream of water sprang.
Another dug her wand into the earth, and there
The god sent up a fountain of wine. Those who desired
Milk had only to scratch the earth with finger-tips,
And there was the white stream flowing for them to
        drink,
While from the thyrsus a sweet ooze of honey dripped.
Oh! if you had been there and seen all this, you would
Have offered prayers to this god whom you now
        condemn.
    We herdsmen, then, and shepherds gathered to
        exchange
Rival reports of these strange and extraordinary
Performances; and one, who had knocked about the
        town,
And had a ready tongue, addressed us: 'You who live
On the holy mountain heights,' he said, 'shall we hunt
        down
Agauë, Pentheus' mother, and bring her back from these
Rituals, and gratify the king? What do you say?'
This seemed a good suggestion; so we hid ourselves
In the leafy bushes, waiting. When the set time came,
The women began brandishing their wands, preparing

To dance, calling in unison on the son of Zeus,
'Iacchus! Bromius!' And with them the whole mountain,
And all the creatures there, joined in the mystic rite
Of Dionysus, and with their motion all things moved.
　　Now, Agauë as she danced passed close to me; and I
At once leapt out from hiding, bent on capturing her.
But she called out, 'Oh, my swift-footed hounds, these
　　men
Are hunting us. Come follow me! Each one of you
Arm herself with the holy thyrsus, and follow me!'
　　So we fled, and escaped being torn in pieces by
Those possessed women. But our cattle were there,
　　cropping
The fresh grass; and the women attacked them, with
　　their bare hands.
You could see one take a full-uddered bellowing young
　　heifer
And hold it by the legs with her two arms stretched
　　wide;
Others seized on our cows and tore them limb from limb;
You'd see some ribs, or a cleft hoof, tossed high and low;
And rags of flesh hung from pine-branches, dripping
　　blood.
Bulls, which one moment felt proud rage hot in their
　　horns,
The next were thrown bodily to the ground, dragged
　　down
By hands of girls in thousands; and they stripped the flesh
From the bodies faster than you could wink your royal
　　eyes.
　　Then, skimming bird-like over the surface of the
　　ground,
They scoured the plain which stretches by Asopus' banks
And yields rich crops for Thebes; and like an enemy
　　force

They fell on Hysiae and Erythrae, two villages
On the low slopes of Cithaeron, and ransacked them
    both;
Snatched babies out of the houses; any plunder which
They carried on their shoulders stayed there without
    straps –
Nothing fell to the ground, not bronze or iron; they
    carried
Fire on their heads, and yet their soft hair was not burnt.
  The villagers, enraged at being so plundered, armed
Themselves to resist; and then, my lord, an amazing
    sight
Was to be seen. The spears those men were throwing
    drew
No blood; but the women, hurling a thyrsus like a spear,
Dealt wounds; in short, those women turned the men to
    flight.
There was the power of a god in that. Then they went
    back
To the place where they had started from, to those
    fountains
The god had caused to flow for them. And they washed
    off
The blood; and snakes licked clean the stains, till their
    cheeks shone.
  So, master, whoever this divinity may be,
Receive him in this land. His powers are manifold;
But chiefly, as I hear, he gave to men the vine
To cure their sorrows; and without wine, neither love
Nor any other pleasure would be left for us.

CHORUS:
I shrink from speaking freely before the king; yet I
Will say it: there is no greater god than Dionysus.

PENTHEUS:
This Bacchic arrogance advances on us like

A spreading fire, disgracing us before all Hellas.
We must act now. [*To the* HERDSMAN] Go quickly to
  the Electran gate;
Tell all my men who carry shields, heavy or light,
All riders on fast horses, all my archers with
Their twanging bows, to meet me there in readiness
For an onslaught on these maniacs. This is beyond
All bearing, if we must let women so defy us.

DIONYSUS:
  You refuse, Pentheus, to give heed to what I say
  Or change your ways. Yet still, despite your wrongs to me,
  I warn you: stay here quietly; do not take up arms
  Against a god. Dionysus will not tolerate
  Attempts to drive his worshippers from their holy hills.

PENTHEUS:
  I'll not have you instruct me. You have escaped your
    chains;
  Now be content – or must I punish you again?

DIONYSUS:
  I would control my rage and sacrifice to him
  If I were you, rather than kick against the goad.
  Can you, a mortal, measure your strength with a god's?

PENTHEUS:
  I'll sacrifice, yes – blood of women, massacred
  Wholesale, as they deserve, among Cithaeron's glens.

DIONYSUS:
  Your army will be put to flight. What a disgrace
  For bronze shields to be routed by those women's wands!

PENTHEUS:
  How can I deal with this impossible foreigner?
  In prison or out, nothing will make him hold his tongue.

DIONYSUS: My friend, a happy settlement may still be
  found.

PENTHEUS: How? Must I be a slave to my own slave-
  women?

DIONYSUS: I will, using no weapons, bring those women here.

PENTHEUS: Hear that, for the gods' sake! You're playing me some trick.

DIONYSUS: What trick? – if I am ready to save you by my skill.

PENTHEUS: You've planned this with them, so that the rituals can go on.

DIONYSUS: Indeed I have planned this – not with them, but with the god.

PENTHEUS: Bring out my armour, there! – That is enough from you.

DIONYSUS [*with an authoritative shout*]:
Wait! [*Then quietly*] Do you want *to see*
Those women, where they sit together, up in the hills?

PENTHEUS: Why, yes; for that, I'd give a weighty sum of gold.

DIONYSUS: What made you fall into this great desire to see?

PENTHEUS: It would cause me distress to see them drunk with wine.

DIONYSUS: Yet you would gladly witness this distressing sight?

PENTHEUS: Of course – if I could quietly sit under the pines.

DIONYSUS: They'll track you down, even if you go there secretly.

PENTHEUS: Openly, then. Yes, what you say is very true.

DIONYSUS: Then shall I lead you? You will undertake to go?

PENTHEUS: Yes, lead me there at once; I am impatient.

DIONYSUS:                                              Then,
You must first dress yourself in a fine linen gown.

PENTHEUS: Why in a linen gown? Must I then change my sex?

DIONYSUS: In case they kill you, if you are seen there as a man.

PENTHEUS: Again you are quite right. How you think of everything!

DIONYSUS: It was Dionysus who inspired me with that thought.

PENTHEUS: Then how can your suggestion best be carried out?

DIONYSUS: I'll come indoors with you myself and dress you.

PENTHEUS:                                        What? Dress me? In woman's clothes? But I would be ashamed.

DIONYSUS: Do you want to watch the Maenads? Are you less eager now?

PENTHEUS: What kind of dress did you say you would put on me?

DIONYSUS: First I'll adorn your head with locks of flowing hair.

PENTHEUS: And after that? What style of costume shall I have?

DIONYSUS: A full-length robe; and on your head shall be a snood.

PENTHEUS: Besides these, is there anything else you'll put on me?

DIONYSUS: A dappled fawnskin round you, a thyrsus in your hand.

PENTHEUS: I could not bear to dress myself in woman's clothes.

DIONYSUS: If you join the battle with the Maenads, blood will flow.

PENTHEUS: You are right; I must first go to spy on them.

DIONYSUS:                                    That way Is better than inviting force by using it.

PENTHEUS: And how shall I get through the town without being seen?

DIONYSUS: We'll go by empty streets; I will show you the way.

PENTHEUS:

 The Maenads must not mock me; better anything
 Than that. Now I'll go in, and think how best to act.

DIONYSUS: You may do so. My preparations are all made.

PENTHEUS:

 I'll go in, then; and either I'll set forth at the head
 Of my armed men – or else I'll follow your advice.

Exit PENTHEUS.

DIONYSUS:

 Women, this man is walking into the net. He will
 Visit the Bacchae; and there death shall punish him.

  Dionysus! – for you are not far distant – all is now
 In your hands. Let us be revenged on him! And first
 Fill him with wild delusions, drive him out of his mind.
 While sane, he'll not consent to put on woman's clothes;
 Once free from the curb of reason, he will put them
  on.
 I long to set Thebes laughing at him, as he walks
 In female garb through all the streets; to humble him
 From the arrogance he showed when first he threatened
  me.

  Now I will go, to array Pentheus in the dress
 Which he will take down with him to the house of
  Death,
 Slaughtered by his own mother's hands. And he shall
  know
 Dionysus, son of Zeus, in his full nature God,
 Most terrible, although most gentle, to mankind.

DIONYSUS follows PENTHEUS into the palace.

CHORUS:

  O for long nights of worship, gay    [*Strophe*
  With the pale gleam of dancing feet,
  With head tossed high to the dewy air –
  Pleasure mysterious and sweet!
  O for the joy of a fawn at play

In the fragrant meadow's green delight,
Who has leapt out free from the woven snare,
Away from the terror of chase and flight,
And the huntsman's shout, and the straining pack,
And skims the sand by the river's brim
With the speed of wind in each aching limb,
To the blessed lonely forest where
The soil's unmarked by a human track,
And leaves hang thick and the shades are dim.

What prayer should we call wise?          [*Refrain*
What gift of Heaven should man
Count a more noble prize,
A prayer more prudent, than
To stretch a conquering arm
Over the fallen crest
Of those who wished us harm?
And what is noble every heart loves best.

Slow, yet unfailing, move the Powers          [*Antistrophe*
Of heaven with the moving hours.
When mind runs mad, dishonours God,
And worships self and senseless pride,
Then Law eternal wields the rod.
Still Heaven hunts down the impious man,
Though divine subtlety may hide
Time's creeping foot. No mortal ought
To challenge Time – to overbear
Custom in act, or age in thought.
All men, at little cost, may share
The blessing of a pious creed;
Truths more than mortal, which began
In the beginning, and belong
To very nature – these indeed
Reign in our world, are fixed and strong.

What prayer should we call wise?                    [*Refrain*
What gift of heaven should man
Count a more noble prize,
A prayer more prudent, than
To stretch a conquering arm
Over the fallen crest
Of those who wished us harm?
And what is noble every heart loves best.


Blest is the man who cheats the stormy sea                    [*Epode*
And safely moors beside the sheltering quay;
So, blest is he who triumphs over trial.
One man, by various means, in wealth or strength
Outdoes his neighbour; hope in a thousand hearts
Colours a thousand different dreams; at length
Some find a dear fulfilment, some denial.
　　But this I say,
　　That he who best
　　Enjoys each passing day
　　Is truly blest.

　　　　*Enter* DIONYSUS. *He turns to call* PENTHEUS.

DIONYSUS:
　Come, perverse man, greedy for sights you should not
　　see,
　Eager for deeds you should not do – Pentheus! Come
　　out
　Before the palace and show yourself to me, wearing
　The garb of a frenzied Bacchic woman, and prepared
　To spy on your mother and all her Bacchic company.

　　*Enter* PENTHEUS *dressed as a Bacchic devotee. He is dazed*
　　　　*and entirely subservient to* DIONYSUS.

　You are the very image of one of Cadmus' daughters.

PENTHEUS:
　Why, now! I seem to see two suns; a double Thebes;
　Our city's wall with seven gates appears double.

DIONYSUS *takes* PENTHEUS *by the hand and leads
him forward.*

You are a bull I see leading me forward now;
A pair of horns seems to have grown upon your head.
Were you a beast before? You have become a bull.

DIONYSUS:

The god then did not favour us; he is with us now,
We have made our peace with him; you see as you
should see.

PENTHEUS:

How do I look? Tell me, is not the way I stand
Like the way Ino stands, or like my mother Agauë?

DIONYSUS:

Looking at you, I think I see them both. Wait, now;
Here is a curl has slipped out of its proper place,
Not as I tucked it carefully below your snood.

PENTHEUS:

Indoors, as I was tossing my head up and down
Like a Bacchic dancer, I dislodged it from its place.

DIONYSUS:

Come, then; I am the one who should look after you.
I'll fix it in its place again. There; lift your head.

PENTHEUS: You dress me, please; I have put myself in your
hands now.

DIONYSUS:

Your girdle has come loose; and now your dress does not
Hang, as it should, in even pleats down to the ankle.

PENTHEUS:

That's true, I think – at least by the right leg, on this
side;
But on the other side the gown hangs well to the heel.

DIONYSUS:

You'll surely count me chief among your friends, when
you
Witness the Maenads' unexpected modesty.

PENTHEUS:

Ought I to hold my thyrsus in the right hand – so,
Or in the left, to look more like a Bacchanal?

DIONYSUS:

In the right hand; and raise it at the same time as
Your right foot. I am glad you are so changed in mind.

PENTHEUS:

Could I lift up on my own shoulders the whole weight
Of Mount Cithaeron, and all the women dancing there?

DIONYSUS:

You could, if you so wished. The mind you had before
Was sickly; now your mind is just as it should be.

PENTHEUS:

Shall we take crowbars? Or shall I put my shoulder under
The rocks, and heave the mountain up with my two arms?

DIONYSUS:

Oh, come, now! Don't destroy the dwellings of the
nymphs,
And the quiet places where Pan sits to play his pipes.

PENTHEUS:

You are right. We ought not to use force to overcome
Those women. I will hide myself among the pines.

DIONYSUS:

Hide – yes, you'll hide, and find the proper hiding-place
For one who comes by stealth to spy on Bacchic rites.

PENTHEUS:

Why yes! I think they are there now in their hidden nests,
Like birds, all clasped close in the sweet prison of love.

DIONYSUS:

What you are going to watch for is this very thing;
Perhaps you will catch them – if you are not first
caught yourself.

PENTHEUS:

Now take me through the central streets of Thebes; for I
Am the one man among them all that dares do this.

DIONYSUS:

  One man alone, you agonize for Thebes; therefore
  It is your destined ordeal that awaits you now.
  Come with me; I will bring you safely to the place;
  Another shall conduct you back.

PENTHEUS:                  My mother – yes?

DIONYSUS: A sight for all to witness.

PENTHEUS:                 To this end I go.

DIONYSUS: You will return borne high –

PENTHEUS:                 Royal magnificence!

DIONYSUS: In your own mother's arms.

PENTHEUS:           You insist that I be spoiled.

DIONYSUS: One kind of spoiling.

PENTHEUS:               Yet I win what I deserve.

*Exit* PENTHEUS.

DIONYSUS:

  Pentheus, you are a man to make men fear; fearful
  Will be your end – an end that shall lift up your fame
  To the height of heaven.
  Agauë, and you her sisters, daughters of Cadmus,
  Stretch out your hands! See, I am bringing this young man
  To his great battle; and I and Bromius shall be
  Victors. What more shall happen, the event will show.

*Exit* DIONYSUS.

CHORUS:

  Hounds of Madness, fly to the mountain, fly     [*Strophe*
  Where Cadmus' daughters are dancing in ecstasy!
  Madden them like a frenzied herd stampeding,
  Against the madman hiding in woman's clothes
  To spy on the Maenads' rapture!
  First his mother shall see him craning his neck
  Down from a rounded rock or a sharp crag,
  And shout to the Maenads, 'Who is the man, you Bacchae,
  Who has come to the mountain, come to the mountain
    spying

On the swift wild mountain-dances of Cadmus' daughters?
Which of you is his mother?
No, that lad never lay in a woman's womb;
A lioness gave him suck, or a Libyan Gorgon!'

Justice, now be revealed! Now let your sword
Thrust – through and through – to sever the throat
Of the godless, lawless, shameless son of Echion,
Who sprang from the womb of Earth!

See! With contempt of right, with a reckless    [*Antistrophe*
   rage
To combat your and your mother's mysteries, Bacchus,
With maniac fury out he goes, stark mad,
For a trial of strength against *your* invincible arm!
His proud purposes death shall discipline.
He who unquestioning gives the gods their due,
And knows that his days are as dust, shall live untouched.
I have no wish to grudge the wise their wisdom;
But the joys *I* seek are greater, outshine all others,
And lead our life to goodness and loveliness:
The joy of the holy heart
That night and day is bent to honour the gods
And disown all custom that breaks the bounds of right.

Justice, now be revealed! Now let your sword
Thrust – through and through – to sever the throat
Of the godless, lawless, shameless son of Echion,
Who sprang from the womb of Earth!
   [*Then with growing excitement, shouting in unison, and
            dancing to the rhythm of their words*]
                  Come, Dionysus!                          [*Epode*
                  Come, and appear to us!
                  Come like a bull or a
                  Hundred-headed serpent,
                  Come like a lion snorting

Flame from your nostrils!
Swoop down, Bacchus, on the
Hunter of the Bacchae;
Smile at him and snare him;
Then let the stampeding
Herd of the Maenads
Throw him and throttle him,
Catch, trip, trample him to death!

*Enter a* MESSENGER.

MESSENGER:

O house that once shone glorious throughout Hellas,
  home
Of the old Sidonian king who planted in this soil
The dragon's earth-born harvest! How I weep for
  you!
Slave though I am, I suffer with my master's fate.

CHORUS: Are you from the mountain, from the Bacchic
rites? What news?

MESSENGER: Pentheus, son of Echion, is dead.

CHORUS: Bromius, lord! Your divine power is revealed!

MESSENGER:

What, woman? What was that you said? Do you exult
When such a cruel fate has overtaken the king?

CHORUS: I am no Greek.
        I sing my joy in a foreign tune.
        Not any more do I cower in terror of prison!

MESSENGER: Do you think Thebes has no men left who can
take command?

CHORUS:        Dionysus commands *me*;
               Not Thebes, but Dionysus.

MESSENGER:

Allowance must be made for you; yet, to rejoice
At the accomplishment of horrors, is not right.

CHORUS: Tell us everything, then: this tyrant king
        Bent on cruelty – how did he die?

MESSENGER:

When we had left behind the outlying parts of Thebes
And crossed the river Asopus, we began to climb
Toward the uplands of Cithaeron, Pentheus and I –
I went as his attendant – and the foreigner
Who was our guide to the spectacle we were to see.
Well, first we sat down in a grassy glade. We kept
Our footsteps and our talk as quiet as possible,
So as to see without being seen. We found ourselves
In a valley full of streams, with cliffs on either side.
There, under the close shade of branching pines, the
    Maenads
Were sitting, their hands busy at their happy tasks;
Some of them twining a fresh crown of ivy-leaves
For a stripped thyrsus; others, gay as fillies loosed
From painted yokes, were singing holy Bacchic songs,
Each answering other. But the ill-fated Pentheus saw
None of this; and he said, 'My friend, from where we
    stand
My eyes cannot make out these so-called worshippers;
But if I climbed a towering pine-tree on the cliff
I would have a clear view of their shameful practices.'
    And then I saw that foreigner do an amazing thing.
He took hold of a pine-tree's soaring, topmost branch,
And dragged it down, down, down to the dark earth.
    It was bent
In a circle as a bow is bent, as a wheel's curve,
Drawn with a compass, bends the rim to its own shape;
The foreigner took that mountain-pine in his two hands
And bent it down – a thing no mortal man could do.
Then seating Pentheus on a high branch, he began
To let the tree spring upright, slipping it through his
    hands
Steadily, taking care he should not be flung off.
The pine-trunk, straightened, soared into the soaring sky,

Bearing my master seated astride, so that he was
More visible to the Maenads than they were to him.
He was just coming into view on his high perch,
When out of the sky a voice – Dionysus, I suppose;
That foreigner was nowhere to be seen – pealed forth:
'Women, here is the man who made a mock of you,
And me, and of my holy rites. Now punish him.'
And in the very moment the voice spoke, a flash
Of dreadful fire stretched between earth and the high
　　　heaven.

The air fell still. The wooded glade held every leaf
Still. You could hear no cry of any beast. The women,
Not having caught distinctly what the voice uttered,
Stood up and gazed around. Then came a second word
Of command. As soon as Cadmus' daughters recognized
The clear bidding of Bacchus, with the speed of doves
They darted forward, and all the Bacchae after them.
Through the torrent-filled valley, over the rocks,
　　　possessed
By the very breath of Bacchus they went leaping on.
Then, when they saw my master crouched high in the
　　　pine,
At first they climbed the cliff which towered opposite,
And violently flung at him pieces of rocks, or boughs
Of pine-trees which they hurled as javelins; and some
Aimed with the thyrsus; through the high air all around
Their wretched target missiles flew. Yet every aim
Fell short, the tree's height baffled all their eagerness;
While Pentheus, helpless in this pitiful trap, sat there.
Then, with a force like lightning, they tore down
　　　branches
Of oak, and with these tried to prize up the tree's roots.
When all their struggles met with no success, Agauë
Cried out, 'Come, Maenads, stand in a circle round the
　　　tree

And take hold of it. We must catch this climbing beast,
Or he'll disclose the secret dances of Dionysus.'
They came; a thousand hands gripped on the pine and
    tore it.
Out of the ground. Then from his high perch plunging,
    crashing
To the earth Pentheus fell, with one incessant scream
As he understood what end was near.

                                His mother first,
As priestess, led the rite of death, and fell upon him.
He tore the headband from his hair, that his wretched
    mother
Might recognize him and not kill him. 'Mother,' he
    cried,
Touching her cheek, 'It is I, your own son Pentheus,
    whom
You bore to Echion. Mother, have mercy; I have sinned,
But I am still your own son. Do not take my life!'
    Agauë was foaming at the mouth; her rolling eyes
Were wild; she was not in her right mind, but possessed
By Bacchus, and she paid no heed to him. She grasped
His left arm between wrist and elbow, set her foot
Against his ribs, and tore his arm off by the shoulder.
It was no strength of hers that did it, but the god
Filled her, and made it easy. On the other side
Ino was at him, tearing at his flesh; and now
Autonoë joined them, and the whole maniacal horde.
A single and continuous yell arose – Pentheus
Shrieking as long as life was left in him, the women
Howling in triumph. One of them carried off an arm,
Another a foot, the boot still laced on it. The ribs
Were stripped, clawed clean; and women's hands, thick
    red with blood,
Were tossing, catching, like a plaything, Pentheus' flesh.
    His body lies – no easy task to find – scattered

Under hard rocks, or in the green woods. His poor head –
His mother carries it, fixed on her thyrsus-point,
Openly over Cithaeron's pastures, thinking it
The head of a young mountain-lion. She has left her
    sisters
Dancing among the Maenads, and herself comes here
Inside the walls, exulting in her hideous prey,
Shouting to Bacchus, calling him her fellow-hunter,
Her partner in the kill, comrade in victory.
But Bacchus gives her bitter tears for her reward.
    Now I will go. I must find some place far away
From this horror, before Agauë returns home.
A sound and humble heart that reverences the gods
Is man's noblest possession; and the same virtue
Is wisest too, I think, for those who practise it.

*Exit the* MESSENGER.

CHORUS:
Let us dance a dance to Bacchus, shout and sing
For the fall of Pentheus, heir of the dragon's seed,
Who hid his beard in a woman's gown,
And sealed his death with the holy sign
Of ivy wreathing a fennel-reed,
When bull led man to the ritual slaughter-ring.
Frenzied daughters of Cadmus, what renown
Your victory wins you – such a song
As groans must stifle, tears must drown!
Emblem of conquest, brave and fine! –
A mother's hand, defiled
With blood and dripping red
Caresses the torn head
Of her own murdered child!

But look! I see her – there, running towards the palace –
Agauë, Pentheus' mother, her eyes wildly rolling.
Come, welcome them – Dionysus' holy company.

AGAUË *appears, frenzied and panting, with* PENTHEUS' *head held in her hand. The rest of her band of devotees, whom the* CHORUS *saw approaching with her, do not enter; but a few are seen standing by the entrance, where they wait until the end of the play.*

AGAUË: Women of Asia! Worshippers of Bacchus!

    AGAUË *tries to show them* PENTHEUS' *head; they shrink from it.*

CHORUS: Why do you urge me? Oh!

AGAUË:   I am bringing home from the mountains
        A vine-branch freshly cut,
        For the gods have blessed our hunting.

CHORUS: We see it ... and welcome you in fellowship.

AGAUË:   I caught him without a trap,
        A lion-cub, young and wild.
        Look, you may see him: there!

CHORUS: Where was it?

AGAUË:             On Cithaeron;
        The wild and empty mountain –

CHORUS: Cithaeron!

AGAUË:   ... spilt his life-blood.

CHORUS: Who shot him?

AGAUË:           I was first;
        All the women are singing,
        'Honour to great Agauë!'

CHORUS: And then – who next?

AGAUË:              Why, Cadmus' ...

CHORUS: What – Cadmus?

AGAUË:         Yes, his daughters –
        But after me, after me –
        Laid their hands to the kill.
        Today was a splendid hunt!
        Come now, join in the feast!

CHORUS: What, wretched woman? *Feast?*

AGAUË [*tenderly stroking the head as she holds it*]:

This calf is young: how thickly
The new-grown hair goes crisping
Up to his delicate crest!

CHORUS: Indeed, his long hair makes him
Look like some wild creature.

AGAUË: The god is a skilled hunter;
And he poised his hunting women,
And hurled them at the quarry.

CHORUS: True, our god is a hunter.

AGAUË: Do you praise me?

CHORUS:                Yes, we praise you.

AGAUË: So will the sons of Cadmus ...

CHORUS: And Pentheus too, Agauë?

AGAUË: Yes, he will praise his mother
For the lion-cub she killed.

CHORUS: Oh, fearful!

AGAUË:             Ay, fearful!

CHORUS: You are happy?

AGAUË:           I am enraptured;
Great in the eyes of the world,
Great are the deeds I've done,
And the hunt that I hunted there!

CHORUS:
  Then show it, poor Agauë – this triumphant spoil
  You've brought home; show it to all the citizens of
     Thebes.

AGAUË:
  Come, all you Thebans living within these towered walls,
  Come, see the beast we, Cadmus' daughters, caught and
     killed;
  Caught not with nets or thonged Thessalian javelins,
  But with our own bare arms and fingers. After this
  Should huntsmen glory in their exploits, who must buy
  Their needless tools from armourers? We with our hands
  Hunted and took this beast, then tore it limb from limb.

Where is my father? Let old Cadmus come. And where
Is my son Pentheus? Let him climb a strong ladder
And nail up on the cornice of the palace wall
This lion's head that I have hunted and brought home.

*Enter* CADMUS *with attendants bearing the body of*
PENTHEUS.

CADMUS:

Come, men, bring your sad burden that was Pentheus.
    Come,
Set him at his own door. By weary, endless search
I found his body's remnants scattered far and wide
About Cithaeron's glens, or hidden in thick woods.
I gathered them and brought them here.

                                    I had already
Returned with old Teiresias from the Bacchic dance,
And was inside the walls, when news was brought me of
My daughters' terrible deed. I turned straight back; and
    now
Return, bringing my grandson, whom the Maenads killed.
I saw Autonoë, who bore Actaeon to Aristaeus,
And Ino with her, there among the trees, still rapt
In their unhappy frenzy; but I understood
That Agauë had come dancing on her way to Thebes –
And there indeed she is, a sight for misery!

AGAUË:

Father! Now you may boast as loudly as you will
That you have sired the noblest daughters of this age!
I speak of all three, but myself especially.
I have left weaving at the loom for greater things,
For hunting wild beasts with my bare hands. See this prize,
Here in my arms; I won it, and it shall be hung
On your palace wall. There, father, take it in your hands.
Be proud of my hunting; call your friends to a feast; let
    them
Bless you and envy you for the splendour of my deed.

CADMUS:

  Oh, misery unmeasured, sight intolerable!

  Oh, bloody deed enacted by most pitiful hands!

  What noble prize is this you lay at the gods' feet,

  Calling the city, and me, to a banquet? Your wretchedness

  Demands the bitterest tears; but mine is next to yours.

  Dionysus has dealt justly, but pursued justice

  Too far; born of my blood, he has destroyed my house.

AGAUË:

  What an ill-tempered creature an old man is! How full

  Of scowls! I wish my son were a great hunter like

  His mother, hunting beasts with the young men of Thebes;

  But *he* can only fight with gods. Father, you must

  Correct him. – Will not someone go and call him here

  To see me, and to share in my great happiness?

CADMUS:

  Alas, my daughters! If you come to understand

  What you have done, how terrible your pain will be!

  If you remain as you are now, though you could not

  Be happy, at least you will not feel your wretchedness.

AGAUË: Why not happy? What cause have I for wretchedness?

CADMUS: Come here. First turn your eyes this way. Look at the sky.

AGAUË: I am looking. Why should you want me to look at it?

CADMUS: Does it appear the same to you, or is it changed?

AGAUË: Yes, it is clearer than before, more luminous.

CADMUS: And this disturbance of your mind – is it still there?

AGAUË:

  I don't know what you mean; but – yes, I feel a change;

  My mind is somehow clearer than it was before.

CADMUS: Could you now listen to me and give a clear reply?

AGAUË: Yes, father. I have forgotten what we said just now.

CADMUS: When you were married, whose house did you go to then?

AGAUË: You gave me to Echion, of the sown race, they said.

CADMUS: Echion had a son born to him. Who was he?

AGAUË: Pentheus. His father lay with me; I bore a son.

CADMUS: Yes; and whose head is that you are holding in your arms?

AGAUË: A lion's – so the women said who hunted it.

CADMUS: Then look straight at it. Come, to look is no great task.

*AGAUË looks; and suddenly screams.*

AGAUË: What am I looking at? What is this in my hands?

CADMUS: Look at it steadily; come closer to the truth.

AGAUË: I see – O gods, what horror! Oh, what misery!

CADMUS: Does this appear to you to be a lion's head?

AGAUË: No! I hold Pentheus' head in my accursed hand.

CADMUS: It is so. Tears have been shed for him, before you knew.

AGAUË: But who killed him? How did he come into my hands.

CADMUS: O cruel hour, that brings a bitter truth to light!

AGAUË: Tell me – my heart is bursting, I must know the rest.

CADMUS: It was you, Agauë, and your sisters. You killed him.

AGAUË: Where was it done? Here in the palace? Or where else?

CADMUS: Where, long ago, Actaeon was devoured by hounds.

AGAUË: Cithaeron! But what evil fate took Pentheus there?

CADMUS: He went to mock Dionysus and your Bacchic rites.

AGAUË: Why were we on Cithaeron? What had brought us there?

CADMUS: You were possessed. All Thebes was in a Bacchic trance.

AGAUË: Dionysus has destroyed us. Now I understand.

CADMUS: He was insulted. You refused to call him god.

AGAUË: Father, where is the beloved body of my son?
CADMUS: Here. It was I who brought it, after painful search.
AGAUË: And are his limbs now decently composed?
CADMUS:　　　　　　　　　　　　　　　　　　Not yet.*
　　We came back to the city with all possible haste.
AGAUË: How could I touch his body with these guilty hands?
CADMUS: Your guilt, my daughter, was not heavier than his.
AGAUË: What part did Pentheus have, then, in my insanity?
CADMUS:

　He sinned like you, refusing reverence to a god.
　Therefore the god has joined all in one ruin – you,
　Your sisters, Pentheus – to destroy my house and me.
　I have no son; and now, my unhappy child, I see
　This son of yours dead by a shameful, hideous death.
　You were the new hope of our house, its bond of
　　　strength,
　Dear grandson. And Thebes feared you; no one dared
　　　insult
　Your old grandfather if he saw you near; you would
　Teach him his lesson. But now I shall live exiled,
　Dishonoured – I, Cadmus the great, who planted here,
　And reaped, that glorious harvest of the Theban race.
　　O dearest son – yes, even in death you shall be held
　Most dear – you will never touch my beard again, and
　　　call
　Me Grandfather, and put your arm round me and say,
　'Who has wronged you or insulted you? Who is unkind,
　Or vexes or disturbs you? Tell me, Grandfather,
　That I may punish him.' Never again. For me
　All that remains is pain; for you, the pity of death;
　For your mother, tears; torment for our whole family.
　　If any man derides the unseen world, let him
　Ponder the death of Pentheus, and believe in gods.

　* This and the three following lines are missing in the text, and are
here conjecturally supplied.

CHORUS:

  I grieve for your fate, Cadmus; though your grandson's
    death
  Was justly merited, it falls cruelly on you.

AGAUË:

  Father, you see how one disastrous day has shattered
  My whole life,* *turned my pride to shame, my happiness*
  *To horror. Now my only wish is to compose*
  *My son's body for burial, and lament for him;*
  *And then die. But this is not lawful; for my hands*
  *Are filthy with pollution of their own making.*
  *When I have spilt the blood I bore, and torn the flesh*
  *That grew in my own womb, how can I after this*
  *Enfold him to my breast, or chant his ritual dirge?*
  *And yet, I beg you, pity me, and let me touch*
  *My son, and say farewell to that dear body which*
  *I cherished, and destroyed unknowing. It is right*
  *That you should pity, for your hands are innocent.*

CADMUS:

  *My daughter, you and I and our whole house are crushed*
  *And broken by the anger of this powerful god.*
  *It is not for me to keep you from your son. Only*
  *Be resolute, and steel your heart against a sight*

---

\* At this point the two MSS on which the text of this play depends
show a lacuna of considerable extent; it covers the end of this scene, in
which Agauë mourns over Pentheus' body, and the appearance of
Dionysus manifested as a god. The MSS resume in the middle of a
speech by Dionysus. A number of quotations by ancient authors,
together with less than twenty lines from *Christus Patiens* (an anonymous
fourth century A.D. work consisting largely of lines adapted from
Greek tragedies) make it possible to attempt a guess at the content of
the missing lines. Since this play is often performed, it seems worth
while to provide here a usable text. In the lines that follow, the words
printed in italics are mere conjecture, and have no value except as a
credible completion of the probable sense; while those in Roman type
represent the sources available from *Christus Patiens* and elsewhere.

*Which must be fearful to any eyes, but most of all*
*To a mother's. [To attendants] Men, put down your burden on*
  *the ground*
*Before Agauë, and remove the covering.*

AGAUË:

*Dear child, how cruel, how unnatural are these tears,*
*Which should have fallen from your eyes on my dead face.*
*Now I shall die with none to mourn me. This is just;*
*For in my pride I did not recognize the god,*
*Nor understand the things I ought to have understood.*
*You too are punished for the same impiety;*
*But which is the more terrible, your fate or mine,*
*I cannot tell. Since you have suffered too, you will*
*Forgive both what I did, not knowing what I did,*
*And what I do now, touching you with unholy hands –*
*At once your cruellest enemy and your dearest friend.*

*I place your limbs as they should lie; I kiss the flesh*
That my own body nourished and my own care reared
To manhood. Help me, father; lay his poor head here.
Make all exact and seemly, with what care we can.
O dearest face, O young fresh cheek; O kingly eyes,
Your light now darkened! O my son! See, with this veil
I now cover your head, your torn and bloodstained limbs.

*Take him up, carry him to burial, a king*
*Lured to a shameful death by the anger of a god.*

*Enter DIONYSUS.*

CHORUS:

*But look! Who is this, rising above the palace door?*
*It is he – Dionysus comes himself, no more disguised*
*As mortal, but in the glory of his divinity!*

DIONYSUS:

*Behold me, a god great and powerful, Dionysus,*
*The son whom Theban Semele bore to immortal Zeus.*
*I come to the city of seven gates, to famous Thebes,*
*Whose people slighted me, denied my divinity,*

*Refused my ritual dances. Now they reap the fruit*
*Of impious folly. The royal house is overthrown;*
*The city's streets tremble in guilt, as every Theban*
*Repents too late his blindness and his blasphemy.*
*Foremost in sin was Pentheus, who not only scorned*
*My claims, but* put me in fetters and insulted me.
Therefore death came to him in the most shameful way,
At his own mother's hands. This fate he justly earned;
*No god can see his worship scorned, and hear his name*
*Profaned, and not take vengeance to the utmost limit.*
*Thus men may learn that gods are more powerful than they.*

*Agauë and her sisters must immediately*
Depart from Thebes; their exile will be just penance
For the pollution which this blood has brought on them.
Never again shall they enjoy their native land;
*That such defilement ever should appear before*
*The city's altars,* is an offence to piety.

Now, Cadmus, hear what suffering Fate appoints for you.
You* shall transmute your nature, and become a serpent.
Your wife Harmonia, whom her father Ares gave
To you, a mortal, likewise shall assume the nature
Of beasts, and live a snake. The oracle of Zeus
Foretells that you, at the head of a barbaric horde,
Shall with your wife drive forth a pair of heifers yoked,
And with your countless army destroy many cities;
But when they plunder Loxias' oracle, they shall find
A miserable homecoming. However, Ares shall
At last deliver both you and Harmonia,
And grant you immortal life among the blessed gods.

I who pronounce these fates am Dionysus, begotten
Not by a mortal father, but by Zeus. If you
Had chosen wisdom, when you would not, you would
    have lived
In wealth and safety, having the son of Zeus your friend.

* Here the MSS resume.

CADMUS: Have mercy on us, Dionysus. We have sinned.

DIONYSUS: You know too late. You did not know me when you should.

CADMUS: We acknowledge this; but your revenge is merciless.

DIONYSUS: And rightly; I am a god, and you insulted me.

CADMUS: Gods should not be like mortals in vindictiveness.

DIONYSUS: All this my father Zeus ordained from the beginning.

AGAUË: No hope, father. Our harsh fate is decreed: exile.

DIONYSUS: Then why put off a fate which is inevitable?

*Exit* DIONYSUS.

CADMUS:
Dear child, what misery has overtaken us all –
You, and your sisters, and your old unhappy father!
I must set forth from home and live in barbarous lands;
Further than that, it is foretold that I shall lead
A mixed barbarian horde to Hellas. And my wife,
Harmonia, Ares' daughter, and I too, must take
The brutish form of serpents; and I am to lead her thus
At the head of an armed force, to desecrate the tombs
And temples of our native land. I am to reach
No respite from this curse; I may not even cross
The downward stream of Acheron to find peace in death.

AGAUË: And I in exile, father, shall live far from you.

CADMUS:
Poor child, why do you cling to me, as the young swan
Clings fondly to the old, helpless and white with age?

AGAUË: Where can I turn for comfort, homeless and exiled?

CADMUS: I do not know. Your father is little help to you.

AGAUË:
Farewell, my home; farewell the land I know.
Exiled, accursed and wretched, now I go
Forth from this door where first I came a bride.

CADMUS:

> Go, daughter; find some secret place to hide
> Your shame and sorrow.

AGAUË:                    Father, I weep for you.

CADMUS: I for your suffering, and your sisters' too.

AGAUË:

> There is strange tyranny in the god who sent
> Against your house this cruel punishment.

CADMUS:

> Not strange: our citizens despised his claim,
> And you, and they, put him to open shame.

AGAUË: Father, farewell.

CADMUS:                    Poor child! I cannot tell

> How you can *fare well*; yet I say, Farewell.

AGAUË:

> I go to lead my sisters by the hand
> To share my wretchedness in a foreign land.

*She turns to the Theban women who have been waiting at
                the edge of the stage.*

> Come, see me forth.

>                         Gods, lead me to some place
> Where loath'd Cithaeron may not see my face,
> Nor I Cithaeron. I have had my fill
> Of mountain-ecstasy; now take who will
> My holy ivy-wreath, my thyrsus-rod,
> All that reminds me how I served this god!

>                *Exit, followed by* CADMUS.

CHORUS:

> Gods manifest themselves in many forms,
> Bring many matters to surprising ends;
> The things we thought would happen do not happen;
> The unexpected God makes possible:
> And that is what has happened here today.

>                *Exeunt.*

# NOTES

\*

## ION

P. 41    *Phoebus Apollo:* also frequently called Loxias, a name applying especially to his prophetic function. In the translation I have generally used 'Apollo' to avoid confusion.

P. 42    *Erichthonius:* the father of Erechtheus the founder of Athens.

P. 49    *Is the common story true . . . ?* If the conversation which occupies the next 25 lines is compared with that on p. 58, beginning for example at 'Ha! another child of the earth!' I think there will be no doubt as to which passage Euripides meant to be accepted as giving the real facts of Ion's birth.

P. 63    *I'm worn out:* it is a convention that old men need help in walking when they arrive; sometimes, as in this instance, the excitement of action later makes them (or their author) forget their feebleness. The same thing happens with Peleus in *Andromache*.

P. 70    *At that time the Earth . . .:* the whole of this passage is 'stichomythia', i.e., the characters alternate with a single line each. The Greek language was at home in such quick exchange; in English it would be tedious, and I have therefore telescoped some of the lines to vary the length of speech.

P. 73    *Look now, you who with . . .:* in this last stanza the Chorus step, as it were, out of the drama and address the audience, and in particular any poet or playwright who may be present. The lines are interesting as coming from one so often called a misogynist.

P. 78    *Enter Ion:* it is sometimes thought that Ion does not see Creusa until near the end of his speech, *See how she weaves*, etc. But I think it more likely that he sees her as soon as he enters; and is at first too overcome with indignation to be able to address her directly.

       *To say nothing of my mother:* it seems that he must here refer to the priestess, who is the only mother he has known.

P. 80    *I am so glad . . .:* the expression is stronger in Greek. It is the sort of moment when understatement is more effective in English.

P. 81    *The Priestess stands by the temple door:* the text gives no indication of her exit; but it would be dramatically right for her to wait to see Creusa and Ion reconciled.

P. 84    *You have another father:* all of Creusa's explanation is in lyric metre; but for an English production the essential note here is intimacy; and this is almost bound to be sacrificed if verse is attempted.

P. 86 *Unless perhaps it is timely:* Ion for a moment reverts to his child-like attitude shown at the beginning of the play; then recollects how much he has learnt, and braces himself to listen with the mind of a man.

P. 87 *Apollo has done all things well:* but when she comes to enumerate these blessings, she finds the list disconcertingly short.


## THE WOMEN OF TROY

P. 89 *Poseidon:* the younger brother of Zeus. *Athene:* the daughter of Zeus. Although Greeks usually referred to Trojans with some contempt for their oriental outlook – love of luxury, acceptance of despotism, and so on – yet it is assumed from Homer onwards that they had the same language, and that at least the principal gods of Hellas were also honoured in Asia.

P. 96 *Peirene:* a spring struck by the foot of Pegasus from a rock at Corinth.

P. 97 *The land of Aetna:* the complimentary reference to Sicily seems to be a protest against the Sicilian expedition, which was in preparation at the time this play was produced.

P. 102 Cassandra's speeches seem to be deliberately made a mixture of pertinent sanity and ironical nonsense. Her warning of the folly of distant military undertakings is only too plainly wise; her superficial arguments of comfort for those bereaved in war, capped by her fatuous praise of Paris's distinguished marriage, equally plainly imply the opposite of their proposed effect.

P. 104 *In his long wandering ... ills innumerable:* This passage is of doubtful authenticity.

P. 105 *Avengers:* the Furies, avengers of blood, who moved Clytemnestra to kill Agamemnon, and later Orestes to kill Clytemnestra.

P. 107 *Good fortune means nothing:* a more literal translation would be: 'Of those (seemingly) blessed with good fortune, call none even lucky until he is dead.'

P. 107 In this Ode the MSS are faulty and confused in several places, so that exactness in translation becomes impossible.

P. 111 *As Hector's wife,* etc.: the sentences which follow here, with their didactic tone regarding the behaviour of women, are not to be regarded as merely another instance of the author's personal views dragged in on an unsuitable occasion. The topicality of Andromache's words serves a dramatic purpose in emphasizing for the audience that this woman being taken off by soldiers to be a slave and concubine is just such a one as themselves; that this is what an Athenian army did to wealthy and cultured women in Melos only two years ago.

P. 120 For the interpretation of Helen's speech see the Introduction.

P. 122 *It's a confusion easily made:* Euripides here refers to *aphrosyne*, 'folly', connecting it with *Aphrodite*. Such puns seemed to fifth-century Athenians to have point; there is, of course, no etymological connection.

P. 124 *On the ensuing attitude . . .:* literally, 'on how the mind of the beloved turns out'. Since Menelaus does not say 'on how she has behaved', it seems that his words may contain already a hint of possible reconciliation with Helen.

P. 125 *Will our home be holy Salamis?:* to an English audience this topographical speculation might seem to come more suitably from their mothers (as before, p. 96) than from the children. A producer would probably wish to close the inverted commas at *rowers ready* and in the following line change *our* to *their*.

P. 126 *Peleus . . . Peleas:* in 'Peleus' the first *e* is long, and *-eus* is one syllable; 'Peleas' has three syllables, and the first *e* is short.

P. 127 *If only you and I both do our best . . .:* if this seems a tactless call for cooperation, surely its purpose is to remind us that a few minutes ago Hecabe was eagerly offering cooperation to Menelaus in the judgement of Helen.

P. 130 *Yet, had not heaven cast down . . .:* this is a difficult passage, made harder by a lacuna of half a line in the text. The thought seems to be: If future ages learn a lesson from what poets shall write about us, perhaps we will not have suffered in vain.

## HELEN

The translation of this play is based, with only occasional exceptions, on the text of A. Y. Campbell.

P. 151 *Once he heard my name:* the subtle absurdity of this argument takes a few moments to work out.

P. 152 *Leave my clothes alone!:* an echo from *Hippolytus*, the scene where the Nurse clings to Hippolytus. Here the word for *clothes* is humorously inappropriate.

P. 156 *The endless chain of tedious days:* this is one of several hints that life with the phantom Helen had not satisfied every aspiration.

*Speak, for my sake:* literally, 'Speak; for it is pleasant to hear of sufferings.' Menelaus means that he wants to hear the story, and explains his wish by this characteristically Euripidean generalization. *For my sake* conveys part of the sense of his appeal while avoiding the impossibly un-English sententiousness.

PP. 159–60 *Tell me about your adventures:* this sudden irrelevance is a parody of a similar moment in *Iphigenia in Tauris*, which had probably been often criticized.

P. 169 *The gods are going to be kind:* an assurance given to the audience that the Apolline fiasco of *Iphigenia in Tauris* will not be repeated.

P. 182 *Darling of Nereus:* the ship. Nereus is a sea-god.

P. 189 *Women, I wish you joy . . .:* the obscurity of the last two lines is surely deliberate. They may be addressed to the Dioscori, to the Chorus, or to the audience. They will satisfy equally the many who insist on regarding Euripides as a misogynist, and the few who perceive the poet's true attitude to women and to Helen as the avatar of her sex. The literal meaning is 'Rejoice in the most noble heart of Helen – a thing not found in many women.'


## THE BACCHAE

P. 191 *Thyrsus:* a light stick of reed or fennel, with fresh strands of ivy twined round it. It was carried by every devotee of Dionysus; and the action of the play illustrates the supernatural power that was held to reside in it.

P. 196 *The celebrant:* Dionysus and the Chorus comprise the typical group of Bacchic worshippers, a male leader with a devoted band of women and girls. The leader *flings himself on the ground* in the climax of ecstasy, when the power of the god enters into him and he becomes possessed.

P. 201 *The ancient word for a pledge:* the translation necessarily expands the original. *Homeros* means 'pledge', and *meros* 'thigh'.

P. 206 *Bromius:* another name of Dionysus, meaning 'noisy' or 'thunderous', and referring probably to the drums used in his worship.

P. 230 *Were singing holy Bacchic songs:* The Greek word is *Bacchic* songs. In English this adjective is too often associated with the 'profane' drinking of wine, whereas in this play it always has a religious or at least a ritualistic meaning. In translation I have been deliberately inconsistent, using either *Bacchic* and *holy* or, as in this line, both.

**P. 230** *As a wheel's curve* ...: a difficult passage of which no satis-factory translation can be made. An emended text gives: 'As a bow by which an untrue wheel, chiselled on a lathe, is swiftly rotated.' This would refer to the use of a bent pole or tree as a source of power.

**P. 235** *And Pentheus too, Agauë?*: the Chorus are physically shocked by the sight of Agauë and her prey, but their attitude does not change to pity. Agauë has been (in their view, justly) punished for her blasphemy against Dionysus, by being tricked into per-forming the usual Bacchic rite of slaughter, not upon the usual victim, a beast, but upon a man, and that her own son. She is now an abhorred and polluted creature, unfit for the company of the 'pure' Bacchae. Hence, though they welcome the punishment of Pentheus, their tone towards Agauë is one not of admiration but of contempt. This line in particular indicates the complete absence of pity.

**P. 235** *Then show it, poor Agauë* ...: if the head of Pentheus had been openly displayed since Agauë entered, these lines would be pointless. To ensure their dramatic power, Agauë must enter carrying the head hidden in her gown; when she shows it to the Chorus ('Look, you may see him: there') she should kneel at front stage with her back to the audience, so that the horror is visibly reflected in the eyes of the Chorus. With 'Come, all you Thebans ...' Agauë gives the audience their first sight of the head; after 'limb from limb' she covers it again.

**P. 239** ... *and believe in gods*: the climax of the play's irony.

**P. 242** *You shall transmute your nature* ...: This puzzling prophecy raises too many questions to be dealt with here; see the excellent note on this passage in Professor Dodds' edition.

# READ MORE IN PENGUIN

In every corner of the world, on every subject under the sun, Penguin represents quality and variety – the very best in publishing today.

For complete information about books available from Penguin – including Puffins, Penguin Classics and Arkana – and how to order them, write to us at the appropriate address below. Please note that for copyright reasons the selection of books varies from country to country.

**In the United Kingdom**: Please write to *Dept. EP, Penguin Books Ltd, Bath Road, Harmondsworth, West Drayton, Middlesex UB7 0DA*

**In the United States**: Please write to *Consumer Sales, Penguin Putnam Inc., P.O. Box 12289 Dept. B, Newark, New Jersey 07101-5289.* VISA and MasterCard holders call 1-800-788-6262 to order Penguin titles

**In Canada**: Please write to *Penguin Books Canada Ltd, 10 Alcorn Avenue, Suite 300, Toronto, Ontario M4V 3B2*

**In Australia**: Please write to *Penguin Books Australia Ltd, P.O. Box 257, Ringwood, Victoria 3134*

**In New Zealand**: Please write to *Penguin Books (NZ) Ltd, Private Bag 102902, North Shore Mail Centre, Auckland 10*

**In India**: Please write to *Penguin Books India Pvt Ltd, 11 Community Centre, Panchsheel Park, New Delhi 110017*

**In the Netherlands**: Please write to *Penguin Books Netherlands bv, Postbus 3507, NL-1001 AH Amsterdam*

**In Germany**: Please write to *Penguin Books Deutschland GmbH, Metzlerstrasse 26, 60594 Frankfurt am Main*

**In Spain**: Please write to *Penguin Books S. A., Bravo Murillo 19, 1° B, 28015 Madrid*

**In Italy**: Please write to *Penguin Italia s.r.l., Via Benedetto Croce 2, 20094 Corsico, Milano*

**In France**: Please write to *Penguin France, Le Carré Wilson, 62 rue Benjamin Baillaud, 31500 Toulouse*

**In Japan**: Please write to *Penguin Books Japan Ltd, Kaneko Building, 2-3-25 Koraku, Bunkyo-Ku, Tokyo 112*

**In South Africa**: Please write to *Penguin Books South Africa (Pty) Ltd, Private Bag X14, Parkview, 2122 Johannesburg*

# READ MORE IN PENGUIN

## A CHOICE OF CLASSICS

| | |
|---|---|
| Aeschylus | **The Oresteian Trilogy** |
| | **Prometheus Bound/The Suppliants/Seven against Thebes/The Persians** |
| Aesop | **The Complete Fables** |
| Ammianus Marcellinus | **The Later Roman Empire (AD 354–378)** |
| Apollonius of Rhodes | **The Voyage of Argo** |
| Apuleius | **The Golden Ass** |
| Aristophanes | **The Knights/Peace/The Birds/The Assemblywomen/Wealth** |
| | **Lysistrata/The Acharnians/The Clouds** |
| | **The Wasps/The Poet and the Women/ The Frogs** |
| Aristotle | **The Art of Rhetoric** |
| | **The Athenian Constitution** |
| | **Classic Literary Criticism** |
| | **De Anima** |
| | **The Metaphysics** |
| | **Ethics** |
| | **Poetics** |
| | **The Politics** |
| Arrian | **The Campaigns of Alexander** |
| Marcus Aurelius | **Meditations** |
| Boethius | **The Consolation of Philosophy** |
| Caesar | **The Civil War** |
| | **The Conquest of Gaul** |
| Cicero | **Murder Trials** |
| | **The Nature of the Gods** |
| | **On the Good Life** |
| | **On Government** |
| | **Selected Letters** |
| | **Selected Political Speeches** |
| | **Selected Works** |
| Euripides | **Alcestis/Iphigenia in Tauris/Hippolytus** |
| | **The Bacchae/Ion/The Women of Troy/ Helen** |
| | **Medea/Hecabe/Electra/Heracles** |
| | **Orestes and Other Plays** |

# READ MORE IN PENGUIN

## A CHOICE OF CLASSICS

| | |
|---|---|
| Hesiod/Theognis | **Theogony/Works and Days/Elegies** |
| Hippocrates | **Hippocratic Writings** |
| Homer | **The Iliad** |
| | **The Odyssey** |
| Horace | **Complete Odes and Epodes** |
| Horace/Persius | **Satires and Epistles** |
| Juvenal | **The Sixteen Satires** |
| Livy | **The Early History of Rome** |
| | **Rome and Italy** |
| | **Rome and the Mediterranean** |
| | **The War with Hannibal** |
| Lucretius | **On the Nature of the Universe** |
| Martial | **Epigrams** |
| | **Martial in English** |
| Ovid | **The Erotic Poems** |
| | **Heroides** |
| | **Metamorphoses** |
| | **The Poems of Exile** |
| Pausanias | **Guide to Greece (in two volumes)** |
| Petronius/Seneca | **The Satyricon/The Apocolocyntosis** |
| Pindar | **The Odes** |
| Plato | **Early Socratic Dialogues** |
| | **Gorgias** |
| | **The Last Days of Socrates (Euthyphro/ The Apology/Crito/Phaedo)** |
| | **The Laws** |
| | **Phaedrus and Letters VII and VIII** |
| | **Philebus** |
| | **Protagoras/Meno** |
| | **The Republic** |
| | **The Symposium** |
| | **Theaetetus** |
| | **Timaeus/Critias** |
| Plautus | **The Pot of Gold and Other Plays** |
| | **The Rope and Other Plays** |

# READ MORE IN PENGUIN

## A CHOICE OF CLASSICS

| | |
|---|---|
| Pliny | **The Letters of the Younger Pliny** |
| Pliny the Elder | **Natural History** |
| Plotinus | **The Enneads** |
| Plutarch | **The Age of Alexander (Nine Greek Lives)** |
| | **Essays** |
| | **The Fall of the Roman Republic (Six Lives)** |
| | **The Makers of Rome (Nine Lives)** |
| | **Plutarch on Sparta** |
| | **The Rise and Fall of Athens (Nine Greek Lives)** |
| Polybius | **The Rise of the Roman Empire** |
| Procopius | **The Secret History** |
| Propertius | **The Poems** |
| Quintus Curtius Rufus | **The History of Alexander** |
| Sallust | **The Jugurthine War/The Conspiracy of Cataline** |
| Seneca | **Dialogues and Letters** |
| | **Four Tragedies/Octavia** |
| | **Letters from a Stoic** |
| | **Seneca in English** |
| Sophocles | **Electra/Women of Trachis/Philoctetes/Ajax** |
| | **The Theban Plays** |
| Suetonius | **The Twelve Caesars** |
| Tacitus | **The Agricola/The Germania** |
| | **The Annals of Imperial Rome** |
| | **The Histories** |
| Terence | **The Comedies (The Girl from Andros/The Self-Tormentor/The Eunuch/Phormio/The Mother-in-Law/The Brothers)** |
| Thucydides | **History of the Peloponnesian War** |
| Virgil | **The Aeneid** |
| | **The Eclogues** |
| | **The Georgics** |
| Xenophon | **Conversations of Socrates** |
| | **Hiero the Tyrant** |
| | **A History of My Times** |
| | **The Persian Expedition** |